THE SACRED EXECUTIONER

Hyam Maccoby

THE SACRED EXECUTIONER

HUMAN SACRIFICE

AND THE LEGACY

OF GUILT

with 12 illustrations

Thames and Hudson

Frontispiece: 'The Wandering Jew Crossing a Cemetery' by Gustave Doré.

Any copy of this book issued by the publisher as a paperback is sold subject to the condition that it shall not, by way of trade or otherwise, be lent, re-sold, hired out or otherwise circulated, without the publisher's prior consent, in any form of binding or cover other than that in which it is published and without a similar condition including these words being imposed on a subsequent purchaser.

© 1982 Hyam Maccoby

All Rights Reserved. No part of this publication may be reproduced or transmitted in any form or by any means, electronic or mechanical, including photocopy, recording or any information storage and retrieval system, without permission in writing from the publisher.

Filmset by Keyset Composition, Colchester, Essex.
Printed and bound by The Pitman Press, Bath.

Contents

1	The Sacred Executioner	7
2	Cain	11
3	The Israelite account of Cain	27
4	Lamech	41
5	The Kenites and the Rechabites	57
6	Abraham and Isaac	74
7	Moses and circumcision	87
8	The sacrifice of Jesus	97
9	Christianity and Hellenistic religion	107
10	Judas Iscariot	121
11	The role of the Jews in the New Testament	134
12	The Church and the Jews	147

13	*The Sacred Executioner in the modern world*	163
14	*Theoretical problems and conclusions*	176
	Notes	187
	Bibliography	198
	Index	203

Chapter One

The Sacred Executioner

A figure in mythology that has received little attention is that of the Sacred Executioner. By this I mean the figure of a person (either a god or a human being) who slays another person, and as a result is treated as both sacred and accursed. Commonly, such a person in myth is ejected from society and condemned to long wanderings; yet he is also regarded as having special privileges, such as being protected from attack and having his life prolonged beyond the average. There are many variations on this pattern; sometimes the person is treated as more sacred than accursed, sometimes as more accursed than sacred. The best-known example in our culture is that of Cain, whose story will begin our discussion, but the discussion will take us to many very different examples, which may not at first seem to fit into the category suggested: Romulus, the founder of Rome; Set, the Egyptian god; Loki, the Scandinavian god; the Wandering Jew (and indeed the Jews as a whole, whose sufferings as the target of anti-Semitism will receive fresh light from this investigation); and examples in literature, such as the Ancient Mariner.

    The historical reality that lies behind all these stories, I shall argue, is the institution of human sacrifice, which was practised throughout the ancient world, though usually only in times of great emergency (it is still practised in certain backward areas of the world today). Very few of the myths we shall be considering actually portray human sacrifice openly; instead, we find stories about accidental deaths on the one hand, or about murders (carried out for merely personal reasons) on the other. Both modulations are intended to absolve society of responsibility for the violent deaths that occur in the stories. For human sacrifice seems almost never to have been unaccompanied by guilt on the part of the society in which it occurred and by a consequent desire to shift the blame, despite the desperate need that was felt to accomplish the deed. (An exception is the society of the Aztecs, which seems to have been almost entirely free of guilt for the institution of human sacrifice, though even here some details are relevant to our purpose.)

    Thus, the myth will rarely admit openly that the slaying in the story was performed as a ritual sacrifice. Instead, it will say that an accident occurred, or alternatively that the slaying was a wicked deed performed by a murderer who was subsequently punished. How do we know then, that ritual sacrifice is the real subject of the myth? This is betrayed by the equivocal character of the story. Some good consequence will be seen to flow from the slaying: a city will be founded, or a nation will be inaugurated, or a famine will be stayed, or a people will be saved from the wrath of the gods, or a threatening enemy will be defeated. Such good consequences are exactly the results that were hoped for by the performance of human sacrifice. If the slaying is blamed entirely on accident, then nobody will be blamed; but more usually the slaying is attributed to malevolence on the part of the slayer. In this case, the hidden character of the story is betrayed by the equivocal nature of the punishment meted out to the slayer. He will be cursed, but not put to death; he will acquire special magic powers; he will be driven out of society, but special pains taken to ensure that he survives. By taking the blame for the slaying, he is performing a great service to society, for not only does he perform the deed, but he takes upon himself the blame for it, and thus absolves society as a whole completely from the guilt of a slaying for which they, in fact, are responsible and by which, in theory at least, they benefit.

A key example may be taken from the religious ritual of Athens. Once a year, at the great Bouphonia (Bull Slaying Feast), a bull representing Zeus, the father of the gods, was sacrificed on the altar of the temple. The custom was that the priests, after sacrificing the bull, fled from the altar in mock panic, crying out a formula absolving them from the guilt of having slain the god. Afterwards, in a special chamber of the temple, a trial was held, in which the blame for the slaying was attributed to the knife that slit the bull's throat. The knife, having been found guilty, was punished by being destroyed.[1]

This ritual is not one of human sacrifice, but it is very instructive even about myths in which the victim is a human being. It shows the desire to shift the blame, and to find some person or even object that can be held guilty and punished for an act which, nevertheless, was regarded as an essential observance, the omission of which would bring disaster upon the state. Actually, the fact that in this instance the victim is an animal, not a human being, does not necessarily mean that the ritual is less primitive than rituals of human sacrifice. In the very earliest times, animals were not regarded as inferior in status to men; on the contrary, they were often regarded as divine beings. Consequently, the killing of an animal would not arouse less guilt than the killing of a man.[2] The era of human sacrifice arrived when human status had increased and the gods were portrayed in human, not animal, form. The myths of human sacrifice with which we are concerned arose in a still later era, when human sacrifice occurred very seldom, only at times of the greatest emergency, and at other times was hardly even mentioned as a possibility. In this period, animal sacrifice mostly took the place of human sacrifice, not because animals were regarded as the most efficacious sacrifices, but because growing civilization and humanitarianism, combined with a higher valuation of human status and a lessened awe of animals, caused a horror of human sacrifice to develop, so that not only was it confined to times of extreme emergency, but references to it in myth were censored and transformed in various ways out of recognition. This is the era when human sacrifice had the character of a great secret, and the myths we shall be examining are therefore all in a coded form.

In general, rituals are earlier than myths. The flight of the Athenian priests at the Bull Feast is a ritual, not a myth, in most versions, though we can imagine how a myth might have arisen from it. Myths often arose in order to explain a ritual; often too, they became detached from the ritual, which had become obsolete, and functioned simply as stories for poets or playwrights, though such stories also had a ritual function, being recited at festivals, and being regarded as holy writ. Ritual is not the only source of myth, which may arise from a historical event; yet in the background of such a transformation the influence of the ancient ritual may often be felt, arising from a fundamental need for placation and expiation in the face of unmanageable fear. Thus a story based on fact, by being interpreted in a way consonant with ancient sacrificial ritual, may actually take the place of that ritual and function in such a way that it is as if the ritual were being perpetually performed. The best example of this is the case of Jesus, whose death was interpreted as the sacrifice of a man-god, the placation of an angry father-god and the expiation of otherwise unpardonable sins; the blame for the shocking but necessary sacrifice was borne by a whole nation, the Jews (though crystallized in the individual form of Judas), who were given the role of a collective Sacred Executioner.

Another possibility, exemplified mainly in the Old Testament, is that a story originally about human sacrifice may be altered to serve a purpose that is the opposite to that intended — to act as propaganda, indeed, *against* the institution of human sacrifice. Perhaps the best example of this is the story of Abraham and Isaac, which extols the willingness of the father to sacrifice his son and nevertheless ends up as validating the substitution of animal sacrifice for human sacrifice. Here the pull towards human sacrifice is still observable, even though it is declared that God, in His mercy, has decided to abolish it. In other stories, however, where the civilizing process has progressed further, a definite polemic against human sacrifice can be discerned, though based on a scenario derived from human-sacrificial ritual. The disguised myth is still further disguised, until not merely guilt about human sacrifice is expressed but a conscious opposition to it as a deplorable pagan practice wholly at variance with the wishes of a merciful God. Here, in analysing the myth, it is necessary to uncover a pre-Hebraic stratum expressive of guilt but not of repudiation of the human-sacrificial institution. A myth of this character, showing the whole complex development from unashamed endorsement to guilty acceptance to indignant repudiation, is that of Cain and Abel, which will therefore repay careful study.

The Bible, indeed, is a fascinating repository of information about a crucial stage in man's development — his slow progress from modes of shifting blame and responsibility through institutions of sacrifice to the acceptance of full personal responsibility for his actions, both as an individual and as a member of a society. The Biblical institution of animal sacrifice should be viewed in this perspective, since its chief characteristic is its deletion of the magical properties of sacrifice, and the substitution of a system of etiquette for the idea of magically efficacious sacrificial rites; that is, the sacrifices are only an *accompaniment* to moral processes of repentance, restitution and punishment.[3] Such a gigantic move towards maturity could not take place in an utterly discontinuous manner; it had to build on previous stages of development, including the institution of sacrifice itself. One of the most important ways in which this process of transformation and sublimation can be traced is in the Biblical myths and stories, which are often basically pagan myths of sacrifice elaborated and essentially transformed to accommodate the new Hebraic insights about moral responsibility and the undesirability of shifting blame by splitting-off devices and excuses of various kinds. Nevertheless, in the basic myth of the New Testament, we shall note a regression to earlier modes of atonement, and, inevitably, a revival of the idea of shifting blame by vicarious atonement, both in the form of a sacrificial victim and in the less understood form of the Sacred Executioner — the main subject of this book — who vicariously undergoes the guilt felt by mankind because of its desperate recourse to sacrificial modes of atonement for its sins.

Chapter Two

Cain

Cain is the archetypal figure of the murderer. The story of Genesis allows him no excuse for his crime, which is actuated by mere jealousy of his brother Abel because the latter's offering to God was accepted with more favour. Nevertheless, I intend to argue that in the original version of the Cain story, Cain was not a murderer at all. He was the performer of a human sacrifice, and in the very earliest form of the story, there was no guilt attached to his deed; on the contrary, it was a meritorious act, just as the sacrifice of Isaac by Abraham would have been, if God had allowed it.

A nearer parallel is the story of Romulus and Remus. This savage tale is the foundation myth of Rome, and contrasts very strongly with the advanced morality of the Hebrew foundation myth of Cain and Abel in its final form; yet I suggest that they have many features in common and can be traced to an identical type. Romulus and Remus were twin brothers who together founded the city of Rome. Their divine parentage and their upbringing by a she-wolf emphasize the utterly new start that they made; they were as if created by nature and were at the dawn of a new world. While they were working on the foundations of the city, they quarrelled over the plans. Remus jumped in derision over a trench that Romulus had dug, and, in anger, Romulus slew him. Nevertheless, he was not punished for the deed, but on the contrary was given a great sign of favour by the gods: a flight of vultures arose over him, showing that he would found a nation as strong and pitiless as the vulture.[1]

Again, this story is not explicitly about human sacrifice; but the disguise here is very thin. Only good consequences flow from the slaying, and it is well attested that a commonly practised form of human sacrifice was at the inauguration of a new city.[2] The purpose of such a sacrifice was manifold: to placate the gods at a moment of *hubris* and avert their jealousy by inflicting a loss upon oneself; and also, possibly, to send an ambassador to the upper world who would act as tutelary spirit of the new city and intercede for it with the gods at closer quarters than any mortal being could command. A human sacrifice was usually over-determined in this way, and could serve multiple and even contradictory purposes.

Cain

The disguise offered in the Romulus-Remus story is that the slaying resulted from a quarrel, and Romulus could not be blamed because he had acted under provocation and insult. Romulus thus comes out as a righteous and innocent party, who merely proved his manhood by his homicide. The legend is thus not far removed from a straightforward unsophisticated account of ritual slaying, in which no guilt is felt for the institution of human sacrifice. An intermediate step between such primeval innocence (which may never have existed in historical fact, but may be taken as an ideal limit) and the Romulus stage is the ritualized combat, as described by Sir James Frazer in *The Golden Bough*. In this form of human sacrifice, the guardian priest of the holy grove was challenged by a rival to the priesthood to mortal combat. Whichever of the combatants was killed, the dead man would be the required victim, and a sacrifice would have been accomplished without the unpleasant and too explicit necessity of slaughtering a passive victim. It is possible that a simulated quarrel was one of the ritualized responsibility-avoidance devices used in one form of human sacrifice, and the Romulus–Remus story may be merely a narrative form of this ritual. Such a simulated quarrel would be yet another intermediate step distancing the horror of a bare slaying; it would require the cooperation of the victim, who would put up a good pretence of offering insult to the executioner. Still another variation on the 'quarrel' theme would be the gladiatorial combat between captured enemy prisoners, by which a victim would be offered to the gods for their granting of victory. The ritual sacrifice elements of the gladiatorial combat were quite openly retained in the triumphal shows of imperial Rome.[3]

In the story of Cain and Abel, we have the quarrel between brothers at the dawn of the world, and even (at a slight distance) the theme of the founding of a city (see Genesis 4:17, where Cain builds a city, which he calls by the name of his son Enoch). But there is no sign of divine favour for the killer, as in the Romulus story. On the contrary, there are great indications of divine displeasure; God pronounces a curse on Cain and condemns him to perpetual wandering. The slaying is not allowed to retain any trace of ritual sacrifice, but is condemned as mere murder, from which no good consequence can flow.

Yet this moral disapproval is not carried through in the way one might expect. After the account of the murder of Abel, the story of Cain is continued (from v. 17) in a quite different style — so much so that scholars have concluded that we are dealing here with a different narrative from a different source. In this new narrative, Cain is not treated as a wandering criminal, but as the respectable founder of a dynasty. Nothing is said about his being a wanderer; on the contrary, he is depicted as the founder of a city, and, most surprising of all, his

The Biblical version of Cain's crime: the horror and violence of fratricide disguise the even grimmer reality of human sacrifice. (Detail of engraving by Lucas van Leyden.)

descendants (whom one would expect to share his curse as wanderers for whom the earth would be infertile) are depicted as the inventors of the civilized arts of music, metal-working and cattle-raising.

This account of Cain as a patriarch and dynast clearly comes from a document in which Cain was regarded with high respect, and not as an archetypal murderer and guilty vagabond. Where could such a document have been found? To answer this question we have to consider the meaning of the name Cain.

The name Cain is explained in Genesis 4:1 as being derived from the Hebrew verb *qanah*, 'to acquire', or sometimes, 'to create' (the second meaning is probably intended, and the New English Bible translation of Eve's pronouncement as 'With the help of the Lord I have brought a man into being' is preferable to the Authorized Version's 'I have gotten a man from the Lord'). This is an interesting derivation (in that it conveys something of the primitive awe felt by men towards women as possessed of divine creative power in their ability to bear children), but etymologically it is wrong. The real meaning of 'Cain' (Hebrew *qayin*) is 'smith', or 'metal-worker'. Now there was actually a tribe whose name was Cain. This tribe is more commonly known as the

Cain

Kenites, but this name is derived from the generic name of the tribe (corresponding to such names as Israel or Ammon or Ashur) which is the name of the mythical hero from which the tribe claimed descent. The Kenites therefore claimed descent from someone called Cain (in Numbers 24:22, where the Authorized Version translates 'the Kenite', the Hebrew has 'Cain' and the New English Bible translates, 'Your refuge is doomed to burning . . . O Cain').

It is probable, in view of their name, that the Kenites were a tribe of smiths, especially as it is known that smith-tribes did exist in the ancient world; and indeed one is known among the Arabs even at the present day. The characteristics of such a tribe are that it is nomadic (since its skills are required over a large area) and that it tends to acquire a reputation for magic, because of the awe aroused by the ability to work metals. Another characteristic of such a tribe is that it tends to be skilled in music and to provide entertainment. Now the descendants of Cain are associated with all these characteristics in the fourth chapter of Genesis; they are described as the inventors of musical instruments and metal-working, as tent-dwellers, and as having some kind of magic about them (if we interpret the protective power of Cain's 'sign' in this way).

Can we say, then, that Cain, the ancestor of the Kenites, and Cain, the son of Adam and murderer of Abel, are one and the same man? If we take the Bible story literally, such an identification is impossible, for the Kenites are described as a tribe that existed after the Flood. The most famous Kenite mentioned in the Bible is Jethro, the father-in-law of Moses, though strangely enough he is not called a Kenite but a Midianite in the story of Moses in Exodus, and it is only from stray verses in the Book of Judges that we learn that Moses' father-in-law was actually a Kenite. In Judges 4:11, we read, 'Now Heber the Kenite, which was of the children of Hobab the father-in-law of Moses, had severed himself from the Kenites'; the New English Bible here deals with the difficulty that the name Hobab contradicts the name Jethro given in Exodus by translating the Authorized Version's 'father-in-law' as 'brother-in-law', a possible translation, but debatable because the Hebrew is the same as that used in Exodus to describe Jethro. In another verse, the father-in-law of Moses is actually called Cain (according to the Septuagint, though in the Hebrew Bible the word is not 'Cain' but 'Kenite'; the Septuagint reading is almost certainly correct, as the Hebrew omits the expected definite article). If Moses' father-in-law was called Cain, in addition to the names Jethro and Hobab, this suggests that the name Cain was a title, rather than an ordinary name, in the Kenite tribe, and that its ruler was always called Cain, or 'smith' (as if to say the 'Smith of Smiths'), rather like the perpetual title Pharaoh in Egypt, or Abimelech in Philistia.

Cain

It seems, then, that the Kenites were one of the tribes of Midian. They became especially associated with the Israelites through their family ties with Moses. Moses invited Jethro his father-in-law to join the Israelites in their journey to the Promised Land, but we are not told whether he accepted. Later, we find the Kenites settled among the Amalekites in North Arabia, but when Saul, king of Israel, attacked the Amalekites, he spared the Kenites, saying, 'Go, depart, get you down from among the Amalekites, lest I destroy you with them: for ye shewed kindness to all the children of Israel, when they came up out of Egypt' (I Samuel 15:6). The Kenites complied, and it seems that they joined the Israelite tribes, since we find them settled in Judah and elsewhere.

The Kenites, then, were a tribe regarded with special friendliness by the Israelites, who eventually absorbed them into their own nation. There is only one hostile reference to the Kenites in the Bible, in the curse or evil prophecy uttered against them by the prophet Balaam (who was of course not an Israelite) in Numbers 24:21–2.[4] How then can we connect this friendly tribe with the murderer Cain, of whom the Bible of the Israelites so strongly disapproves?

The Bible itself certainly does not make any such connection, and even seems to be covering up the fact that Moses married the daughter of a Kenite, since we gather this only from stray verses in another context, not from the main story of Moses. The chronological scheme of the Bible quite rules out any connection between the Kenites and Cain, son of Adam. For according to the Bible all the descendants of Cain died in the Flood. The only survivors of the Flood were the family of Noah, who was descended not from Cain but from Seth, the son born to Adam and Eve after the murder of Abel. So the Kenites, on the Biblical scheme, were descended, like all other nations, from Noah. No special genealogy is given for the Kenites, but since Jethro is called a Midianite (Exodus: 3:1) and later a Kenite, we are presumably intended to regard the Kenites as a subdivision of the Midianites. The genealogy given for the Midianites (Genesis 25:2) makes them a tribe of very late origin, being descended from a son of Abraham by Keturah, the wife he took after the death of Sarah; through Keturah Abraham is represented as being the progenitor of many of the tribes of Arabia. According to this scheme, then, the Kenites were a tribe of relatively recent origin, even more recent than that of the Israelites, who began with Abraham himself (dated, according to the Biblical chronology, at about 1900 BC). The Kenites, then, like the Midianites, were a Semitic tribe (i.e. descended from Shem, the son of Noah), and were closely related to the Israelites, according to the Bible, which is actually reticent and unexplicit about the origin of the Kenites themselves.

Cain

The friendliness felt by the Bible towards the Kenites is in marked contrast to the hostility expressed towards the Midianites, who were accused of putting sexual temptations before the Israelites (Numbers 25:18) and against whom religious war was waged (Numbers 31). The Kenites were regarded with friendship not just because of one man, Jethro, who was allied by marriage to Moses, but because of their conduct as a community towards the Israelites; when Saul expresses Israelite gratitude towards the Kenites, he does not even mention Jethro, but refers, as we have seen, to their 'kindness to all the children of Israel'. All this suggests that the Kenites were in some way very different from the Midianites, to whom they supposedly belong.

Jethro, Moses' father-in-law, is described in Exodus as the 'priest of Midian' (the Hebrew word here for 'priest' is *kohen*, the same word used later for the Aaronite priesthood of the Israelites). Some scholars have suggested that *kohen* in this context means only 'leader' or 'ruler', but this is unlikely; the word in cognate languages always has reference to religious leadership, though sometimes combined with kingship. The only other person mentioned in Genesis who is called 'priest', *kohen*, is Melchizedek, the priest-king of Salem (Genesis 14:18), who is expressly assigned a religious function as 'priest of the Most High', and who blesses Abram (later Abraham) in religious terms. It should be noted that the Bible does not confine religious status to functionaries of the Israelites. Not only priests were allowed to exist outside the Israelite religious community, but even prophets, such as Balaam; and a whole book of the Bible, Job, is devoted to a non-Israelite sage and his friends. Both in the Bible and in later Jewish writings, it was considered that belief in monotheism long preceded the foundation of the Israelite nation and had existed from the earliest period of human history; for example, Adam, Enoch, Noah and Shem, all pre-Israelite figures, were considered to have been monotheists of high stature.

In view of the religious status of Jethro, scholars since the nineteenth century have suggested that he, or the Kenites in general, may have had a great influence on the religion of Israel.[5] Indeed, the Bible itself admits that Jethro influenced the development of Israelite religion. According to Exodus (18:14–26), it was by the advice of Jethro that Moses set up a system of courts of justice instead of judging all cases himself. This system was of the utmost importance in the administration of religious law in Israel, and it is strange to think that the origin of such an institution as the Sanhedrin is traced in the Biblical source not to divine ordination but to the advice of a non-Israelite priest and sage. On the other hand, in what seems to be an alternative account of the origin of the Council of Seventy Elders (Numbers 11:14–18), the institution is attributed to the direction of God Himself.

Cain

It seems that the earlier account of Exodus ascribing the development to the intervention of Jethro was felt to be unsuitable, as not in accordance with the doctrine that the entire Torah was given by direct revelation of God. But the earlier account was still allowed to stand, and is interesting evidence of a tradition that there had been Kenite influence on the basic institutions of Israel.

The question, then, arises whether this influence was in fact much greater than is indicated by this surviving fragment of tradition. Many scholars have thought so. Some have even thought that the God of the Israelites, YHWH, came to them from Kenite worship. This theory takes various forms: Sigmund Freud's book *Moses and Monotheism* has popularized the version that YHWH was a volcano-god of the Kenites, and that a fusion was made between this god and the universal God of monotheism, derived from Egyptian religion (i.e. from the ideas of the 'heretic' Pharaoh, Akhnaton), thus resulting in an uneasy combination of monotheism and tribalistic worship. This theory has not worn well, for it is no longer thought that Akhnaton was a monotheist, and the so-called evidence for tribalist worship among the Israelites (except on the level of dissidence and backslidings from monotheism) has not stood up to further research, including the study of archaeological evidence.

On the other hand, the idea that there has been Kenite influence on Israelite religion is still very much alive, but this takes the form of an influence on the Bible itself. For many of the Biblical myths and legends can be understood better on the hypothesis that they are adaptations of stories taken from Kenite tradition. The most important adaptation of this kind is the story of Cain himself.

Though Cain, according to the Bible, was an antediluvian figure, and therefore could not have been the ancestor of the post-diluvian Semitic tribe, the Kenites, there can be little doubt that the Cain of the Bible is derived from the Cain whom the Kenites regarded as their ancestor and the founder of their tribe. Indeed, there is good reason to suppose that the whole history of the pre-Flood era, and even the story of the Flood itself, was taken from a Kenite saga describing the early history of the Kenite tribe.

The chief reason for this conclusion is that close examination of the early chapters of Genesis shows that Cain is a far more important person in the story than appears at first. On the surface, Cain seems to have a fairly minor role; he is the guilty progenitor of a rejected line of humanity that ceased to exist at the time of the Flood, and had no influence on post-diluvian history. Infinitely more important than the line of Cain is the line of Seth, the true heir of Adam because of his freedom from Cain's guilt. This is the line to which the Bible gives honour, by recounting it in more detail, giving the length of life of each figure and even the age at which he begat the next figure in the line. The line of Cain, however, is given as a bare succession of names. Thus the chronology of the Bible, by which the length of time between the Creation and the Flood is calculated, depends on the line of Seth.

Yet this is mere appearance. The truth is that the line of Seth has no real existence at all, but is a shadow or reflection of the line of Cain. For it requires little enquiry to see that the two lines of Seth and Cain are really one line, and that the line of Seth was derived from the line of Cain and not vice versa. If we examine the names in both lists, we see that there is only one list with slight variations, for the names are basically the same in both lists. This can be seen in the form of a table:

	Adam and Eve
Cain	Seth
Enoch	Enosh
Irad	Kenan
Mehujael	Mahalalel
Methushael	Jared
Lamech	Enoch
Jabal, Jubal, Tubal-Cain	Methuselah
	Lamech
	Noah
	Shem, Ham, Japheth

Comparing the two columns, we see that two of the names (Enoch and Lamech) appear in both columns. Four names are the same with slight variations (Cain, Kenan; Irad, Jared; Mehujael, Mahalalel; Methushael, Methuselah). Another similarity (which will prove important in the argument below) is that each list ends with a trio of names, even though those names are not identical. There are some variations in the order of the names, the chief displacement being that of Enoch.[6]

Three names appear in the Sethian line but not in the line of Cain: Seth himself and his son Enosh, and, at the end of the line, Noah (setting aside the final trios for the moment). The name Enosh is significant, because the meaning of this name is simply 'man'. It seems very likely, then, that this is an alternative name for Adam, which also means 'man'. Thus the only redundant names are Seth at the beginning and Noah at the end. So it looks as if these names have been added to the line of Cain in order to create a new succession, the blameless line of Seth.

The most remarkable duplication is that of Cain himself, who appears in the Sethian list as the wholly innocuous figure of Kenan. The similarity between the two names Cain and Kenan is more marked in the original Hebrew, where they differ only in the doubling

Cain

of the last consonant. This concealment of the dreaded figure of Cain in innocent disguise shows clearly the derivation of the Sethian list from that of Cain, the motive being to provide a line for mankind free of Cain's crime.

The name Seth is derived from the verb *shith*, meaning 'to put'. The etymology given in the Bible (Genesis 4:25) is forced, and the name seems very colourless compared with the other names in the chronicle. It could almost be translated, 'he who was added' or 'he who was put in', though literally it might be regarded as the imperative, 'put (him) in'. As for the other extra name in the Sethian list, Noah, see below, p. 54, for a discussion of its meaning.

One difficulty is that the line of Cain is shorter than that of Seth. The three sons of Lamech (in Cain's line) are presumably intended to be the last generation before the Flood, and therefore contemporary with Noah, but this makes only eight generations for Cain's line, as opposed to ten for Seth. Even supposing that Cain's descendants were just as prodigiously long-lived as Seth's, this is a great discrepancy. The gap could easily have been bridged by omitting two names in the Sethian list: Enosh could have been omitted, as a mere duplicate of Adam, and Kenan as a too-revealing duplicate of Cain. Why then were these names not omitted? The answer lies in the desire of the compilers of the Sethian line to produce a neat symmetry by having ten generations before the Flood and ten generations up to the advent of Abraham after the Flood. This desire for symmetry is seen also in the ages assigned to the patriarchs of Seth's line, which form part of a carefully calculated numerical pattern, as often pointed out by scholars.[7]

The upshot of this argument is that the Biblical chronicle of the generations before the Flood is based on a chronicle of the line of Cain only. Such a chronicle must have come from a tribe to whom Cain was a revered ancestor. This tribe must be the Kenites, who were called after Cain and among whom his was a royal or priestly name.[8] We conclude, therefore, that the Israelite writers who compiled the early chapters of Genesis used as one of their main sources a Kenite saga, which recounted the sacred history of the Kenite tribe, tracing it back to its ancestor, Cain. This is inherently probable in that Israelite tradition preserves the memory of Kenite influence on the origins of Israelite religion in the form of the figure of Jethro, the 'priest of Midian', later identified as a Kenite and even called by the title 'Cain'. It would seem that the Israelites, a parvenu nation formed by Moses out of a caste of slaves whom he liberated from Egypt, and endowed by him with a universalist vision that required a universal history going back to the Creation of the world, had no traditions of their own going back so far, and had to borrow them from another community with which they had strong connections (Moses himself having lived among the Kenites and acquired their culture). It would seem probable that the Kenites traced their own ancestry back to the beginning of the world. Most ancient tribes did this; the Israelites were in fact unusual in *not* regarding their tribal ancestor (Abraham, or more correctly, Jacob, since it was his alternative name, Israel, that gave the Israelites their name) as belonging to the dawn of human history. To see one's own tribe as the oldest tribe in existence and the genealogical source of all mankind is in fact a parochial view; it was part of the new universalism of the religion of Israel *not* to see Israel as the basic ingredient of humanity but as a small and relatively late nation, coming into existence when the civilizations of Babylonia and Egypt were already old. God, out of His mercy and loving kindness, had decided to make this weak, small and apparently insignificant nation the instrument of His purposes: 'The Lord did not set His love upon you, nor choose you because ye were more in number than any people, for ye are the fewest of all peoples' (Deuteronomy 7:7). Yet a vast stage was required in which this insignificant yet chosen people could play its awesome role; so a panorama of universal history was provided by utilizing records of a tribe which had no such universalist vision; and this background of a wide concourse of nations ensured that the Israelites always looked beyond their own borders and saw themselves as having a mission to the whole world, as expounded in the internationalist writings of the prophets.

But what about Cain's murder of Abel? What place did this have in the original Kenite saga? On the one hand, it is most unlikely that the Kenites would have traced their ancestry to a murderer; but on the other hand, it is also unlikely that the story of Cain's crime was merely added to the story of Cain that the Israelite compilers found in the Kenite sources. Cain's crime must be based on something that they found there. The probable answer is that the Kenite saga did contain a slaying performed by Cain, but that it was not a murder but a ritual human sacrifice.

In the original Kenite saga, the slaying of Abel by Cain may well have been a story similar to the founding legend of Rome, the slaying of Remus by Romulus. Just as Romulus slew Remus as an inauguration sacrifice for the building of a new city and nation, so Cain, who 'builded a city', performed the necessary human sacrifice that would ensure the future welfare of the city and the Kenite nation, and the care and goodwill of its gods. So, too, Abraham was prepared to sacrifice his son at the inauguration of the new nation of the Israelites, though in a later version of the legend, after human sacrifice had become abhorrent, God was represented as preventing the sacrifice from taking place.

Cain

The Kenite saga may have disguised the story to the extent of representing the slaying as the result of a quarrel, as in the Roman foundation story. If so, as in the case of Romulus, there would have been little or no guilt attached to the slaying, since the Kenites would regard their first ancestor as a great hero, not as a guilty man. It is quite possible that a certain ritual impurity, following the slaying, was attached to the slayer, even though he was innocent of murder, and Cain, for this reason, had to retire to the desert for a while until purged of his defilement. This would have been the case even if the Kenite legend, as encountered by the Israelites, was still at the primitive stage when Cain was openly acknowledged to have killed his brother as a human sacrifice; ritual impurity would nevertheless ensue. In the Babylonian New Year festival ceremony, the two priests who sacrificed a sheep and smeared the walls of the shrine with its blood were obliged to flee into the desert until the festival was over, because, even though their ritual sacrifice was essential to purify the shrine, they became polluted by their act.[9] A remnant of this impurity of the sacrificer is found in Hebrew religion, in which the priest who slaughtered the 'Red Cow' (whose ashes were essential for purifying purposes) became unclean through performing the sacrifice (Numbers 19:7), as did the other officiants involved in burning the corpse and gathering the ashes. The Red Cow sacrifice was a more primitive rite than the other Hebrew sacrifices (as is shown by the fact that it was sacrificed outside 'the camp', and not in the Temple), so it retained this primitive feature too.[10]

We have thus isolated two possible stages of the Cain legend: (i) an acknowledged human sacrifice, followed by purification in the desert; (ii) a quarrel, also followed by purification in the desert, but purification from the pollution of justified homicide, not human sacrifice. A third stage (or an alternative second stage) might be: a human sacrifice, after which the sacrificer is banished permanently to the desert, where he carries with him the guilt of the tribe for performing the human sacrifice. This stage can be discerned in the Biblical account of Cain's slaying of Abel, yet it cannot be derived from the Kenite saga itself, in which Cain must have been ultimately purified and allowed to resume his place as patriarch. The traces of the third stage in the Hebrew account must come from some other source, or arise by a natural development. It is this third stage that is of greatest interest for us, as it is the characteristic stage of the Sacred Executioner – the figure of guilt who is banished from society, yet carries with him society's gratitude for taking upon himself the burden which would be too heavy for his fellows to bear. The third stage is not characteristic of Hebrew religion, which bypassed it by outlawing human sacrifice itself. Yet there are still traces of it in the Hebrew Bible, not only in the

Cain

story of Cain, but also in the ritual on the Day of Atonement, when the Scapegoat is sent into the desert as the last vestige of the Sacred Executioner motif, in which the Executioner was banished after his essential act (see Leviticus 16, and further discussion on p. 34ff.).

By comparison between the Sethite and Cainite chronicles as given in Genesis, it may be possible to throw light on a mysterious passage in the Bible that has given rise to many conjectures, and also to uncover a hidden feature of the original Kenite saga. The passage about Enoch in the Sethite chronicle runs as follows:

And Enoch lived sixty and five years, and begot Methuselah, and Enoch walked with God after he begot Methuselah three hundred years, and begot sons and daughters. And all the days of Enoch were three hundred sixty and five years. And Enoch walked with God, and he was not; for God took him. (Genesis 5:21–4)

Enoch is thus the only antediluvian patriarch who died before his time, at the tender age (for those times) of 365 years, whereas the others lived to an average of about 900 years. Later legend made much of the figure of Enoch, who became the subject of apocalyptic writings. It was thought that after his early death he was so beloved of God that he was made into an angel; even, according to some accounts, into the highest of the angels, Metatron. Enoch became a special object of veneration in the Christian Church, because he was an example of a non-Jew who reached the highest stage of prophecy and nearness to God, thus proving the right of the Gentile Christian Church to take over the prerogative of the Jews as people of God, and also to challenge the primacy of the Jewish Church of Jerusalem over Christendom. In the Synagogue, however, Enoch became a suspect figure, probably because of the Christian overtones he had acquired, and his importance was denied. (Similar developments took place in relation to Seth and to Melchizedek, both non-Jewish figures of high religious stature. Seth became the centre of heretical Christian Gnostic sects, while Melchizedek was exalted in orthodox Christian doctrine, notably in the Epistle to the Hebrews, as the type of a priesthood superior to the Levitical Jewish priesthood. Surprisingly, however, Jethro, the non-Jewish 'priest of Midian', does not seem to have been utilized for a similar purpose, perhaps because of the well established Jewish tradition that he was converted to Judaism.)

Modern scholars have noted that the age of Enoch when 'God took him' was the same as the number of days in a solar year, and have speculated as to the meaning of this. One may also wonder what exactly is the meaning of the statement that Enoch 'walked with God', and what is meant by the bare mysterious statement, 'and he was not, for God took him.' Does this mean that he disappeared from sight, or that he was taken up to heaven in a chariot, like Elijah?

Cain

Particularly interesting, from the standpoint of the present enquiry, is the dislocation of Enoch's position in the order of the Sethite chronicle. Here he is placed as the great-grandson of Kenan, while in the Cainite chronicle he is actually Cain's son. If Enoch were put back as Kenan's son in the Sethite chronicle, only one slight displacement would be left, namely the reversal of the order of Mahalalel and Jared (for Irad and Mehujael). The displacement of Enoch is thus by far the largest displacement in the Sethite chronicle (which, as we have argued, is later than the Cainite chronicle), and we are bound to ask what is the motive for this change of the genealogical order.

I suggest that the Cainite chronicle is right and Enoch was Cain's son, not his great-grandson.[11] We can now collate what we know about Enoch from the Cainite chronicle with what we know about him from the Sethite chronicle, and we are left with the following information: (i) Enoch was Cain's son; (ii) Cain built a city and called it by the name of his son Enoch (Genesis 4:17); (iii) Enoch died young. What is suggested by this sequence of events?

It is hard to resist the conclusion that Enoch was sacrificed by his father Cain when he built the city, which he then named after his sacrificed son, whose spirit would act as guardian deity of the city and who would expect the honour of giving his name to the city for which he had willingly given his life.

Some support is given to this theory by Enoch's name, which comes from a word meaning 'to dedicate', or 'to inaugurate'. He was the dedicated one, whose willing sacrifice inaugurated the founding of the Kenite nation and the building of their city. The number 365, preserved in connection with Enoch's name, perhaps indicates that sun-worship was involved in this act of ritual sacrifice; the soul of Enoch may have gone to replenish the sun-god (as in the case of Aztec sacrifices) and the sun-god may have been worshipped from then on under the name of Enoch. He was 'with God' in the sense that the sun-god had incorporated him, thus making the Kenite nation kin to the sun-god and under his special protection. The later monotheistic legends, in which Enoch became the highest of the angels, were a reflection of this apotheosis.[12]

To the compilers of the Sethite chronicle, this was appalling primitivism and could not be allowed to appear openly in the pure Sethian line. Enoch was removed far from Cain in the line in order to minimize the connection between them, and the early death of Enoch was refined into the translation to heaven of a saint.

But according to this interpretation what has become of the slaying of Abel? If Cain's deed was in fact the sacrifice of his first-born son Enoch, why does it appear in the Cainite chronicle of the Bible as the murder of his brother Abel?

Cain

The sacrifice of a son is a more primitive rite than the sacrifice of a brother. Psychologically, it represents a deeper submission to the father-god, as if to say, 'You only are entitled to be a father. It is presumption on my part to be a father at all.' The sacrifice of a brother, however, makes no such utter submission; it is the sacrifice of a spare person, so to speak, not required for the continuance of the line. The sacrifice of a first-born son (the most usual form of the more primitive rite) constitutes a pathetic appeal to the god: 'See, I am prepared to destroy my own succession. I throw myself on your mercy, and in consideration of my preparedness for extinction, my utter reliance on your grace, grant me another son to continue my line.' It may well be that in the Kenite saga, in the form in which it reached the Israelites, a brother sacrifice had already taken the place of a son sacrifice as the inauguration rite of the Kenite tribe. This would be a sign of advancing civilization, and the beginning of the search for substitutes by which animals or captured prisoners or convicted criminals took the place of the original son sacrifice.

That there has been here the conversion to a brother sacrifice of a previous son sacrifice (whether in the Kenite saga itself or in its Israelite adaptation) is indicated by the very name of the sacrificed brother, Abel. For this name (more correctly, *hevel*; the transliteration 'Abel', like many other somewhat misleading forms, comes from the Septuagint) means literally 'vapour'. It is often used to mean simply 'emptiness'; it is the word used in Ecclesiastes in the repeated phrase, 'All is vanity'. That the victim of the first murder, the prototype of all innocent sufferers and martyrs, should have such a shadowy and even derogatory name is surprising; but this tells us that Abel never really existed and is a mere wraith substituted for a more substantial and shocking reality.

A number of questions about the Kenite saga present themselves to which there may be some possibility of giving an answer. First, we may ask the question, 'Who was the First Man in the Kenite saga?' Was it, perhaps, Cain himself? Did the Kenites regard their ancestor as not only the founder of the Kenite tribe or nation, but as the common ancestor of mankind? A good case might be made out for giving the answer 'yes' to this question. For several of the details given about Cain echo the details given about Adam in the Hebrew account of the early days of creation.

When Cain sinned (according to the Israelite account) by murdering Abel, he was cursed by God, and the terms of this curse are strikingly similar to the curse pronounced against Adam for his sin of eating the fruit of the Tree of Knowledge in the Garden of Eden. To Cain, God said, 'When thou tillest the ground, she shall not henceforth yield unto thee her strength' (Genesis 4:12). To Adam, God had already said, 'Cursed is the ground for thy sake; in toil shalt thou eat of it all the days of thy life. Thorns also and thistles shall it bring forth to thee' (Genesis 3:17–18). One could easily patch up some ad hoc explanation on the lines that, while Adam's curse made the ground infertile unless he expended labour on tilling it, in Cain's case, even labour would produce no results. Consequently, Adam, as a result of his Fall, became an agriculturist, gaining his living by 'the sweat of his brow' (Genesis 3:19), while Cain, after his sin, became a nomad, eating wild plants, since the earth would not respond to his agriculture: 'a fugitive and a wanderer shalt thou be in the earth' (Genesis 4:12). This, no doubt, is how the compilers of Genesis as we have it meant the matter to be understood. But it cannot have been so in the Kenite saga, for we soon find Cain building a city, which must have been sustained by agriculture, not by gathering wild plants. So if the curse against Cain was actually in the Kenite saga, and not entirely inserted by the Israelite compilers as part of their portrayal of Cain as a murderer, it must have been as part of a story of the Fall similar to that which we now find ascribed to Adam, only with Cain playing the part of the First Man, instead of Adam. If this is so, then it was Cain and his unnamed wife who were in the Garden of Eden, who ate the fruit of the forbidden tree and were expelled to gain their livelihood by hard tilling of the earth. This would make more sense too in sociological terms, for a transition from agriculture to nomadism is most unusual, while a transition from nomadism (idealized in the shape of the Garden of Eden, giving its fruits without the necessity of labour, and requiring only to be gathered) to agriculture is quite common.

A possible confirmation of the picture of Cain as the First Man is given by two telling phrases. After his sin, the Bible tells us, Cain 'dwelt in the land of Nod, on the east of Eden'. Why this sudden reintroduction of the name of Eden, supposedly by now left far behind since the expulsion of Cain's father and mother, Adam and Eve, many years before? But if Cain, in the Kenite saga, actually was the First Man himself, the introduction of the name of Eden is quite understandable. Having just been expelled from the Garden of Eden, Cain settles down in the land of Nod, eastward of Eden and adjacent to it. We have previously indeed come across the phrase 'east of Eden' (in the Hebrew almost, but not quite, identical to the phrase used here of Cain) precisely in the context of Adam's expulsion from Eden, saying that God posted cherubim and a flaming sword 'east of Eden . . . to guard the way to the tree of life' – presumably because Adam could be expected, if he decided to make a raid on Eden, to come from that direction. So both Adam and Cain are found 'east of Eden' after their sin, and a plausible conclusion is that Cain, like Adam, was once actually in Eden.

Cain

What then is the 'land of Nod' to which Cain was banished? The word *nod* in Hebrew means 'the aimless wandering of a fugitive'. The same word is used in the curse pronounced by God against Cain, when He condemns him to be 'a fugitive and a wanderer' (*na' va-nad*). Yet there is a strange paradox here, for it is in the 'land of wandering' that Cain settles down and builds a city. Moreover, the curse pronounced against Cain never comes into effect, for he does *not* become a 'fugitive and a wanderer', but, on the contrary, a city-patriarch of a most respectable kind. The solution of this paradox is very simple. The expression the 'land of Nod' does not mean the 'land of wandering', but the 'land of exile' – that is, exile from the Garden of Eden. Every land other than Eden is the 'land of Nod', and however much we settle down, we can never quite forget our first home or quite suppress the longings of the refugee. Thus, in the Kenite saga, Cain the First Man entered the land of Nod in this sense, but there was no contradiction in the fact that he then proceeded to build a city and to become a settled person, in so far as such a condition is possible to fallen man, in exile from the Garden of Eden. But in the Biblical account of Cain, in which Cain had become not the First Man but the first murderer, the graphic word *nod*, originally descriptive of Cain's sense of exile from Eden, was used to describe the wanderings of the guilty murderer, expelled from the settled habitations of man, and Cain became a literal wanderer – a description that turned out to be contradictory when it became necessary to incorporate in the chronicle further details of the Kenite saga showing Cain to have been a city-patriarch.

A further tell-tale echo showing Cain to have been the First Man in the Kenite saga relates to Cain's wife. Genesis tells us that, after Cain settled in the land of Nod, 'Cain knew his wife; and she conceived and bore Enoch' (4:17). About Adam, the Bible tells us that, after the expulsion from Eden, 'Adam knew Eve his wife, and she conceived and bore Cain' (4:1). Now of all the names in the Sethite and Cainite chronicles, Adam and Cain are the only ones of whom this is said. Even of Seth, the founder of the Sethian line, it is not said that he 'knew his wife'. Indeed, no wives are mentioned at all, after Adam and Cain, until we come to Noah in the Sethian line and his counterpart (as it will be argued later) Lamech in the Cainite line, both regarded as the initiators of a fresh start for humanity. So this impressive phrase, 'knew his wife', signifying an especially important occasion of sexual intercourse, is reserved for initiators, and the use of it in the case of Cain, supposedly a reprobate and the ancestor of an abortive line, reinforces the view that in the original Kenite saga he had the place occupied in the Hebrew Bible by Adam.

Chapter Three

The Israelite account of Cain

We now turn to a closer examination of the Cain story as it was developed by the Israelite compilers of the Bible, who made Cain into a murderer. In the religion of Israel, human sacrifice had been declared an abominable sin by the time these early chapters of Genesis reached their present form (though there is some question whether human sacrifice was completely outlawed at an earlier period of Israelite religion).[1] For example, Psalm 106:37 indicts those who 'sacrificed their sons and their daughters to demons, and shed innocent blood, the blood of their sons and of their daughters'. The Torah (Deuteronomy 12:31) solemnly bans human sacrifice: 'Thou shalt not do so unto the Lord thy God; for every abomination to the Lord, which He hateth, have they [the pagans] done unto their gods; for even their sons and their daughters do they burn in the fire to their gods.' The prophets too inveigh against human sacrifice: 'They have built the high places of Topheth, which is in the valley of Hinnom, to burn their sons and their daughters in the fire; which I commanded not, neither came it into My mind' (Jeremiah 7:31).

In Israelite religion, the place of human sacrifice was taken by the sacrifice of animals. Even this, however, did not carry with it the full connotation that had belonged to human sacrifice; for the animal sacrifices of the Israelites had no magical saving power, but were merely gifts to God on the Sabbaths and festivals, or (in the case of sin-offerings) marked the fact that repentance had taken place on the part of the offerer, and acted as the formal completion of his atonement. Thus the system of animal sacrifices represented not merely a form of substitution for human sacrifice, but a denial of the very principle of human sacrifice, namely that such sacrifice produced magical effects, either in the form of physical protection or of atonement for offences against the god quite independently of a process of repentance.[2]

The Israelite compilers of Genesis found in the Kenite saga a story of a human sacrifice of the type known as a 'foundation sacrifice', that is, one offered at the foundation of a city or nation. Possibly, as argued above, the story was already somewhat disguised, and had become a homicide for which ritual purification was required. If so, the Israelite compilers still sensed in the story a defence and justification of the institution of human sacrifice, for they changed the story not only into one of plain murder, but into a polemic in favour of animal sacrifice.

It has often been argued that what we have in the Cain and Abel story is an example of an ancient conflict between the agriculturist and the shepherd.[3] Certainly the Bible says explicitly that Cain was a 'tiller of the ground', while Abel was a 'keeper of sheep'. Nevertheless, if our argument so far has been correct, this contrast is not part of the earliest form of the story, in which Abel did not figure at all, and the victim of Cain's slaying was his son Enoch. If the contrast between Cain's tilling of the ground and Abel's sheep-rearing dates from the Israelite recasting of the story, no fundamental rivalry between these activities can be intended, as the Israelites respected both sheep-rearing (the occupation of their ancestors Abraham, Isaac and Jacob) and tilling the ground (the main activity of the Holy Land, and the basis of the tithes by which the Temple and the priesthood were maintained). If anything, tilling the ground was the more respected during the period of occupation of the Holy Land, and there even came a time (in the post-Biblical period) when sheep-raising was banned, except in semi-desert regions, because of its bad effect on agriculture.

It seems unlikely, therefore, that the point of the story is the conflict between shepherds and farmers, told from the point of view of the shepherds. After all, Adam himself, in the previous chapter, was told by God to till the ground, and this is evidently regarded as the normal lot of mankind, even though resulting from the curse incurred by the primal sin.

It has been argued, consequently, that the contrast is not between farming and sheep-rearing but between Cain's meanness and Abel's generosity.[4] There is some ground for this interpretation in the text, since Cain, it is said, merely 'brought of the fruit of the ground an offering unto the Lord', while of Abel it is said that he brought 'of the firstlings of his flock and of the fat thereof'. However, this reduces the story to a rather trivial level, making Cain into a petty-minded villain compounding stinginess with violence. It is much more likely that the contrast between the offerings is meant to bring out the inherent superiority of animal offerings over vegetable offerings, since the former have features that the latter necessarily lack, i.e. firstlings and fat. Animals, considered as a substitute for human sacrifice, are clearly much closer to the real thing than plants. In particular, the all-important place of the first-born in sacrifice can be retained. True, there is such a thing as the 'first fruit', but this is a very pale imitation compared with the first-born of an animal. As for the 'fat', this refers not to subcutaneous fat, but to the intestinal fat, which played a great

The Israelite account of Cain

part in all Near Eastern sacrifice as being especially sacred to the gods; it is forbidden as food to Orthodox Jews to this day.[5] It must have been important in human sacrifices, for some reason not easy to recover.

The contrast between the sacrifices of Cain and Abel, then, is between the types of sacrifices they offered, not between the inherent quality of their offerings, or between the occupations of the sacrificers. Animal sacrifice, the story is telling us, is better than vegetable sacrifice, and better fitted to please God. That Cain was a tiller of the earth is told us not to denigrate him on that account, but to explain the fact that he brought a vegetable sacrifice; he ought to have brought an animal sacrifice, like his brother Abel, and if he did not have any animals, he should have procured them from Abel, just as so many farmers in later Israel procured animals from shepherds or dairy-farmers in order to fulfil the requirements of the Jewish law of animal sacrifice, without in any way being regarded as inferior in their occupation.

It has been argued (especially by the noted scholar S.H. Hooke[6]) that a contrast between animal sacrifice and vegetable sacrifice cannot be the point of the story, since in later Israel vegetable sacrifices were offered as well as animal sacrifices. But a study of the Israelite sacrifices shows that the vegetable element was always subordinate to the animal element, and acted, so to speak, as an accompaniment to the main dish, except in the case of some relatively unimportant types of sacrifices.

The recognition that the story of Cain and Abel is mainly about the superiority of animal sacrifice (as the story has been worked up by the Israelite compilers) helps us to make sense of a very baffling passage which has defeated all commentators. This is the speech of God to Cain, after observing that Cain's 'countenance had fallen', because of the lack of favour shown to his vegetable sacrifice. This is translated in the Authorized Version as follows:

If thou doest well, shalt thou not be accepted? and if thou doest not well, sin lieth at the door. And unto thee shall be his desire and thou shalt rule over him. (4:7)

The expression 'sin lieth at the door' has been taken to refer to a personified figure of evil, lying in wait to trap mankind. In support of this interpretation, modern scholars have cited the use in certain Babylonian texts of an expression meaning 'the croucher' (a word cognate to the Hebrew term *rovetz* used in this passage, meaning 'crouching' or 'lying'), signifying a kind of malignant demon.[7]

Against this well established interpretation is the fact that the Hebrew Bible does not personify evil or ascribe ill-doing to the influence of demons. If this passage refers to such an idea, then it is

The Israelite account of Cain

unique in the whole Hebrew Bible, and should be regarded as the intrusion of an uncharacteristically dualistic philosophy of morality. There is no Devil (in the Christian sense of the word) in the Hebrew Bible. The Fall of Adam is not ascribed to the machinations of the Devil, or Satan, but to the ill-will of one of the animals, the serpent. (The idea that the serpent was merely the outward guise of Satan is a much later development, found in certain Apocryphal books rejected from the Jewish canon, but fully accepted into Christianity.) Satan is mentioned in the Book of Job, but as one of the 'sons of God', i.e. as one of the angels, whose task it is to accuse human beings and bring their faults before God (this idea is continued in the Talmud, which calls Satan the 'counsel for the prosecution' – *meqatreg*). Only once in the whole Bible is temptation ascribed to an 'evil spirit', and that is in the very late, post-Exilic work Chronicles, where David's temptation in the matter of the census is explained as due to the activity of Satan (I Chronicles 21:7), though in the corresponding passage in the earlier account in Samuel, Satan is not mentioned (II Samuel 24:16). The appearance of dualism in the latest book of the Bible and in the Apocrypha (possibly owing to the influence of Persian religion) is one thing; its appearance in Genesis in the form of a demon lying in wait to tempt mankind to sin is another – such an interpretation, however well established, of the passage before us is surprising and suspect.

Fortunately, another interpretation is possible. The Hebrew word for 'sin', in the phrase 'sin lieth [or croucheth] at the door', can equally well mean 'sin-offering'.[8] The whole phrase can therefore mean 'the sin-offering [i.e. the sheep] is crouching at the door'. The word here meaning 'crouching' (*rovetz*) is that regularly used in the Bible for a crouching animal (see Genesis 49:9, 'lion'; 49:14, 'ass'; Isaiah 11:6, 'the leopard shall lie down with the kid'), though it is true that the same verb can sometimes mean 'to lie in wait'. The hostile meaning of the verb is here quite unnecessary; all that is meant is that if means of atonement are required, the sheep or goat that lies down or crouches at the door (i.e. is easily available) will serve this purpose. If the word *rovetz* is taken to be a noun, rather than a participle (as seems required by the fact that the word for sin-offering – *hat'at* – is feminine) then the meaning 'crouching beast' fits the sin-offering far better than the demon.

Consequently, the cryptic saying that has been regarded as a theological apophthegm of a dualistic kind quite uncharacteristic of the Hebrew Bible turns out, on inspection, to be something much more simple and direct: a recommendation of animal sacrifice as a means of atonement for sin.

In support of this interpretation, we may now turn to consideration of the final section of v.7: 'And unto thee shall be his desire, and thou shalt rule over him.' This has been taken to refer to the demon, whose desire is to destroy man by tempting him to evil; but this desire can be frustrated, with the result that man rules over the demon instead. This interpretation is open to several objections, but the main one is that it ignores the strong similarity of this saying, supposedly about a demon, to the saying made previously about woman in relation to man. Eve was told by God, after the Fall, 'Thy desire shall be to thy husband, and he shall rule over thee' (Genesis 3:16). The expression 'Thy desire shall be to thy husband' does not signify any destructive feeling of woman towards man; it simply means that woman (as a result of the Fall) has become subordinate to man, and naturally suppresses her own ambitions in favour of those of her husband, or finds her chief happiness in ministering to him (as Milton put it, 'He for God alone, she for God in him'). The expression 'and he shall rule over thee' does not signify that man conquers and subdues the aggressive assaults of woman, but only completes the meaning of the first part of the sentence; because woman now subordinates her desires to his, he becomes her natural lord and rules over her. (It should be noted also that this implies that in an unfallen state of mankind no such subordination exists.)

Using the model of the identical phrasing in relation to man and woman, we can now understand the meaning of God's saying to Cain about the sin-offering. He is saying, 'You need not scruple to use animals as sacrifices, for animals are subordinate to man.' The sentence is thus an expansion of the previous formulation, 'Have dominion over the fish of the sea, and over the fowl of the air, and over every living thing that moveth upon the earth' (Genesis 1:28). The principle that animals are subordinated by divine decree to man implies that man may kill animals for purposes of sacrifice (not, apparently, for purposes of food, as the Talmud points out;[9] this right was not given to man until after the Flood; see Genesis 1:29 and 9:3). The general formula of the subordination of animals to man is the same as the formula of the subordination of woman to man. The general formula points to the psychological sense of subordination implanted by God in animals, i.e. their inborn fear of man and willingness to be domesticated by him, and what is regarded as a similar inborn sense of inferiority felt by women towards men after the Fall.

Thus a paraphrase of God's saying to Cain would run as follows: 'Why has your countenance fallen? You should learn from this incident that vegetable offerings are unacceptable to God, not that you personally are unacceptable. Just bear the lesson in mind and bring Me animal sacrifices in future. They are easily obtainable and they are of great benefit to you, as they can bring about the atonement of any

The Israelite account of Cain

sins you may commit. Do not be worried about the apparent cruelty of depriving animals of life, for it is My divine decree that animals may be used for this purpose, and you may see that animals regard themselves as inferior to man.'

Cain, however, did not listen to this advice, and the result was that he killed Abel. The moral of the whole episode, therefore, is: 'He who refrains from sacrificing animals ends by murdering (sacrificing) human beings.' This moral is in fact a historical truth, for it was through the substitution of animal sacrifice that human sacrifice was gradually abolished.

The Israelite compilers have thus transformed a story originally about a human sacrifice into propaganda in favour of animal sacrifice. This does not mean that the above analysis exhausts the meaning of the story or its function in the total Biblical scheme. Another aspect of the story is the rival-brothers motif, which is of great importance in the Bible, for several reasons: it forms an integral part of the narrowing-down process by which God's election finally lights on the Israelites, after passing over various other strands of humanity; it is a theme of the younger brother triumphing over the elder (i.e. securing the favour of the father); e.g., besides Abel and Cain, there are Isaac and Ishmael, Jacob and Esau, Joseph and his brethren, David and his brothers – a theme that, among other purposes, validates the claim of the parvenu nation, the Israelites, to usurp the position of 'God's firstborn'; as a psychological theme, it marks the strongly established patriarchy of Israelite culture, by which the chief struggle is not between father and son (as it was in the mythology of the Greek culture, where patriarchy was somewhat weakly established) but between brothers competing for the succession in the patriarchal line; and, on the more positive side, it marks the theme of reconciliation and love between brothers (here initiated by the basic principle of being one's 'brother's keeper'), which is the chief problem and preoccupation of a progressive patriarchal society, finding its Biblical expression in the reconciliation of Joseph and his brothers, but also in the 'band of brothers' theme throughout Jewish history (e.g. the Maccabaean revolt).

Such multiplicity of meaning in the Cain and Abel story warns us against a narrow concept of interpretation in the understanding of any Biblical story. Nevertheless, the interpretation outlined above, in terms of propaganda for animal sacrifice, is valid within the local context of the story (and not necessarily without connections with the wider themes of the story in the total Biblical context).

We may now turn again to the aspect of the Israelite version of the Cain and Abel story that is of special interest for the main enquiry of this book: the banishment of Cain. The chief difficulty here, from a

The Israelite account of Cain

literal standpoint, is: why did not Cain suffer death as punishment for his crime of murder? The Bible is most explicit elsewhere that only death can atone for murder: 'Whoever sheds the blood of man, by man shall his blood be shed; for God made man in His own image' (Genesis 9:6); 'Ye shall take no ransom for the life of a murderer that is guilty of death; but he shall surely be put to death' (Numbers 35:31). Israelite religion differs here from other ancient religions of the Near East, which laid down provisions for the paying of blood-money;[10] life, in Israel, could never be regarded as a commodity. Yet in the case of Cain, the first murderer, where one would have thought the application of the principle 'a life for a life' was especially important as a guiding example, Cain is let off with a sentence of banishment and even given protection to prevent him from suffering death for his crime. The Midrash offers the legal solution that Cain had not been warned not to commit murder, and therefore by Mishnaic law could not be executed;[11] but this applies only to capital punishment carried out by a human court, and does not preclude execution by the hand of God, which was expected to occur in cases of premeditated murder in which the conditions for human punishment were unfulfilled.

On the basis of previous argument we can reply that Cain's sentence of banishment, in the original Kenite story, was not a punishment for murder or a condemnation to wandering, but expulsion from the Garden of Eden in the manner ascribed in the Hebrew Bible to Adam. This, however, does not answer our question completely, for there are features in Cain's banishment that do not belong to the Garden of Eden story and suggest that there is another source in the background of the banishment.

When Cain was banished, he was given protection by God against possible attackers. This does not form part of the story of the expulsion from Eden, but is clearly part of a different type of story, in which a criminal is condemned to banishment, but, because of the nature of his crime, is given divine protection. There has been some telescoping here, by which the banishment of Cain from Eden is made to combine with a different kind of banishment more appropriate to the ritual killing now ascribed to Cain. Cain, in the Hebrew account, has become a murderer, but the characteristics of his banishment show traces of an intermediate stage in which he was a Sacred Executioner.

The Sacred Executioner is banished to the desert because he has performed a human sacrifice, of which society, at this stage, disapproves, only resorting to it at times of great desperation. By banishing the Executioner to the desert, society excommunicates him, saying, in effect, 'He is not one of us. We are not responsible for what he did.' He becomes an outlaw and is not protected by the laws of society, so that it is no crime to kill him; indeed, it is a meritorious act,

The Israelite account of Cain

not only because of the horror of his crime, but because, being an outlaw, he is to be feared, and can only make a living through violence; he has become a creature of the desert and a devotee of the demons of the desert. At the same time, it cannot be forgotten that he performed an act that saved society. It cannot be forgotten, either, that in performing the sacrifice, he played a priestly role. Consequently, he is given protection, not by society, but by the god who demanded the sacrifice and whose cruel anger he thus appeased. The form of protection is not that which society affords, i.e. the protection of the law, but a reversion to the primitive law of vengeance. Anyone who kills him will suffer a dreadful vengeance – seven lives for one; the god himself undertakes that this vengeance will be carried out on the family of the killer of the Executioner. In token of this protection, the Executioner wears a sacred sign, whose significance is known to all.[12]

Two questions may be dealt with summarily. It has often been asked why Cain was afraid of being killed, since the only people in the world at the time were his father and mother. The Midrash answers that he was afraid of the animals, whose awe of man had been removed in his case by his crime.[13] On a similar level, one might reply that he was afraid of future generations of men. The real answer, however, is that the story at this point is not concerned with Cain but with the Sacred Executioner and his role in ancient religion. The story of privileged banishment has become attached to Cain, but was doubtless told of many other mythical figures, as a validation of a tribal institution, the rarely performed rite of human sacrifice and its attendant modes of shifting of responsibility.

The other point is the often repeated view that the story of Cain marks the foundation of the institution of the blood-feud.[14] This view can be safely rejected. The blood-feud never required sevenfold revenge, and, in any case, the Cain story does not concern the duty of the kindred of a murdered person to avenge him, but rather the intention of God to carry out sevenfold vengeance. If the story concerned the origin of the blood-feud, its purpose would be far better served by portraying Cain as being killed in retaliation for his murder of Abel than by showing him being protected; the so-called blood-feud apparently applies only to the killer of Cain, but not to the first murderer, Cain himself in relation to his murder of Abel. The story thus has nothing to do with the blood-feud, which applied in the case of a normal, straightforward murder; it is concerned with a very special case, the performance of a ritual sacrifice, where the Executioner was expressly exempted from the blood-feud by his token of divine protection.

Considerable light can be thrown on the Sacred Executioner and on the story of Cain by considering the ritual of the Scapegoat on the Day

The Israelite account of Cain

of Atonement (Leviticus 16). A distinctive feature of this day of purging from sin was the offering of two goats, one of which was killed, and the other sent out into the desert. The roles of the two goats were not fixed beforehand, but decided by lot on the actual day. The goat that was killed was said to be 'for the Lord', and the other, which was sent into the desert, was said to be 'for Azazel'. The Bible says:

> And Aaron shall present the goat upon which the lot fell for the Lord, and offer him for a sin-offering. But the goat, on which the lot fell for Azazel, shall be set alive before the Lord, to make atonement for him, to send him away for Azazel into the wilderness. (Leviticus 16:9–10)

In the second sentence, what is the meaning of the phrase 'to make atonement for him'? The English preposition 'for' here is ambiguous. Does it mean 'for his sins' or 'for what was done to him'? In the Hebrew, this ambiguity does not exist, for throughout the passage when the meaning 'to atone for someone's sins' is required the preposition *be'ad* is used (see, for example, v.17: 'and he shall make atonement for (*be'ad*) himself and for (*be'ad*) his household and for [*be'ad*] all the assembly of Israel'); while if the sense 'to atone for what was done to something' is required, a different preposition, *'al*, is used (for example v.16: 'and he shall make atonement for [*'al*] the holy place, because of the uncleannesses of the children of Israel').

In the case of the Scapegoat (i.e. the goat that was sent into the desert: the translation 'scapegoat' is that of the Authorized Version based on a mistaken Septuagint etymology of the word 'Azazel'[15]) quoted above, it is said that he 'shall be set alive before the Lord, *to make atonement for him*, to send him away for Azazel into the wilderness'. In the phrase that I have italicized, the preposition used is *'al*, and the phrase ought therefore to mean 'to make atonement for what was done to him'. For what was done to whom? The phrase has been found very puzzling by commentators, who have suggested various explanations (e.g. that the preposition should be translated here as 'on' or 'over' or 'by means of', so that the pronoun 'him' refers to the Scapegoat himself, through whom atonement is being made in general for the community). These, however, are strained interpretations; one would expect explicit mention to be made either of the person or persons whose sins are being expiated or of the person, institution or thing which, being sinned against, necessitates expiation. But the use of the preposition *'al* does suggest that we are being told the latter. What then is the reference of the pronoun 'him'? I suggest that it can be regarded very naturally as referring to the *other* goat, the one that was killed (mentioned in the previous verse). What is being said is that the Scapegoat is sent into the wilderness to atone for what was done to 'him', i.e. to the sacrificed goat.

It seems then that an ancient formula explaining the function of the Scapegoat has survived in the text of the Hebrew Bible, even though the redactors of the final version of the text did not understand the formula, and explained the function of the Scapegoat in a different way. For, later in the passage, the Scapegoat is represented as bearing *all* the sins of the congregation, not merely the guilt of sacrificing the other goat: 'And Aaron shall lay both his hands upon the head of the live goat, and confess over him all the iniquities of the children of Israel, and all their transgressions, even all their sins; and he shall put them upon the head of the goat, and shall send him away by the hand of an appointed man into the wilderness' (16:21). If the function of the Scapegoat was really so all-embracing in its atonement, it is difficult to see why the other goat needed to be sacrificed at all; but this difficulty is actually covered in the passage by making the sacrificed goat atone only for offences against the sanctity of the shrine (v.16), while the Scapegoat atones for all other sins. This division of labour, however, is likely to be an ad hoc explanation brought forward at a time when the original reason why there had to be two goats was no longer understood or had been forgotten.

Originally, then, the two goats represented two men, one of whom was sacrificed and the other sent into the desert, where he was no longer a member of the community of the god, but instead became a devotee of the desert demon, Azazel. And the reason why he was sent away was that he was the man who had acted as Executioner of the human victim who died for the sins of the community in order to avert the wrath of the god. An interesting detail that we can glean from the Scapegoat ritual is that the victim was chosen by lot. This was yet another distancing device, by which responsibility could be shifted from the community. It was not any human member of the community who singled out this man to be sacrificed, but the god himself, who made the lot fall upon him. Perhaps, originally, the whole community submitted to the casting of lots; and it was only at a later stage that the lot chose between only two men, one of whom died while the other acted as the Executioner. Where the lot was cast wider, it was not necessary to have a Sacred Executioner at all, since the whole responsibility could be placed on the god. There is Biblical evidence of such a stage in the story of Achan (Joshua 7). While the Israelites were invading the Holy Land they suffered an unexpected defeat at Ai, which caused a catastrophic loss of morale at a critical juncture. The crisis was solved by the sacrifice of Achan of the tribe of Judah, chosen by lot (as it appears, though not quite explicitly) from the whole nation of Israel. This is, of course, not represented as a human sacrifice, which to the compilers of the narrative would have been an abomination, but as a punishment for hidden sacrilege.

The Israelite account of Cain

In the ritual of the Scapegoat, then, we have a later, uncomprehending account of a very primitive rite, one not far removed from the performance of human sacrifice itself. Animals had taken the place of human beings in the sacrificial system, but enough of the old guilt remained to make necessary an animal substitute even for the figure of the banished Executioner in the old murderous ritual, an animal who was sent into the desert just as the Executioner had been. In time, the reason for this strange rite was forgotten, and new meanings were attached to it. The name Azazel, originally that of a desert demon,[16] was retained in the rite and in the Biblical account, but its meaning was forgotten, and had become incompatible with the monotheistic faith of Israel. Some interpreted it to mean 'the goat who escaped' (i.e. scapegoat), as if the name were formed from the combination of *ez*, meaning 'goat' and *azal*, meaning 'to go', or 'to escape'. Others interpreted it to mean 'hard mountain'; this interpretation arose at a time when it had become customary to kill the Scapegoat in the desert by throwing it over a cliff, a rite not prescribed in the Bible and flatly contradictory to the original meaning of the ritual, if the above analysis is correct.[17]

The Scapegoat should not be regarded as the equivalent of the animal in the Babylonian spring New Year festival to which it has often been likened.[18] This animal was loaded with the evil exorcized from the temple, and then thrown into the Euphrates, after which all those who had handled it became impure. The Scapegoat, on the contrary (in the original rite as described in the Bible), was sent away to wander free in the desert, not killed. There is something casual about the way it is sent away 'by the hand of an appointed man' (Leviticus 16:21). The word translated as 'appointed' here is in Hebrew '*itti*, which means literally 'timely'. The rendering 'appointed' is probably incorrect, indeed almost the opposite of the correct rendering, which is 'someone who happens to be there at the time'. This man did not even have to be a priest.[19] The reason for this casualness is that the Scapegoat is really supposed to wander away of his own volition, like the lonely figure of the Executioner, so only the minimum escort is provided, in an ad hoc manner, to see that he actually does go into the desert, and the man who acts as escort is treated as if he had not played an important part in the rite. For in the original role of the Sacred Executioner, it is probable that after performing the sacrifice, the Executioner actually fled away from the altar with every appearance of guilt. Any assistance given to him in his flight would mar the appearance of lonely individual guilt by implicating the assembled community in his act.

A better simulation of the flight of the Executioner is to be found in another rite, in which a certain similarity to the Scapegoat ritual has been noted by scholars (Leviticus 14).[20] This is the ceremony of the purification of a leper, after he has been cured of his illness. The ceremony involves two birds, one of which is killed and the other loosed 'into the open field' (14:7). It is noteworthy that the living bird, before being released, is dipped in the blood of the sacrificed bird. The man to be purified is then sprinkled with the blood of the sacrificed bird seven times and becomes clean, and then the living bird is released. This puzzling ceremony can be fully understood if the living bird is regarded as representing the Sacred Executioner, who, in more primitive times, cleansed a whole tribe – the leper-cleansing ceremony is probably derived from the more serious rite involving the whole community – by sacrificing a human being and then taking flight.

Another feature of the leper-cleansing ritual is of some importance to our enquiry. This is the use of 'cedar-wood, and scarlet thread, and hyssop'. These too are to be dipped into the blood of the sacrificed bird (14:6). No-one has been able to explain the meaning of these symbols. Jewish tradition, as found in the Mishnah and other writings, stated that these three substances, cedar-wood, scarlet thread (wool), and hyssop, were to be bound together, not used separately. The binding material was the thread, which was called the 'strip' – literally 'tongue' – 'of crimson' (*lashon shel zehorit*).[21]

The same combination of cedar-wood, scarlet thread and hyssop is found in connection with the burning of the Red Cow. While it was burning to ashes (which would later be used for purification purposes) the officiating priest was told to 'take cedar-wood, and hyssop, and scarlet thread, and cast it into the midst of the burning of the Cow' (Numbers 19:6). According to Jewish tradition (Mishnah, Parah 3:11), the cedar-wood and hyssop had to be bound together, as in the rite of the leper, the scarlet thread again being used as the binding material.

In the case of the Scapegoat, the Bible makes no mention of the 'crimson tongue' as forming part of the ceremony. But in Jewish tradition it played a prominent role. We are told in the Mishnah that the 'crimson tongue' was tied between the horns of the Scapegoat. Another piece of red thread was hung in the porch of the Temple (according to a late and Apocryphal tradition), and, at the moment when the Scapegoat died (by being thrown over a cliff), the red thread in the Temple turned white, as a token of God's forgiveness. More reliable is the tradition that a red thread was also bound between the horns of the goat that was slaughtered.[22]

The probable explanation of all this is that the combination of cedar-wood and hyssop, bound together by scarlet or crimson thread, formed an implement for sprinkling used in sacrifice. The Bible pre-

The Israelite account of Cain

serves the use of hyssop alone for this purpose (Numbers 19:18). Hyssop was also used as a brush for daubing the lintels of the doors of the Israelites with blood from the sacrificed lamb on the occasion of the tenth plague in Egypt (Exodus 12:22). The Sacred Executioner used this implement to sprinkle the blood of the human sacrifice on the altar, and when he embarked on his ritual flight, he took this sprinkling implement with him and bound it permanently on his person as a sign of his identity and immunity as a sacred being. This was the 'sign' that God gave to Cain 'lest any finding him should smite him'. Long years later, the Israelites, sending the Scapegoat into the desert, bound a thread of scarlet on the head of the animal, not knowing why they did it, and having to invent a fanciful explanation of it. In the two other most primitive purification rites of the Israelites, that of the Red Cow and that of the leper, the old sprinkling implement was included, but without any functional purpose.

The hyssop itself was the truly functional part of the implement, being a natural choice for sprinkling because of its shape. The cedarwood was no doubt included in these special sacrifices because it was at the upper limit of the vegetable kingdom, just as the hyssop was at the lowest limit: King Solomon, says the Bible, 'spoke of trees, from the cedar that is in Lebanon even unto the hyssop that springeth out of the wall' (I Kings 4:33). The woollen thread, on the other hand, represented the animal kingdom together with its animal dye. The complicity of all nature was thus secured in the sacrifice; all the universe was guilty, but not the community. In fleeing to the desert with the blood-stained and blood-coloured sprinkler, the Executioner became a creature of the wild, part of nature; thus the execution became a natural event, what we would call an 'accident'.

Thus the story of Cain's crime and punishment has many layers of meaning, deriving from different historical epochs and different literary sources; but the most compelling aspect and level of the story has always been that of the Sacred Executioner, banished from society for an appalling crime, which yet is so equivocal in nature that his life is spared and even protected by a sign given to him by God and recognized by all men. We may ask how this aspect entered the Biblical story; for it seems incompatible either with Kenite reverence for Cain as their ancestor, or with Israelite dismissal of human sacrifice as mere murder, for which the punishment is death. I have suggested that even in the Kenite saga, Cain may have had to retire to the desert for a while after his slaying of his son Enoch, in order to be purified from the effects of the sacrifice. This could well have been the germ of a story of Cain, circulating not in the Kenite tribe itself but in neighbouring, sometimes hostile, tribes, in which Cain was depicted as a murderer, but of some awesome equivocal kind that made him an

The Israelite account of Cain

outlaw and yet put him under the protection of a savage desert god. It was from such a source that the Israelites, at that time themselves not quite free from belief in the occasional terrifying necessity of human sacrifice, derived a story that was sufficiently denigratory to dislodge Cain from his place in the Kenite saga as honoured hero and original patriarch of all humanity, but still allowed him some status as the progenitor of a tribe to whom they owed a cultural debt.

Chapter Four

Lamech

In Chapter 4 of Genesis we find, compressed into only two sentences (vv. *17–18*), the genealogy of the descendants of Cain that, as has been argued above, really forms the basis for the whole Biblical narrative of the pre-Flood era. The two sentences run as follows:

And Cain knew his wife; and she conceived, and bore Enoch; and he builded a city, and called the name of the city after the name of his son Enoch. And unto Enoch was born Irad; and Irad begot Mehujael; and Mehujael begot Methushael; and Methushael begot Lamech.

The rest of what remains of the Kenite saga in the Hebrew Bible consists of five sentences, partly very cryptic, concerning Lamech and his three sons (vv. *19–24*). These sentences are of extraordinary interest, and a close examination of them will throw light on the interconnections between the Israelite story of the Flood and the Kenite saga. It will also throw further light on the theme of human sacrifice and its treatment by the Israelite compilers of the Hebrew narrative.

The five sentences in question are as follows (Jewish Publication Society of America translation):

And Lamech took unto him two wives; the name of the one was Adah, and the name of the other Zillah. And Adah bore Jabal; he was the father of such as dwell in tents and have cattle. And his brother's name was Jubal; he was the father of all such as handle the harp and pipe. And Zillah, she also bore Tubal-Cain, the forger of every cutting instrument of brass and iron; and the sister of Tubal-Cain was Naamah. And Lamech said unto his wives:

> Adah and Zillah, hear my voice;
> Ye wives of Lamech, hearken unto my speech;
> For I have slain a man for wounding me,
> And a young man for bruising me;
> If Cain shall be avenged sevenfold,
> Truly Lamech seventy and sevenfold.

As indicated by the Jewish Publication Society (JPS) lineation, the speech of Lamech is in verse, a fact that is important for its interpretation.

Lamech

A question that it is natural to ask at once is 'Was there an account of the Flood in the Kenite saga?'. Since the Israelites, as we have seen, took so much information about the early history of mankind from the Kenites, it seems probable that they took their information about the Flood from the same source, combined, perhaps, with information from other sources. But what is left of the Kenite saga in the Bible says nothing whatever about the Flood. It stops abruptly with Lamech's speech to his wives, the import of which has been an age-old puzzle. We are not told explicitly that Lamech, his wives and his three sons died in the Flood, but since the line of Cain is traced no further, and since Noah and his family, descended not from Cain but from Seth, were the only survivors of the Flood according to the Biblical narrative, we are evidently intended to regard the three sons of Lamech as the final generation of the line of Cain.

If this is so, it immediately becomes an enigma that they are described not as the last of their line but as founders and patriarchs. For Jabal, the eldest, is described as the 'father of such as dwell in tents and have cattle'; Jubal is described as the 'father of all such as handle the harp and pipe; while the youngest son, Tubal-Cain, is described as the pioneer of the art of metal-working. (The description in Hebrew of Tubal-Cain is difficult, and is translated by the New English Bible as the 'master of all coppersmiths and blacksmiths'.) If the three sons of Lamech taught mankind the arts of cattle-rearing, music and metal-working, they had very little time to give such instruction and could only have handed on their knowledge by transmitting it to Noah, with whom it is unlikely that they were acquainted.

This leads us to ask another question, which is obvious enough, yet seems to have escaped the attention of all Bible commentators. Why did it take mankind so long to develop the arts of cattle-rearing, music and metal-working? According to the Bible account, these arts were first invented by the sons of Lamech at the very end of the first era of human history, and not near its beginning, as one would expect. Why was it that during those long generations before the Flood (comprising 1,656 years, according to the Sethite chronicle in the Masoretic text, though the Samaritan text makes it less, at 1,307 years, and the Septuagint makes it more, at 2,242 years) no-one thought of living in tents, or rearing cattle, or playing music, or working metals? But is it indeed the case that the sons of Lamech were the first to develop these arts? As far as cattle-rearing is concerned, the Bible itself tells us that Abel was a rearer of sheep. Also, we are told that Cain built a city, and he is hardly likely to have been able to do this without some knowledge of metal-working. Why indeed is his name Cain, which means 'smith', if he knew nothing of the arts of the smith? Finally, we may ask why Jabal was the pioneer tent-dweller when his remote ancestor Cain was a city-dweller. This seems to be a retrogression, rather than an advance, in civilization as it is evidently meant to be, since it is mentioned together with inventions of primary importance.

There is a very simple answer to all these questions. It is that in the original Kenite saga the three sons of Lamech were not the last generation before the Flood, but the first generation after it, or, rather, they were the counterparts of that other trio, the three sons of Noah – Shem, Ham and Japheth – who lived through the Flood in the Ark, and became the three patriarchs of the world after the Flood, fathering the three main branches of mankind. This explains not only the symmetry of the three sons in each case, but also why we find that the sons of Lamech were all pioneers. They had to be pioneers because they were starting a new world; this makes much more sense than being pioneers while winding up an old one. It is now easy to understand why Jabal was the 'father of those who dwell in tents', despite the fact that he came from a long line of city-dwellers. In a brand new world a new and more primitive start had to be made, before mankind could work its way back to city-building once more.

The strange dislocation that we find in the Hebrew Bible, by which pioneers come at the end of an epoch instead of at its beginning, is a by-product of the Bible's drastic adaptation of the Kenite saga, by which the line of Cain, instead of being the main line of humanity, was diverted into a blind alley. But once we discover what has happened, an important corollary appears. This is that Lamech himself was the Kenite Noah.

That there is something remarkable about Lamech, apart from the fact that he addressed a cryptic speech to his two wives, is shown merely by the space given to him, as opposed to the bare mention given to all the Cainite line since Cain himself. Lamech is the first Cainite since Cain whose wife is mentioned, just as Noah is the first Sethite since Adam who is given this honour. Evidently there was a great deal of information in the Kenite saga about Lamech, so that the Israelite compilers could not exclude this material completely, though they pared it down to a minimum and left it almost unintelligible.

If we now look at Lamech's speech to his wives, using the guiding thread that, in the Kenite saga, Lamech is the counterpart of the Sethite Noah and that it was Lamech who built the Ark and escaped from the Flood together with his two wives and three sons, we shall perhaps begin to understand this enigmatic and poetic remnant of a very ancient chronicle.

We may note at once that Lamech brings the name of his ancestor Cain into his speech, or song, when he says, 'If Cain shall be avenged sevenfold,/Truly Lamech seventy and sevenfold.' Commentators have explained this as 'the cry of a vengeful tribesman who has triumphed over his enemy'.[1] In other words, it is regarded as a declaration by Lamech that he will exact terrible revenge against anyone who attacks him or his family; a declaration whose savage confidence has been fuelled by the sight of the freshly killed enemy lying before him: 'I have slain a man for wounding me,/And a young man for bruising me.' (It is generally agreed that this refers to only one killed man, not two, the apparent duplication being a literary device used in Hebrew poetry known as 'parallelism', which consists of the rhythmic repetition of a statement in different words.) Some commentators see the insertion of this song at this point as intended to highlight the moral degradation of the generation before the Flood and its recourse to violence: 'And the earth was corrupt before God, and the earth was filled with violence' (Genesis 6:11). Lamech has succumbed so much to the violent spirit of the age that he is prepared to kill many times ('seventy and sevenfold') in revenge for having been only bruised or wounded. Others see significance in the juxtaposition of Lamech's 'savage' song to the previous verse about his son Tubal-Cain's invention of iron-working. Lamech, according to this interpretation, is delighted with the new iron weapons forged by his son, and declares that with their aid he will be able to repeat Cain's crime of murder on a large scale. According to these interpretations, the point of comparison between Lamech and Cain is that they are both violent murderers, and Lamech is vaunting his own ability to emulate and even much surpass the crime of his ancestor.[2]

This kind of interpretation is wrong, I suggest, because it does not attend sufficiently carefully to the comparison that Lamech is making between himself and Cain. When Cain was told that he would be avenged sevenfold, this was not in connection with any revenge that he himself would take. It was a promise by God (Genesis 4:15) that if Cain himself were killed, God would see to it that sevenfold punishment would come upon the family of his killer (i.e. seven lives would be taken for one). The real point of this threat was that it was a *protection* for Cain. It was something that was to be publicly known, and in token of its publication, God gave a sign to Cain; the meaning of the sign – that Cain was under the protection of God who would punish severely anyone who ignored it – must have been known to all, for otherwise it would have been inefficacious.

So Lamech is not boasting about his intention to take murderous revenge on his enemies; he is invoking from God the same protection that was given to Cain. He is saying, 'Cain killed someone, and instead of dying for this deed he was given a special protection by God. I too have killed someone, and in my case protection from God is also to be expected. Indeed, my protection should be far greater than that given to Cain. If Cain was protected by a public undertaking

'And Noah builded an altar unto the Lord; and took of every clean beast, and of every clean fowl, and offered burnt offerings on the altar': this was the ideal ordering of ritual sacrifice laid down by the Israelites in their version of the story of the Flood. In the original version of the story the sacrifice was a human one. (17th-century engraving.)

that his killer would be punished sevenfold, then I should be protected by an undertaking that my killer will be punished seventy and sevenfold.' In other words the deterrent offered should be greater; the sevenfold killing mentioned in connection with Cain, and the seventy and sevenfold killing mentioned in connection with Lamech are killings which are not intended to be carried out unless it becomes unfortunately necessary; their main object is to prevent the death of Cain and Lamech respectively by the fearsomeness of the *threat*.[3]

The important question to ask, then, is the nature of the deed to which Lamech refers when he says, 'I have slain a man'. What kind of killing must it have been if Lamech felt entitled to claim protection for it, if he expressly invoked the example of Cain, and if he felt entitled to claim even greater protection than was afforded to Cain?

The answer must be, if there is any validity in the argument set out in the previous chapter about the deed performed by Cain, that Lamech had just performed a ritual human sacrifice. The likelihood of this is all the greater if Lamech was the Kenite Noah. For, if so, his position was directly analogous to that of Cain. For just as Cain, the Kenite Adam, performed a human sacrifice to inaugurate the first era in history and mark his situation as the patriarch of all humanity, so Lamech, the Kenite Noah, performed a similar sacrifice to inaugurate the new beginning of history after the Flood. We find, indeed, in the

Lamech

Hebrew Bible, that the first thing that Noah did when he emerged from the Ark after the Flood was to build an altar and offer a mighty sacrifice which had crucially beneficial consequences for mankind:

And Noah builded an altar unto the Lord: and took of every clean beast, and of every clean fowl, and offered burnt offerings on the altar. And the Lord smelled a sweet savour: and the Lord said in His heart, I will not again curse the ground any more for man's sake; for the imagination of man's heart is evil from his youth; neither will I again smite any more every thing living, as I have done. While the earth remaineth, seedtime and harvest, and cold and heat, and summer and winter, and day and night shall not cease. (Genesis 8: 20–2)

This sacrifice, however, is an animal sacrifice, not a human one, in keeping with the views of the Israelite compilers, who regarded human sacrifice as wicked, and would certainly not portray the blameless Noah, the figure whom they had substituted for Cainite Lamech, and whose descent they traced from the fictitious line of Seth, as performing any sacrifice except one in accordance with their own ethical code. As if to underline the artificial nature of Noah's sacrifice, it is described as having been made of only 'clean' animals, though according to the Hebrew Bible's own account the distinction between 'clean' and 'unclean' animals did not exist at this time. This distinction was first made in the Law given to the Israelites in the desert after their Exodus from Egypt about a thousand years after the time of Noah (Leviticus 11). The writers of the Priestly source of the Pentateuch (P), however, could not imagine that so saintly a man as Noah, even though not an Israelite, could offer unclean animals in sacrifice. We can discern in their account how they even altered the number of animals taken into the Ark in order to provide Noah with clean animals for his great sacrifice (the non-Priestly source, J, says that two of every living thing, male and female, were to be taken in, Genesis 6:19, but the Priestly source in the next chapter, v.2, says that seven each are to be taken of clean beasts and two each of unclean beasts).

We see, then, that the account of Noah's sacrifice has been edited in accordance with Israelite ideas. In the original Kenite version, as we see from Lamech's song, the sacrifice was a human one. Can we further discern whom it was that Lamech sacrificed? The song does give us some clues. For, rightly translated, it tells us that the person whom Lamech sacrificed was someone near and dear to him. The Authorized Version here gives a more accurate translation than the modern versions, one of which (the JPS translation) was quoted above. The Authorized Version translates: 'For I have slain a man to my wounding, and a young man to my hurt.' In contradiction to this, but in approximate accord to the JPS version, the New English Bible translates, 'I kill a man for wounding me,/a young man for a blow.'

The latter translation alters the plain past tense of the Hebrew verb (*haragti*) to a present tense ('I kill') in order to fit in better with the 'boasting of blood-revenge' theory. The most literal translation is that of the Authorized Version, and this makes it clear that the speaker is lamenting the killing that he has been obliged to perform although it has caused him much suffering to do so. The only criticism that can be offered against this translation is that the word translated as 'young man' really means 'child' or at most 'boy' (*yeled*). The most accurate translation would be: 'I have killed a man to my own wounding, a child to my own bruising.' Bearing in mind the poetic device of parallelism that is being employed, we can say that Lamech is lamenting that he has killed a man who is also a child; that is, he has killed his own grown-up son, who is also a child, because a person is always a child to his own parents. We can understand now why Lamech is making this speech to his wives. It is a self-justifying speech by which he defends himself from their sorrowful reproaches: he tells them that he has killed his and their son most reluctantly and to his own wounding and bruising of spirit, but with such justification that if Cain was protected by God with a sevenfold threat, then he, Lamech, should be protected with a seventy and sevenfold one.

There is some corroboration of this reading of the Lamech passage in a strange story found in the Midrash, according to which Lamech killed his own son Tubal-Cain by accident. The story is found in the Midrashic work known as *Midrash Tanhuma*, the earliest version of which (no longer extant) was probably written in the fourth century AD, but which is now extant in a version dating from the eighth or ninth century AD. This may seem a very late work to adduce for the understanding of a Biblical passage which may have originated, in its Kenite form, in the second millennium BC. But the Midrashic writings were compilations of very heterogeneous materials, some of them handed down by oral tradition from remote times. Some of these materials, from their naive savagery, seem to derive from a period earlier than the composition of the Hebrew Bible, and indeed to belong to the body of folk-tales that were excluded from the Bible because of their primitivism but survived in popular tradition, of which the Midrashic literature is a repository. The Midrash can therefore be used sometimes as evidence of what lies behind the monotheistic and civilized surface of the Bible, though such use of the Midrash must of course be made with due caution.[4]

The story found in *Midrash Tanhuma* is as follows. Lamech was a blind man. He used to go hunting, however, with his son Tubal-Cain acting as his guide. When Tubal-Cain sighted a deer, he would indicate the direction to his father, who would point his bow in that direction and shoot. One day, Tubal-Cain saw what he thought was a deer in the distance and pointed his father in that direction. The arrow hit the quarry, but on coming up to it, Tubal-Cain found that it was not a deer but a dead man, who had a horn protruding from his forehead. He informed his father of this, and Lamech cried out in horror that it could be no-one other than Cain, his own great-great-great-grandfather, whose protruding horn was the 'sign' of protection given to him by God. This horn had now proved the cause of his death, since it had deceived Tubal-Cain into thinking him a deer. Lamech was so overcome with dismay that he clapped his hands together in grief. Unfortunately, however, Tubal-Cain was standing between his hands at the time and Lamech thus struck his son's head with great force with both hands. This blow caused Tubal-Cain's death. Lamech stood on the scene of the double tragedy until the evening, when his two wives, Adah and Zillah, came in search of him and led him home. His wives, however, now refused to have intercourse with him, as they did not wish to bear children who would be under a curse (the curse pronounced against anyone who killed Cain). Lamech then argued with his wives, saying, 'Even Cain, who killed with murderous intent, was allowed to be the progenitor of seven generations before God took vengeance on him; surely, then, I, who killed accidentally, will be allowed to be the progenitor of seventy-seven generations.'

The last part of this story is an attempt to interpret Lamech's statement, 'For Cain will be avenged sevenfold, and Lamech seventy and sevenfold', taking it to mean, 'For if Cain had to suffer God's vengeance after seven generations, Lamech's punishment will be postponed for seventy-seven generations.' This is not a plausible interpretation and is evidently a late editorial addition to the story; yet the motif that Lamech was making his speech in order to appease his wives for the slaying he had just committed may well be an earlier and more authentic element.

The doubling of the slaying in this Midrashic story is probably due to a misunderstanding of the parallelism 'For I have killed a man to my wounding and a boy to my bruising'. It is understandable that this should be taken to mean that Lamech has just killed two people, one a man, and the other a boy, and that the man should be identified as Cain because of the mention of Cain in the next verse. Such an interpretation satisfies a natural curiosity about what happened to Cain in the end.

It may be thought that the whole story is merely an ingenious piece of exegesis, by which a man and a boy (as required by the parallelism literally understood) are killed by Lamech through the narrative device of his blindness. But there is something so archetypal about the story that it cannot quite be dismissed in this way.[5] Further, a point

Lamech's blindness, the accidental nature of his act, and his use of a bow and arrow are all distancing devices which disguise the event that is actually taking place and which remove responsibility for it from a single individual. (Lamech and Cain: engraving by Lucas van Leyden.)

that cries out for deeper understanding may be provided by the Midrashic story, if the latter is taken seriously; that is, the curious fact that Lamech's son is called in the Bible not just Tubal (in keeping with the similar names of his brothers Jabal and Jubal), but Tubal-Cain, a name that somehow links him with his first ancestor Cain, whose name appears so obscurely in the utterance of Lamech.

If we decide, then, to take the Midrashic story seriously as a possibly genuine ancient tradition rather than a by-product of Biblical exegesis, we may begin by noting certain striking parallels in general mythology. The theme of a blind man killing with an arrow is paralelled in the Norse myth of the death of Balder. This story, as found in the prose *Edda*, is as follows. Balder was a good and beautiful god, the son of Odin, the greatest god. Once Balder dreamt that his death was at hand. He told the other gods, who were dismayed and decided to protect him. They arranged with the goddess Frigg that she would take an oath from all beings and substances on earth, animal, vegetable and mineral, that they would not harm Balder. They all gave this undertaking, so the gods now regarded Balder as invulnerable.

Consequently, they amused themselves by putting him in their midst and throwing and shooting all kinds of substances at him, to see how nothing could harm him. The evil god, Loki, however, sought to bring harm to Balder. To this end, he went to Frigg in the guise of an old woman and asked her whether there was anything in the world from which Frigg had not bothered to require an oath not to harm Balder. Frigg revealed that there was one thing so insignificant that she had not troubled to require an oath from it: the mistletoe. Loki went and plucked the mistletoe and went back to the assembly of the gods, where the game of hurling things at Balder was still going on. Standing on the edge of the circle was the blind god Hother. Loki asked Hother why he too did not join in doing honour to Balder by shooting at him. Hother replied that he could not join in as he was blind and had no weapon. Loki then put a bow into his hand, and inserting the mistletoe as an arrow, directed Hother where to shoot. Hother shot the mistletoe, which struck Balder and killed him. Balder's body was then burned on a great funeral pyre, together with his wife and his horse, amid scenes of great sorrow.[6]

Frazer has proved with a wealth of examples that the myth of Balder's death was derived from an actual ritual in which an effigy of Balder (earlier, a human representative of the god) was burned at a fire festival. If we examine the myth itself, we note a number of distancing devices by which the human-sacrificial meaning of the story is disguised. The killing is made as indirect as possible: firstly, it is done accidentally, by a blind man; secondly, it is done at long range, by an arrow; thirdly, so far from being done by the general will of the community, it is done through the malice of one individual; fourthly, the event is greeted with sorrow and mourning.

It is a good rule when considering the meaning of a myth (or a dream, as Freud explained[7]) to attend to its main scene, ignoring secondary details which may be suspected as being intended to divert the mind from the plain meaning of the scene before us. In the Balder myth, the main scene is plain enough: it consists of a ring of people with a man standing at its centre, at whom the people are flinging missiles of all kinds; the man falls dead, and then his body is burned. The 'secondary elaboration' of the story, however, tells us that this scene is not as it appears: it is as if the community as a whole is saying, 'None of our missiles did the man any harm. The missile that killed him came from one man only, standing outside our circle. Even he was not responsible, for he was blind and knew not what he did. It happened through the evil plotting of a villain who is not one of our community at all.' The Balder myth is thus a prime example of the devices by which a community disguises from itself what it is doing when it performs, or celebrates through the imaginative medium of

Lamech

myth, human-sacrificial expiation. Frazer and other enquirers do not seem to have considered this aspect of the Balder myth, to which we shall be returning at later stages of our investigation.

We note, however, that the Balder myth does not contain a Sacred Executioner, because the role of the executioner is divided entirely between accident and malice, without any admission that the sacrifice had to occur for the good of the tribe (this refusal to admit the necessity of the sacrifice, which is treated as a wholly regrettable event, comprises a fifth distancing device). The evil plotting of Loki corresponds to the murderous motive of Cain and similarly draws attention away from the necessity of the sacrifice, though Loki's role as plotter and betrayer corresponds more closely to that of Judas in the Christian myth. It seems that the Balder myth represents a stage when the sacrifice was performed not by a deputed figure, the Sacred Executioner, who was then driven out with a mixture of hatred and respect, but by the tribe itself, by communal stoning, but with the fiction that this stoning was ineffective and death had come about by other means. The apotheosis of the whole scene, by which it is represented as taking place among the gods instead of on earth among the tribe, may be regarded as a sixth distancing device.

The chief point of contact between the Balder myth and the Midrashic story of Lamech is the scene of a blind man drawing the bow by the direction of another figure and thus killing the victim. The existence of this graphic scene in both myths forms a striking parallel. No diffusionist theory can account for it, since there was no connection between Norse mythology and that of the Near East. It is best accounted for by the postulation of a similar psychological mechanism operating in both cases: the desire to shift reponsibility for a ritual killing. The evidence of the Balder myth thus suggests that the Lamech story is something more than an exegetical extravagance and that it has genuine mythical quality.

Who was it that Lamech killed, then? Was it Cain or his son Tubal-Cain, or both? The Midrash says both, and this may be due, as we have seen, to a misunderstanding of a parallelism. Yet there is the complication that Lamech's son also bore the name Cain as his second name, so the tradition that Lamech killed both Tubal and Cain may have arisen through a misunderstanding of the double name of the son. Yet this too may be a superficial solution. Why, indeed, did Lamech's son bear the name Cain as well as the name Tubal? If, as previously argued, the name Cain was also used as a title among the Kenites, it is possible that the person who in every generation bore the name was regarded as the incarnation of the original Cain, the ancestor of the tribe, just as in Egypt the Pharaoh was regarded as the incarnation of previous Pharaohs. No doubt Cain, among the Kenites, was regarded as a divine or semi-divine figure, like Romulus among the Romans. At a time of supreme crisis, therefore, such as military catastrophe or the foundation of a new epoch in the history of the tribe, the most suitable person to be sacrificed would be the human representative of the god, he who bore the name Cain and thus embodied the very spirit of the tribe. In a mystical sense, then, Lamech, in sacrificing his son, would be sacrificing both Tubal and the original Cain, for Tubal, as his name Tubal-Cain shows, was the individual in whom Cain was at that time incarnate. The fact that it was Tubal who, of Lamech's three sons, was regarded as embodying the spirit of the tribe is shown by the attribution to him of the re-invention, after the Flood (according to the present chronological theory), of the art of metal-working, which was the main pride of the Kenite tribe and the very meaning of the word 'Cain'.

Alternatively, it could be that it was only after his death as a sacrifice for the tribe that Tubal was given the name Tubal-Cain, i.e. he was elevated to deity, as a human sacrifice so often was, and identified with the divine figure of his tribal ancestor Cain. Such a conception could lead, at a later time, to the idea that his name had been Tubal-Cain even when he was on earth, and also that when he was sacrificed this was a double sacrifice in which he shared death with Cain himself.[8]

The conclusion proposed, then, is that the Midrashic legend does have value in the interpretation of the mysterious song of Lamech; that, in this song, Lamech was indeed appeasing his wives, as the Midrash says, for having killed his son Tubal; but that the element of accident introduced by the Midrash through the motif of the blindness of Lamech is one of those masking devices characteristic of myths based on a ritual of human sacrifice. The reality behind the mask is that Lamech sacrificed his son in gratitude for his deliverance from the Flood and as a foundation sacrifice for the new epoch that was beginning. The masking device may itself be very ancient, being part of the Kenite saga itself, which was composed at a stage when open acknowledgment of human sacrifice was reluctantly, if ever, made. From there, the legend, together with its disguises, entered into extra-Biblical oral tradition among the Israelites, and was eventually collected and recorded by the compilers of the Midrash.

It may be asked why, if this is so, Tubal-Cain is represented in the Biblical account as being the youngest of the three sons of Lamech. Surely it would be more in keeping with ancient patriarchal custom to sacrifice the eldest, rather than the youngest, son?

We may attempt to answer this question by pointing out that there is in any case something strange about the names of the three sons of Lamech. Jabal, Jubal and Tubal – these do not sound like three

Lamech

genuinely separate names, but like variations on one name, like Tweedledum and Tweedledee. I am not suggesting that Lamech had only one son, whose name was expanded into three: this is not a viable solution, because the threeness of the sons is well established by the parallel trio, Shem, Ham and Japheth, the sons of Noah, who would not have been three in number unless the Kenite saga had contained the same number. But if we are to find a solution to the riddle of the unlikely sounding variations-on-a-theme in the names of the sons of Lamech, it is probably to be sought in the exigencies of adapting the Kenite saga for Israelite purposes. I suggest that in the Kenite saga the names of the three sons of Lamech were Tubal, Ham and Japheth. Now the Israelite compilers, in their earlier manufacture of a Sethite line to oust the Cainite line from its primacy, had, as we have seen, taken over the Cainite names and merely changed them very slightly and also made some changes in their order, in order to disguise their provenance. If, however, they had given Noah three sons called Tubal, Ham and Japheth, or names very similar to these, the coincidence of names, all in one generation, would have been too obvious to avoid remark. They therefore adopted a different method. They left one of the names, Tubal, where it was in the Cainite line, replacing the other two names, Ham and Japheth, with fictitious names based on assonances with Tubal. They then transferred Ham and Japheth, the two names thus gained, to the Sethite line. They were thus left with one name to supply in the Sethite line, and they provided this in the form of Shem, which means in Hebrew simply 'name'. This is in accordance with their policy, probably forced upon them by the extreme difficulty of inventing a name without the help of tradition, of giving colourless names to fill-out characters in the chronicle (as we saw previously in the case of Abel and Seth).

If this analysis is correct, Tubal in the Cainite line corresponds with Shem in the Sethite line. As a consequence, Tubal must be regarded as the eldest of Lamech's three sons, not the youngest as the Biblical record represents him to be. For Shem is unequivocally represented by the Bible as the eldest of Noah's three sons.[9] The displacement of Tubal from eldest to youngest in the Cainite chronicle of the Bible may thus have been a by-product of the dislocation of the record in order to provide material for the Sethite line of Noah. That Tubal was the eldest son accords with the choice of him to act as the victim in the sacrifice offered by Lamech (in the Kenite saga) after the Flood. For although in matriarchal societies it was not unusual to regard the youngest son as the heir, and therefore as a candidate for sacrifice, in a patriarchal society such as that of the Kenites, the natural choice would be the eldest son. Again, it is more in accordance with patriarchal practice that the eldest son should be given the chieftain's title (in this case,

Lamech

Cain), whether this was given to Tubal during his lifetime, as heir-apparent, or after his death, as tutelary deity of the tribe.

It is interesting, however, that there is a discussion in the Talmud (Sanhedrin 69b) as to whether Shem really was the eldest of Noah's three sons, or the youngest. The doubt purportedly arises out of chronological considerations, but it may be that the doubt already existed, and the chronological reasons were adduced to account for it. If so, some vague memory may have persisted in Israelite oral tradition that the primogeniture of Shem was somehow cast in doubt through the dislocation of the Cainite register. If Tubal, Shem's analogue, was demoted from eldest to youngest, a shadow of a memory that Tubal was the *alter ego* of Shem may have affected the tradition about Shem, despite the plain Biblical record that he was the eldest.[10]

A confirmation that Tubal was a real name, while Jabal and Jubal were not, is that Tubal turns up again in the record, as the name of a son of Japheth (Genesis 10:2), while Jabal and Jubal never appear again.[11] Tubal was also the name of a nation mentioned by the Hebrew prophets (Isaiah 55:19 and Ezekiel 27:13; 32:26; 38:2), identified by the Talmud as Bithynia, but in Jewish medieval tradition regarded as identical with Italy (which may account for Shakespeare's choice of the name in *The Merchant of Venice* for a character who was an Italian Jew).

It may be as well, at this point, to consider the name Noah. According to our theory, Noah was the Sethite figure corresponding to Lamech himself, and one would expect, therefore, that his name would turn out to be as colourless and lacking in content as the other fill-in names we have examined. The Bible itself attempts to provide an explanation of the name as follows:

And Lamech lived a hundred eighty and two years, and begot a son. And he called his name Noah, saying: 'This same shall comfort us in our work and in the toil of our hands, which cometh from the ground which the Lord hath cursed.' (Genesis 5:28–9).

The etymology suggested here for the name Noah is that it is derived from the Hebrew verb *nahem*, meaning 'to comfort'. However, this is impossible, as the final 'm' is an integral part of the verb. Instead, the name Noah must be derived from the verb *nuah*, meaning 'to rest', or 'to be at a certain spot' (as, in English, 'his foot rested there'). The name, therefore, is remarkably analogous to the name Seth, in its generalized sense of location. Just as Seth means 'he who is put there', Noah could mean 'he is located there', or, if we take it as an imperative form, 'be there' or 'stay there'. Thus the name fits in well with the other fill-in names, being colourless and vacuous in content, and

Lamech

giving clues to its own status as an inserted name. All the other names in the genealogies given in Genesis, however, are unlike this; either they are not explicable at all because not derivable from any known Hebrew word (e.g. Lamech, Hebrew *lemekh*; the form Lamech derived from the Septuagint transliteration is based on the pausal form, as in the case of Abel), or else they have an easily understood and non-vacuous Hebrew meaning (e.g. Enoch, meaning the 'dedicated one'). (The name Adam, however, is in a different category altogether. This too is a made-up name, since the Kenite saga began with Cain, but the name Adam is not vacuous, since it was not put in merely to fill up an empty space. It was inserted for ideological reasons, for it marks the universalism of the Israelite compilers, who wished to provide a genealogy of all mankind, not a glorification of the Kenite tribe: mankind therefore had to begin with Adam – whose name means simply 'humanity' – and not with any tribal name.)

It is natural here to ask about Kenite influence on the genealogies given in the Bible for mankind after the Flood. We have seen that the apparent discontinuity marked by the complete dissimilarity of the Sethite trio – Shem, Ham and Japheth – from the Cainite trio – Jabal, Jubal and Tubal – is illusory. Can we see, then, whether there is any evidence of Kenite influence on the genealogy leading from Shem to Abraham, or from the other two patriarchs, Ham and Japheth, to their descendants?

One point of importance has already been noted: that the name Tubal appears among the descendants of Noah, showing that the allegedly extinct line of Cain was still alive after the Flood. There is, however, an even more striking point. This is that the name Cain itself appears in the line of Shem (called Sem in the Greek, from which we derive the words 'Semite', 'Semitic', etc.). This is not observable in English translations, which are all made from the Masoretic text (the received Hebrew text, finalized about the beginning of the Christian era). The name Cain, in its variant form Cainan, appears in the Septuagint version, as follows:

And to Sem himself also were children born, the father of all the sons of Heber, the brother of Japheth the elder. Sons of Sem, Elam, and Assur, and Arphaxad, and Lud, and Aram, and Cainan. And sons of Aram, Uz, and Ul, and Gater and Mosoch. And Arphaxad begot Cainan, and Cainan begot Sala. (Genesis 10:*21–4*)

In the next chapter, we find a further genealogy stemming from Shem:

And Sem lived after he had begotten Arphaxad five hundred years . . . and Arphaxad . . . begot Cainan. And Arphaxad lived after he had begotten Cainan four hundred years . . . and Cainan . . . begot Sala . . . and Cainan lived after he had begotten Sala, three hundred and thirty years. (11:*11–13*)

In these two passages, the name Cainan is cited seven times. Yet in the received Hebrew Bible, the name does not appear even once. A whole generation that appears in the Septuagint, that of Cainan the son of Arphaxad, is omitted. It looks as if there has been some censorship by the redactors of the Masoretic text, though at the time of the translation of Genesis into Greek at Alexandria (about 200 BC) the references to Cainan still formed part of the text. It cannot be the case that, at this late date, the Masoretic redactors were conscious of obliterating traces of the Kenite saga; they may simply have felt that the name did not quite fit their list comfortably, especially as they wished to reduce the generations before Abraham in accordance with a symmetrical chronological scheme. Actually, the name Cainan forms part of the Sethite line, and might therefore have been regarded as a respectable Sethite name (as opposed to the name Cain, of which it is in fact merely a variant). Yet some residual uneasiness must have impelled the deletion of all references to Cainan.

It is interesting that the Septuagint itself (in the text quoted above[12]) contains an uncomfortable anomaly in relation to Cainan. For the name is given as that of the youngest son of Shem, but this son disappears from view, being given no descendants; instead, Cainan is given again as the grandson of Shem, and from this second appearance, a line of descent is given. Scholars have agreed, therefore, that the text that contains this anomaly must be incorrect, and the first mention of Cainan should be deleted in accordance with other texts of the Septuagint. However, in view of the foregoing discussion, this textual emendation does not look unquestionable after all. We would expect uneasiness about the appearance of Cainite names in a supposedly Sethite chronicle to affect the text, causing lacunae and anomalies. It may well be, then, that the text that includes *two* characters by the name of Cainan in the line of Shem is after all correct. If Cain (Cainan) is not only a name, but a title, as argued above, we would expect it to appear rather frequently in any Kenite genealogy.

We may conclude, then, that Kenite influence can be detected in the genealogical record even after the Flood. The line of Shem, purporting to show the descent of Abraham, the progenitor of Israel, from Shem the eldest son of Noah, is actually based on a Kenite record showing the post-diluvian descent of their tribe from Tubal, the eldest son of Lamech, the Kenite figure from whom the Biblical Noah is derived.

Chapter Five

The Kenites and the Rechabites

As we have noted, the Bible has preserved part of the Kenite saga concerning the period after the Flood, quite apart from the traces of Kenite genealogy just discussed. For the attribution of pioneering skills to the three sons of Lamech, though now purportedly referring to the period just *before* the Flood, has been removed by the Biblical redactors from its true place, which, in the original Kenite saga, was in a narrative describing the rebirth of civilization *after* the Flood.

Let us turn back to this important passage, and consider its implications:

And Adah bore Jabal; he was the father of such as dwell in tents and have cattle. And his brother's name was Jubal; he was the father of all such as handle the harp and pipe. And Zillah, she also bore Tubal-Cain, the forger of every cutting instrument of brass and iron; and the sister of Tubal-Cain was Naamah. (Genesis 4:10–2, JPS translation)

It is somewhat remarkable here that, though pioneering activities are described, their total range is not very wide. The full conspectus of activities – tent-dwelling, cattle-rearing, music-playing and metal-working – is such as might be ascribed to a single tribe, of a particular kind, rather than to mankind as a whole. We may infer from this that the Kenite saga of the post-Flood era was narrower in scope than is the Hebrew Bible. The Kenite saga was concerned only to give an account of the post-Flood history of the Kenite tribe itself. The tenor of this account was that, while before the Flood the patriarchs of the line of Cain were city-dwellers, the renewal of the tribe that took place after the Flood was in the form of a special way of life, that of a nomadic tribe of smiths, living on the proceeds of cattle-rearing, as well as on their skills in metal-working, and also acquiring fame, in the manner of such tribes, in the arts of music and entertainment. It may well be that the Kenite saga did not represent Lamech and his family as the sole survivors of the Flood, in the way that the Hebrew Bible represents Noah. If so, the Kenite saga had no need to trace the entire population of the post-Flood world from one man. All the Kenite chroniclers were concerned to show was the nobility of their descent, for Lamech was represented as in the main line of primogeniture descending from Cain himself, the supreme patriarch of all humanity.

The Kenites and the Rechabites

Like the Hebrew Bible (which gives the name of the eldest son and then adds that the patriarch in question 'begot sons and daughters', without detailing their names), the Kenite saga envisaged many inferior lines of descent, which were also represented after the Flood by other surviving families. How these other families developed to form all the nations of the world was not the concern of the Kenite chroniclers. Their own tribe was derived from the senior survivor of the Flood, and was therefore the 'first-born' and aristocracy of all tribes. While the Hebrew Bible does not narrow down its scope to the history of the Israelite tribe until it comes to the time of Abraham (and even then does not concentrate on Israel alone until it comes to Jacob), this narrowing-down occurred in the Kenite saga at the time of the Flood itself.

Whereas the Kenite chroniclers regarded the three sons of Lamech as fathering three subdivisions of the Kenite tribe, the Biblical chroniclers had a universal scheme of humanity in mind, and therefore used two of the sons, Ham and Japheth, as patriarchs of the non-Semitic nations. Similarly, within the line of Shem itself, they were concerned not merely to detail the line from which Abraham emerged, but to give an account of the origins of all nations related to the Israelites, or of what we today call the Semitic nations. The genealogy tables of the post-Flood period in the Bible thus comprise a magnificent attempt at a comprehensive ethnology, by which the Biblical chroniclers sought to explain the connections and divisions of all the nations known to them, with an intended scope covering the entire population of the world.

Clearly, in constructing their record of the genealogy of all mankind, the Israelite chroniclers had recourse to documents other than the Kenite saga. What these documents were that enabled them to arrive at a surprisingly accurate assessment of the affinities of the various great families of mankind we have no means of knowing. Since an influence from Babylonia is discernible in the story of the Flood, it may be that Babylonian lore was influential here too. Having used the Kenite saga exclusively for the period before the Flood, the Israelite chroniclers found that record too parochial for the post-Flood period and adapted it for very much wider purposes.[1]

We have now arrived at a picture of the Kenites as a tribe consisting of three clans with specialized functions, comprising in their totality a nomadic cattle-raising community with a special interest in metal-working and the art of music. Is there any other means by which we can confirm all or part of this picture? The Kenites are mentioned here and there in the Bible, but no mention is made of them as either metal-workers or musicians. Some clue as to their nomadic or semi-nomadic character may be gleaned from the scattered and varied

The Kenites and the Rechabites

localities of their settlement, since they are found at one time in Midian (Jethro himself, whose Kenite status is discussed above on p. 14), at another time in Amalek (in the time of Saul) and at another time in several different locations in Israel.[2] Their metal-working activities we have so far gleaned only from the name Cain, meaning 'smith', and from the specific remark about Tubal-Cain that he was a pioneer of working in iron and brass, and their musicianship only from the remark about Jubal.

A general confirmation of the tribal picture may be gathered from ethnological data from various countries. Even today there exists an Arab tribe, known as the Sleib, who act as travelling smiths, following regular trade routes with their asses and tools, and supplementing their somewhat meagre income by acting as musicians and fortune-tellers. This tribe, however, have a character more similar to the gipsies than to the proud Kenite tribe with its wealth of tradition and self-aggrandizing myths; yet perhaps the Sleib have declined from a previously high status.[3] A tomb at Beni Hasan dated to the nineteenth century BC portrays a group that has been credibly identified as nomadic metal-workers.[4] Both copper and iron are known to have been mined at around this date in the Jordan Valley. The date of the Flood, according to the Biblical chronology, was about 2500 BC. So there is nothing inherently unlikely about the inauguration of a tribe of metal-workers shortly after that time. The working of iron for tools and weapons is dated considerably later, in the twelfth and eleventh centuries BC (though the beginning of the Iron Age is lately a matter of renewed question, and there seems to be considerable variation in its introduction in different areas). A tribe that began as bronze-workers, and perhaps making iron ornaments, would later add large-scale iron-working to its repertoire, and then anachronistically ascribe this to the early days of its history.

The fact that there are smith-gods in several pantheons (e.g. Hephaestus, Vulcan, Wayland the Smith) shows the high esteem in which smiths were held. Metal-working is regarded as a kind of magic in primitive communities (see, for example, the Fan tribe cited by Frazer[5]), and its techniques were closely guarded secrets confined to a particular family that would eventually grow into a tribe. The nomadic character of such a tribe would arise from the need to visit clients, but also from the very freedom from attachment to the soil given by the possession of a portable skill. Hephaestus was a cripple, and it has been suggested that this defect (matched by crippled smith-gods in other mythologies) arose from a practice of crippling smiths to prevent them from wandering away to another tribe.[6]

An important piece of archaeological evidence points to the existence of a tribe of metal-workers, with a distinctive religion and system of symbols, whose work is found all over the countries bordering the Mediterranean. Their centre is thought to have been Asia Minor.[7] Greek writers also refer to a people called the Chalybes, who were a tribe of iron-workers.[8]

There is thus some general corroborative evidence for our picture of the Kenites as a tribe of metal-workers. The degree of their nomadism requires some further remarks. As we have seen, it seems from the references in the Bible that they had no fixed territory of their own, but had settlements in various countries simultaneously. This accounts for the fact that the Kenites are mentioned at one point as one of the nations living in Canaan and requiring to be driven out by the invading Israelites (Genesis 15: 19) – even though we know that they also lived in Midian and Amalek. It seems clear that the Kenites also built cities in their adopted countries. One such city is referred to as a stronghold, 'set in the rock' (Numbers 24:21). There was even a town in Judaea called Kain, or Cain (Joshua 15:57), a strange fact in a nation that was supposed to regard the name of Cain, the murderer, with abhorrence. In connection with the story of David, there is a reference to the 'cities of the Kenites' in the Negeb (I Samuel 30:29). Such settling down, however, did not erode the separate identity of the Kenites; nor did it destroy their essentially nomadic character. They were always liable to revert to a tent-dwelling mode of life. We see this from the example of Heber the Kenite, whose wife Jael became a heroine in Israel when she killed Sisera, the commander of the invading Canaanites. Heber lived in a tent (Judges 4:11) and had a band of tent-dwelling followers.

So much we can gather from the explicit Biblical references to the Kenites. But there is also another, less explicit, source of information in the references found in the Bible to a group known as the Rechabites, who were in some way connected with the Kenites.[9]

The Rechabites are described by the prophet Jeremiah, who regarded them with great respect (Jeremiah 35). When Jeremiah offered them wine, they refused, citing the commands of their ancestor Jonadab, son of Rechab: 'You shall not drink wine, neither you nor your sons for ever; you shall not build a house; you shall not sow seed; you shall not plant or have a vineyard; but you shall live in tents all your days, that you may live many days in the land where you sojourn.' Jeremiah commended the loyalty of the Rechabites to these commands, contrasting them favourably with the ordinary Israelites, who had neglected the commands of Moses.

Jeremiah does not connect the Rechabites with the Kenites in any way, but this connection can be made through a single passage that has survived in the latest book of the Bible, the Book of Chronicles. This passage is as follows:

The Kenites and the Rechabites

And the families of scribes that dwelt at Jabez: the Tithrathites, the Shimeathites, the Sucathites. These are the Kenites that came of Hammath the father of the house of Rechab. (I Chronicles 2: 55)

This passage, introduced into a context where its relevance is problematic, is clearly a fragment of tradition which the Chronicler found on his hands and fitted in as he could. The information it gives is intriguing. The descent of the Rechabites from Rechab we knew from Jeremiah, who gives their chief ancestor and law-giver as Jonadab, son of Rechab, though why they were named after Rechab and not after the more important Jonadab is not clear. Jonadab, indeed, is known to us as a significant figure in Israelite history, for it was he who was associated with Jehu in his extirpation of the worship of Baal (II Kings 10:15-27). From the account in Kings, it seems that Jonadab was a person of high religious and political stature, whose support the new king Jehu was anxious to enlist. Yet it should be noted that the narrative in Kings does not mention that Jonadab was a Kenite; this is typical of the Biblical reticence on the Kenites generally, the motive for which may be their descent from Cain, and the unacknowledged extent of their contribution to Israelite religion.

Most intriguing of all is the information that the ancestor of the house of Rechab was someone called Hammath. Scholars have been considerably puzzled by this name, since it is not found elsewhere as a personal name, but it is found as a place-name, i.e. the town Hammath in the territory of Naftali. This city was at the northernmost limit of the land of Israel and was often under independent pagan rule. Its name derived from a time before the Israelite conquest. Scholars have made several suggestions as to the origin of the name ('fortress', 'sacred enclosure', or 'place of hot springs'), but it does not seem to have been suggested that it may be associated with the name Ham, though the Bible makes Ham the father of Canaan (the name has nothing to do with Cain, to which, in Hebrew, it is very dissimilar, though in English transliteration the two names appear superficially similar), the eponymous founder of the land Canaan, in which the city Hammath was situated. If indeed Hammath and Ham are related names, it is no longer a puzzle that the ancestor of the Rechabites, according to Chronicles, was someone called Hammath; this is simply an occurrence in the background of the Rechabites of a name derived from the Kenite saga, for, as argued above, the name Ham originally belonged not to the Sethite line to which the Bible assigns it, but to the line of Cain. Since the same passage in Chronicles states explicitly that the Rechabites were Kenites, the name Hammath in their background is not at all inappropriate. What has prevented recognition of this is the assumption that the Kenites were a Semitic tribe related to the Midianites. This is the impression the Bible wishes to give, and, consequently, most of the evidence of their high ancestry from antediluvian times has been suppressed. If the Kenites were a junior branch of the line of Shem, we would not expect to find them numbering Ham, Shem's brother, as one of their ancestors. We can now understand another surprising tell-tale verse (Genesis 15: *19*), in which the Kenites are listed as the senior branch of the Canaanites, though in parallel lists of the Canaanite tribes they are omitted altogether.[10]

The information given to us about the Rechabites tells us how the Kenites reacted to their incorporation within the Israelite fold. They preserved their separate identity not only by building cities of their own (as we have seen) but by preserving a separate way of life that made them into a kind of religious élite, or dedicated order. The Rechabites did not, of course, comprise the whole of the Kenite tribe; they probably represented an élite within the Kenites, making it their aim to oppose the tendency to assimilation. They achieved this aim by stressing the original character of the Kenite way of life, that is, by remaining tent-dwelling nomads and by eschewing agriculture, these traits now acquiring the aura of a religious covenant. As a result, the Rechabites indeed remained an independent entity within Israel, not by rebelling in any way against the demands of Israelite religion, but by the opposite course of adopting a more severe form of it, similar in some ways to the rigorous vows undertaken by the Nazirites. The Rechabites thus gained high status among the Israelites as dedicated ascetics, and it seems from later Jewish tradition that they were regarded as equal in status to the Levites, and, like them, were accorded the privilege of serving in the Temple.[11] They partook particularly in the musical part of the Temple services, thus transmitting in its final form the musical heritage derived from their Kenite ancestor 'Jubal'. Eventually, however, the Kenites disappeared from history, the Rechabite section being absorbed into the Levites, and the remainder of the tribe into the general body of Israel. The last glimpse of the Kenites, possibly, is in the Arab tribe the Banu-Qayin, whom we find mentioned in the fourth century AD, though this section was probably never included in the community of Israel, preserving its identity until this late date among the pagan tribes of Arabia.[12]

The strong link now established between the Rechabites and the Kenites may now enable us to recover even more of the Kenite saga, buried beneath the adaptation of it which we know as the Bible. For there is surely some significant connection between the Rechabites' abhorrence of the drinking of wine and the extraordinary and little-understood story of the drunkenness of Noah. An analysis of this story in the light of the connections so far made may also enable us to understand further the sacrificial themes which lie beneath the surface of the Bible narrative, and also the great moral advances which that narrative embodies.

The story of Noah's drunkenness is given in the Bible as follows:

And Noah began to be an husbandman, and he planted a vineyard. And he drank of the wine, and was drunken: and he was uncovered within his tent. And Ham, the father of Canaan, saw the nakedness of his father, and told his two brethren without. And Shem and Japheth took a garment, and laid it upon both their shoulders, and went backward, and covered the nakedness of their father; and their faces were backward, and they saw not their father's nakedness. And Noah awoke from his wine, and knew what his younger son had done unto him. And he said, Cursed be Canaan; a servant of servants shall he be unto his brethren. And he said, Blessed be the Lord God of Shem; and Canaan shall be his servant. God shall enlarge Japheth, and he shall dwell in the tents of Shem; and Canaan shall be his servant.

There are many difficult problems in this account; for example, the apparently trivial nature of Ham's offence, which hardly seems to deserve the curse pronounced as a result of it; and the fact that the curse is pronounced not against Ham, the perpetrator of the offence, such as it is, but against his son Canaan. Leaving aside such questions for the moment, we may note that the story as a whole, in its original form, is likely to have been directed against the cultivation of the vine and against the vice of drunkenness. This aspect is ignored in the Biblical story, which passes over Noah's drunkenness without moral comment, and reserves its censure for Ham's failure to show respect for his helpless father by averting his eyes from his nakedness. But if we consider the story as a foundation myth of the Kenite tribe, which it originally was, we can see how it could have acted as explanation and justification for the tribe's ban on the drinking of wine. There is also a moral reflection on the degeneration caused by agriculture itself, for it was only when Noah 'began to be a husbandman' that he was tempted to plant vines and to become a drunkard. We see here a common tendency of nomadic tribes, priding themselves on their superior hardiness and freedom from sedentary vices, to eschew the drinking of wine as symptomatic of the effeminacy induced by agriculture. Thus the ban on wine and other alcoholic beverages still in force today in Islamic countries represents a devotion to the ideals of the desert and the scorn of an agricultural life that still remains the basis of Islamic religion; and this is an inheritance from pre-Islamic asceticism in the Arabian peninsula.[13] It was from the practice of the Rechabites that we gleaned that a ban on wine was part of the ethos of the Kenites; but it is also necessary to note that this ban is bound up with the other vow of the Rechabites, to 'live in tents all your days'.

The Kenites and the Rechabites

The Bible in general is not opposed to the drinking of wine or the planting of vineyards. On the contrary, the Biblical ideal includes wine and the vineyard as necessary ingredients, with 'every man under his vine and under his fig tree from Dan even unto Beer-Sheba' (I Kings 4:25; see also Micah 4:4; Zecharia 3:10). Wine formed an essential part of the Temple service, being used as a libation in the sacrifices. Moreover, wine is continually spoken of favourably: 'Wine that maketh glad the heart of man' (Psalms 104:15), and 'Wine which cheereth God and man' (Judges 9: 13). In later Judaism, wine was an indispensable part of the Kiddush ceremony, ushering in Sabbaths and festivals, and thus entered the Christian sacrament of the Eucharist. The Talmud regards wine as a sovereign remedy for all bodily ills.[14] This high estimation of wine is a measure of the agricultural emphasis of Israelite religion, which (contrary to the opinions of certain mainly anti-Semitic scholars) gave no veneration to nomadic ideals except in a peripheral way, as in the respect accorded to the Rechabites. There are warnings in the Bible against drunkenness, but only as a misuse of something essentially good and beneficial, not as a fundamental vice. The positive function of wine in the Israelite imagination is perhaps best shown in the poetry of the Song of Songs, where wine is a symbol of sexual energy and the sweetness of life. The institution of the Nazirites, by which a person could voluntarily forswear wine for a period as an act of asceticism (see Numbers 6), is a remnant of nomadic practice, but was kept within strict limits and regarded with reserve (one Talmudic rabbi said that the reason why the Nazirite had to bring a sin-offering after completing his vow was to atone for the sin of depriving himself of wine).[15]

It is thus an anomaly that the story of Noah's drunkenness occupies such a prominent and crucial place in the Biblical narrative, and it is not surprising that the main feature of the story is glossed over and made to give way to a moral that was not part of the original version. Yet there is another Biblical story that presents a similar anomaly: that of the drunkenness of Lot (Genesis 19: 30-8). This somewhat disreputable story tells how Lot, after the destruction of Sodom and Gomorrah and the other cities of the plain, was made drunk by his two daughters (who thought that the world had come to an end and they were the only survivors), so that they could lie with him and thus continue the human race. This is told as a foundation myth for the tribes of Moab and Ammon but, as several scholars have pointed out, it has the features of a more generalized foundation myth, and may be a displaced alternative version of the renewal of the human race after the Flood or some other worldwide catastrophe.[16] Here the part played by the motif of drunkenness seems more equivocal than in the story of Noah; it acts as a kind of excuse for the motif of incest, rather than as something reprehensible. We are forced to consider more deeply what the role of drunkenness and of sexual transgression may be in a narrative of a renewed beginning of the human race.

We may achieve a deeper dimension of interpretation by considering the myths of Bacchus and of Osiris, after which we shall be drawn into discussing other myths: those of Attis, Adonis, Cronus and Uranus, and others that may appear even more remote from Genesis. The story of the drunkenness of Noah will be seen to be far from a mere anecdote, but part of an important mythological complex, with sacrificial connotations of a type not hitherto discussed in this enquiry.

But before making comparisons between the story of Noah and the savage myths of pagan mythology, it is necessary to turn once more to the Midrash, which, as in the case of Lamech, will give us a glimpse into the primitive violence underlying the Biblical account. For the Midrash, commenting on the verse, 'And Noah awoke from his wine, and knew what his younger son had done unto him' (a verse that is indeed puzzling, since, if Ham's offence was voyeurism, Noah would not have been aware of it on recovering from his drunkenness), says bluntly that what Noah discovered was that his son Ham had castrated him.[17] Further proof of this is found in the verse, 'And Noah lived after the flood three hundred and fifty years', which does not add 'and he begat sons and daughters', as in the previous Sethite genealogy (Chapter 5). So, once more, the Midrash, despite the late date of its redaction, gives us a version of the story that is more primitive and authentic than the civilized Biblical story whose moral is merely that children should look away when a parent happens to appear before them undressed. The Midrash further alleges that Noah was engaged in sexual intercourse with his wife in the tent (as the Midrash points out, the Hebrew of v. 22 'and he was uncovered within his tent' actually reads consonantally 'within her tent', though the Masoretic vocalization makes the pronominal suffix masculine). We have here, then, a very much more lurid picture: one of drunken intercourse followed by castration. The motive assigned to Ham in his violent intrusion on the parental bed is one of power: he wished to prevent the birth of more brothers who would claim a share of the world from the present triumvirate of brothers. But this is no doubt a rationalization: we think instead of such myths as the castration of Uranus by Cronus, for the incident as it appears in the Midrash is clearly of mythical status.

We are now in the realm to which the myths of Dionysus (Bacchus) and Osiris belong. The myth of Dionysus is essentially one of drunken revelry and orgiastic sexual activity followed by the dismemberment of the god and his consequent resurrection. The god is closely associated with the realm of the female; both in the legend of his upbringing among women, and in his portrayal as an effeminate youth with deliberately emphasized female attributes. The worship of Dionysus is thus very old (despite the attempt of Greek patriarchalism to demote him by representing him as a recent arrival and as no more than a demi-god), and derives from a matriarchal or partly matriarchal form of society in which the gods were acolytes of the goddess, whom they served sexually and by their deaths and mutilations. The ritual that lies at the root of these myths is a spring-time celebration of orgiastic wine-drinking (formerly beer-drinking) and sexual licence (in which normal taboos are broken) followed by the tearing of a male victim by female Maenads or a male deputy, and the scattering of his limbs over land and sea to ensure the fertility of the earth.[18]

In the myth of Osiris, the wine-drinking element is not prominent (though not entirely absent, since Osiris like Dionysus was accompanied by a rout of Satyrs), but the dismemberment of the body is similarly accomplished, while special attention is given in the myth to the castration and disposal of the genitals. Osiris's wife, Isis, is represented as chief mourner and avenger, but, as we saw in the myth of Balder, the chief mourner is really the chief perpetrator of the deed. She works, however, through a male figure, Set (or Typhon), who, as rival of the doomed king and his slayer, represents the earliest, matriarchal form of the Sacred Executioner. The Osiris myth has been much overlaid with patriarchal modifications, but is essentially, like that of Dionysus, the outcome of a sacrificial fertility ritual by which the mother-goddess, earth, is fructified. Other versions of the myth are that of Attis (whose devotees or priests castrated themselves as an act of devotion to the goddess), of Adonis (castrated by a male rival in the shape of a boar and mourned annually by women on behalf of the goddess), of Pentheus (torn to pieces by wild women, or Maenads), of Orpheus, and so on.

The myth of the castration of Uranus by Cronus is particularly interesting because of the evidence it shows of the transition of a myth from a matriarchal to a patriarchal setting. The story describes how mother earth instigated the revolt of the Titans, led by the youngest, Cronus, against their father (and her husband) Uranus. It was mother earth who gave Cronus the flint sickle with which he then castrated his father, after which he threw the severed genitals into the sea (just as Set threw the genitals of Osiris into the sea). According to one version, it was because of this impregnation of the sea that the sea-born Aphrodite was brought to life, for which reason at her greatest centre of worship, Paphos, her priestess bathed every spring in the

The Kenites and the Rechabites

sea in order to renew her vital force. Drops of blood from the castration wound also fell on the earth, giving birth to the Three Erinnyes, or Furies (who, like Aphrodite, are simply another aspect of the goddess herself). In other words, the purpose of the castration of the god is to revivify the goddess, and the male slayer or castrator is merely acting as instrument and agent of the goddess. Yet this aim is disguised and denied in the fully developed patriarchal form of the story, in which the ambition of Cronus to be king of the gods is stressed. In the Hittite version of the legend, the equivalent of Cronus (Kumarbi) actually swallows the seed of his castrated father, thus conceiving the goddess of love within his own body, whence she has to be cut out from his side (like Adam producing Eve from his rib, and Zeus producing Athene from his head).[19] Thus the male slayer moves to the centre of the stage and becomes the progenitor of the goddess whom he previously served. In the process, the conflict between king and rival for the favour of the goddess becomes a male power-struggle.

With the mythological background sketched above, we may turn back to the story of Noah's drunkenness. It is now possible to discern three layers of development in the story: a matriarchal agricultural myth, overlaid by a Kenite patriarchal adaptation, overlaid once more by an Israelite patriarchal adaptation.

In the original matriarchal myth, the element of drunkenness was not a peccadillo but a divine frenzy of the kind induced in Bacchic rites and also found in the Ugaritic literature and ascribed to the god El.[20] In this frenzy, a copulation takes place between the goddess and her husband, who is then destroyed by the new young lover and destined king-consort of the goddess, the body of the slain king being scattered over the fields, and his genitals thrown into the vivifying waters of the sea or river. The hero of this myth is likely to have been Canaan, the eponymous ancestor of the Canaanites, who by slaying the old king established himself as consort of the goddess and thus as rightful founder of a new nation (here a patriarchal element is already entering, for in a true late-matriarchal setting, Canaan too would have to be slain after a while by a new supplanter; Canaan, however, remains to found a dynasty, which is validated, in the manner of early-patriarchal dynasties generally, by a matriarchal myth).

In the Kenite version of the story, the emphasis has been shifted to make a point validating the Kenite ethos and self-identifying code. The main moral is that tents and wine do not go together; Noah introduced wine into his tent and thus got into serious trouble. Canaan has become the villain, though not such an accursed figure as in the Israelite version. He stands for the kind of agricultural community that the Kenites reject, the community based on orgiastic rites,

The Kenites and the Rechabites

in which the men become effeminate and emasculated in their devotion to the mother-goddess earth (for it was when Noah 'began to be a husbandman' that he met his downfall). The hero of the Kenite story is likely to have been Ham (since, on the Rechabite evidence, it was from Ham, or 'Hammath', that the Kenites traced their post-diluvian descent), who dissociated himself both from Noah's drunkenness and from Canaan's crime of impiety, and founded a patriarchal tribe in which orgiastic rites were abolished and the agricultural dependence on mother earth was severed by the adoption of a nomadic life based on an industrial skill, inherited from the antediluvian ancestor, Cain the Smith.

In the Israelite form of the story as it finally appears in the Bible, Ham has been made to share in the crime of Canaan.[21] In this way, the claims of the Kenites to precedence are denied as well as those of the Canaanites, just as the claim of Cain himself was denied by making him the villain of the story of the slaying of Abel. In the Israelite story, the drunkenness of Noah is neither an orgiastic frenzy nor a surrender to the effeteness of agricultural life; for the distinctiveness of the Israelites was that they combined patriarchy with a reverence for agriculture. The drunkenness of Noah is a mere indiscretion caused by inexperience as a husbandman. The crime of Ham is the infringement of a delicate point of etiquette in the code of respect for parents, the savagery of the original castration and dismemberment being censored (remaining only as a folk-memory in the Midrash). A tell-tale clue to the substitution of Ham for Canaan remains in the verse (9: 24) 'And Noah awoke from his wine, and knew what his youngest son had done to him'. Ham was not his youngest son, but Canaan was the youngest son of Ham (10: 6). (The Authorized Version tries to reconcile the contradiction by translating 'his younger son', but the New English Bible quite correctly changes this to 'his youngest son'). This immediately recalls the deed of Cronus, the youngest son of Uranus. In matriarchal myth, the youngest son, the favourite of the mother, is the inevitable champion of the mother in her bloody struggle with the father.

Thus the Israelite story stands in contrast both to the Canaanite version and to the Kenite version, marking a new development in the religious consciousness in its relation to agriculture. The belief in a father-god, transcendent and superior to the rhythms of the earth, released the Israelites from the persistent anxiety of paganism of the Canaanite type, which regarded every springtime as a crisis requiring a magical renewal of nature by means of sacrifice. This release from anxiety and its consequent cruelty is magnificently expressed in the speech given to God after the Flood; 'While the earth remaineth, seedtime and harvest, and cold and heat, and summer and winter, and day and night shall not cease' (Genesis 8: 22). Here the need for cyclic magic is abjured; for God Himself requires no renewal, being able by His steadfast power to guarantee the continual succession of the natural cycles. This aspect of monotheism is alone able to account for the qualitative leap it provided into a new region of human confidence and progress towards freedom. The Flood thus assumes the character of the final crisis, in Hebrew mythology, though in pagan mythology it merely symbolizes in a graphic form the state of perennial and recurring crisis; that is why there is flood imagery in the portrayal of a crisis-figure such as Dionysus, who is associated with an icon of sailing in a boat with animals, while Deucalion, the Greek equivalent of Noah, is given characteristics similar to those of Dionysus.[22]

The Kenites too secured their release from cyclic anxiety, but only at the cost of severing themselves from the earth and agriculture. They became a nomadic tribe, but not in the most primitive sense of nomadism, in which there is indeed complete dependence on the nature goddess, like that of a child at the breast. The Kenites' nomadism was that of skilled artisans, freed from the necessity to till the ground, and thus from the necessity of placating the goddess for injuries done to her or for favours required of her. They were thus city-dwellers as well as nomads, being actually parasitic on the agricultural toil of their customers, to whom they nevertheless offered indispensable service in the manner of all city-dwellers and skilled artisans. They thus portrayed their ancestor Cain as both a nomad and a city-builder, as they themselves were in building cities in lands that were not their own, and keeping contact with the life of the tent, to which they were always ready to have recourse. Their god was thus an inhabitant of a desert volcano (the very word 'volcano' is derived from the name of the smith-god Vulcan whose smithy was inside a volcano), and was specialized in function, serving the other gods by his skill. He was a god who imparted knowledge to his devotees, the knowledge of their craft, which freed them from the land and from the goddess.

The Israelites too had a special knowledge derived from their father-god in His aspect as volcano-god of the desert, but, instead of being a specialized knowledge, it had a universal character. It was the Torah, or 'teaching', which made them free of the caprices of the goddess, but also made them turn back to the earth as its masters or 'husbands' (the expression about Noah could even be translated 'husband of the earth', and the Authorized Version translation 'husbandman' is full of apt resonance). The knowledge given by their God was how to master the land and turn it into an expression of His will. He directed them, therefore, away from His desert residence towards the Promised Land, where, He told them, His own true dwelling place

The Kenites and the Rechabites

lay. Thus the Israelites acquired from the Kenites some of the characteristics that have marked them throughout their history: their search for wisdom and sense of transcendence over earthly matters, enabling them to achieve detachment and mobility; but they, unlike the Kenites, used this freedom of intellectual movement to solve the problems of the 'settlement of the earth' in a paradigmatic section of it, the Holy Land (though in times of exile, they have been forced to revert to something very like the Kenite pattern).

From the above discussion of the story of Noah's drunkenness, we have learnt something important about the figure of the Sacred Executioner: that he was originally, in matriarchal society, or in proto-patriarchal society still basing itself on matriarchal forms, the agent of the goddess, carrying out her will by slaying the outgoing consort and then taking his place. He may be regarded as a positive figure, as in the case of Cronus, or as a negative figure, as in the case of Set, who becomes the prototype for the later dark figure of the banished Sacred Executioner in patriarchal society where the victim is a son – rather than a father-king figure – whose function is to take the place of his father on the altar and enable him to continue his reign in feigned obedience to the demands of the goddess. As patriarchal society develops, the victim becomes a tribute to the father-god instead, and the goddess is forgotten. But the compulsion to sacrifice is never so strong in patriarchal society as it was in late matriarchy, except in times of crisis or panic when the matriarchal pattern reasserted itself in many interesting and subtly disguised ways, which we shall later investigate.

The outcome of the above analysis of the story of Noah's drunkenness, in relation to our main theme of the Sacred Executioner, is as follows. The story, as found in the Bible, is not a Sacred Executioner story, since the execution has been altogether censored out, unlike the story of Cain, in which the censorship took the form of a conversion of the sacrifice into a murder. But *behind* the Bible story we have discerned a Sacred Executioner story of a type earlier than that underlying the story of Cain. This underlying story is of a matriarchal type, in which the sacrifice was demanded by a goddess, and the slayer was originally the goddess's new consort, though as guilt developed he became a dark figure (such as Set or Typhon). Earliest of all the slayers were priestesses of the goddess, acting in a frenzy induced by drugs or wine.

As a further summary of the rather complicated argument, I append two tables, one showing the comparison between the versions of the Bible and the Midrash from which the argument takes its start, and the other the full development of the story from matriarchal ritual to Biblical legend.

1 Comparison between the Biblical and the Midrashic accounts of Noah

BIBLE	MIDRASH
Noah becomes a husbandman	Noah becomes a husbandman
Noah plants a vineyard	Noah plants a vineyard
Noah becomes drunk	Noah becomes drunk
Noah becomes naked in his tent	Noah has intercourse with his wife in her tent
Ham enters the tent and looks at his father's nakedness	Ham enters the tent and castrates Noah to prevent the birth of rival brothers
Ham tells his brothers, Shem and Japheth	
The brothers enter the tent with eyes averted and cover their father	The brothers enter the tent to succour Noah
Noah awakes and becomes aware of what his 'youngest son has done to him'	Noah awakes from drunkenness and becomes aware that Ham has castrated him
Noah blesses Shem and Japheth, and curses Ham's youngest son, Canaan	Noah blesses Shem and Japheth and curses Ham's fourth son (since Ham has prevented him from having a fourth son)

Table 2 overleaf >

2 From matriarchal ritual to the

Matriarchal rituals and myths

Early matriarchal ritual	Early matriarchal myth	Late matriarchal ritual	Late matriarchal myth
(promotes fertility)	(cosmic myth validating matriarchal system)	(promotes fertility and female domination)	(validates late matriarchal system)
Wine orgy	Young god (Dionysus) in continual wine orgy	Wine orgy at wedding of new consort at end of year or half-year	
Triumphant procession of new king	Triumphant progress of Dionysus over the world	Triumphant procession of new king	Triumphant progress of god (Osiris) through world, accompanied by Satyrs
Sexual union of queen and consort		Sexual union of queen and new consort	Marriage of Osiris to Isis
Killing and dismemberment of consort by priestesses	Dionysus-worship involves tearing to pieces of males by female Maenads (e.g. Pentheus Hippasus, Orpheus)	Old consort previously slain and castrated by new consort, acting under orders of queen, who pretends to mourn	Osiris dismembered by evil god, Set, his brother. Isis mourns for him. (Or slayer may be youngest son of goddess, e.g., Cronus)
Genitals of victim thrown in sea. Other limbs scattered over fields			Isis searches for genitals of Osiris, thrown in sea, but cannot find them. She finds his limbs and distributes them to various parts of Egypt

NOTE Matriarchal myths have all been transmitted with patriarchal modifications. The myths of Dionysus and Osiris have been cited simply because they have retained more matriarchal features than most.

Bible story of Noah's drunkenness

Patriarchal foundation myths

Canaanite myth	Kenite myth	Israelite myth (as found in Bible)
(early patriarchal foundation myth of Canaanite nation)	(patriarchal, anti-agricultural foundation myth of Kenite nation)	(patriarchal, pro-agricultural; Canaanite foundation myth in reverse, showing Canaanite nation to have originated in a curse, thus validating Israelite conquest of Canaan)
Old king in wine orgy	Old king forgets nomadic ideal and succumbs to matriarchal wine orgy	Noah, inexperienced agriculturalist, drinks wine and becomes drunk, helpless and naked
King copulates with queen in tent	King has drunken sexual union with queen	
Canaan (youngest son) enters tent, kills and castrates king	Canaan castrates king and takes his place, thus confirming matriarchal pattern	Noah's son Ham enters tent and fails to turn away his eyes from his father's nakedness
Canaan marries queen permanently, thus founding Canaanite nation as patriarchy, but validated by matriarchal forms and practices	Canaan thus founds an effete nation, the Canaanites, still bound to agriculture and matriarchal forms	
	Ham repudiates his son Canaan's action by cursing him. He renounces wine and agriculture, giving his special blessing to his eldest son, who founds the Kenite nation	On waking, Noah curses Ham (thus disqualifying Kenites from primacy) but the curse falls mainly on Canaan, Ham's son, thus dooming the Canaanites to conquest by the Israelites

Chapter Six

Abraham and Isaac

We have seen in the last chapters how the Hebrew Bible transforms the stories of Cain, Lamech and Ham by divesting them of human-sacrificial content. In the case of Lamech, the result is merely a version so truncated and obscure that it serves no new purpose in the narrative, but survives only like an archaeological relic, giving clues about the stratum to which it originally belonged. In the case of Cain and Ham, however, a true transformation has been achieved, by which the stories have been made to serve new purposes. The Cain story becomes a parable of human brotherhood, pointing the moral with the Israelite redactor's great query, 'Am I my brother's keeper?' While condemning violence against one's fellow-man, the story also provides a justification of the institution of animal sacrifice, by which the craving for shedding human blood was to be diverted. In the case of Ham, the crude castration-wish of the son against the father has been transformed into a political message, justifying the Israelite conquest of Canaan. At the same time, on the moral level, a new kind of father-son relationship is inculcated, in which the father is regarded not as a tyrant but as a human being who requires protection by his sons. Ham's defect, in the Israelite story, was not just lack of respect but lack of love towards his father, whose dignity should be safeguarded even when he fails to uphold it himself.

Perhaps the most interesting story of all in this connection, however, is the story of Abraham and Isaac, for here we find not complete transformation, made from an anti human-sacrificial standpoint, but a phase of transition, in which the yearning for human sacrifice is still struggling with the desire to abolish it. The purpose of the story is to show that God Himself ordained that animal sacrifice should be substituted for human sacrifice. At the same time, the story contains no moral revulsion from the very idea of human sacrifice. On the contrary, it is imputed to Abraham as extraordinary merit that he was willing to sacrifice his favourite son, Isaac, at the behest of God. We see here the dynamics of the historic move from human to animal sacrifice: on the one hand, this is a revolutionary step, by which a higher morality is brought into effect; on the other hand, the benefits of human sacrifice cannot be lightly relinquished, and the transition from human to animal sacrifice must appear plausible in the sense that animal sacrifice must acquire the same aura of reverence and holiness that previously belonged to human sacrifice. So Abraham's willingness to perform human sacrifice is in a way a validation of the animal sacrifice that takes its place; if he had not been willing, animal sacrifice would appear only an evasion or inadequate second-best that might not, perhaps, prove an effective substitute, especially in times of emergency. The danger of this method of transition, of course, is that since human sacrifice is not disowned in principle, there is always a possibility that it may return. Nevertheless, once the difficult transition has been made, there is the possibility (actually fulfilled in the Biblical record) that the practice of animal sacrifice may defuse the whole issue and lessen the tension and fear underlying human sacrifice, so that eventually sacrifice becomes divested to a large extent of its magical aspects and becomes a mere sacred meal or gift; at this stage, a genuine moral denunciation of the idea of human sacrifice becomes possible, since the psychological need for it has been transcended.

There can be little doubt that the original story of Abraham and Isaac was one of actual human sacrifice (as argued by various scholars, principally M. J. Bin Gorion[1]). Like other nations, the Israelites traced the foundation of their tribe to a foundation sacrifice. The paradox that Isaac was the promised and miraculously born child through whom the perpetuation of the tribe was to be secured, and yet at the same time the inevitable victim of the sacrifice, was one that could be solved in various ways, but in any case it is typical of the dilemma of founding a nation, a city or a tribe. The device of having twin-founders, one of whom is sacrificed (as in the case of Romulus and Remus, variants of the same name) is one way of solving the dilemma. Another way could be that the next child born could be given the same name as the child sacrificed, thus being regarded as the resurrected or reincarnated lost one. But the success of the new tribe could only be assured by complete surrender to the will of the god, thus abjuring the hubristic position of setting out to fulfil the dictates of an individual will or decision. Thus the chief hope of the new nation must be destroyed, and it must be left to the god to renew the hope in some unlooked-for and miraculous way.

In the Abraham-Isaac story as we have it in the Bible, the double aim is secured by having a father willing to sacrifice, but a merciful God who forgoes the sacrifice, allowing the substitution of an animal. In the original story, in which the sacrifice actually took place, there was no doubt some resurrection motif, by which the foundation of the tribe was miraculously renewed. Some traces of this original story, as we shall see, have been preserved in the Midrashic legends.

Abraham and Isaac

The important point to notice, in relation to the main theme of this book, is that the sacrifice, or attempted sacrifice, of Isaac is accomplished without recourse to a Sacred Executioner figure. There is an extraordinary directness and lack of guilt about the sacrificial theme in the Biblical story. The slayer is Abraham himself, and he is represented as a wholly good figure. Such directness, we may say, was possible only because the decision had been made once and for all to abolish human sacrifice. If there had been some reservation in the minds of the redactors of the Bible, some idea that human sacrifice must be preserved as a secret resource for a time of great trouble, the actual death of Isaac on the altar would have been retained, but the story would have been disguised. By showing that, in the supreme moment of crisis (the actual founding of the nation, and no subsequent crisis could ever equal this moment in poignancy), the sacrifice was abrogated, no excuse was left for its reinstitution in any lesser emergency. The founding of the nation and the abrogation of human sacrifice are associated together in a manner that is decisive. It is as if, in the story of Balder discussed above, the dream devices by which the story is disguised were dissolved and the evil figure of Loki and the blind deluded figure of Hother were to disappear, revealing the scene in its full horror as the slaying of Balder by the assembled crowd of worshippers as a spring sacrifice for the fertility of the crops – only for a voice from heaven to announce that the slaying, now revealed in its true colours, is to be cancelled. Or (to anticipate the argument of a later chapter), it is as if, in the story of the Crucifixion of Jesus, the disguising trappings of malevolent Jews were to disappear, leaving the allegedly Jewish crowd in its true identity as the assembled worshippers of the Christian Church itself, crucifying Jesus for their own salvation and as a foundation sacrifice for Christendom, and then, at this point, as if the Crucifixion were cancelled, since anything so plain and obvious would be impossible to proceed with.

The sheer explicitness, then, of the Biblical story of Abraham and Isaac is an essential part of its function as a myth validating the permanent substitution of animal for human sacrifice. Not that this explicitness is unique to the Bible story: other legends can be found in the ancient world by which nations other than the Israelites marked the substitution of animal for human sacrifice. Among the Greeks, there is the well-known story of Phrixus, first-born son of Aeolus king of Athamas, as it is told by Apollodorus, Herodotus and Plutarch.[2] In a time of great drought, the people decided to offer up Phrixus to the god Apollo. Phrixus was led out to be sacrificed, but the god sent a ram, which carried him off to safety. Phrixus then sacrificed the ram as a *thanksgiving* offering. What happened about the drought we are not

Abraham and Isaac

told. Such a story tells us that the gods can sometimes be merciful, but it does not validate a general and permanent substitution of animal for human sacrifice.

Even more celebrated is the Greek story of the sacrifice of Iphigenia. According to the best-known version of this legend (as recounted by Homer and Aeschylus), Iphigenia was actually sacrificed by her father Agamemnon, in obedience to the god-inspired demand of the prophet Calchas, in order to ensure a good wind to carry the Greek fleet to Troy. But according to another version of the legend (recounted by Euripides[3]), Iphigenia was rescued by the goddess Artemis, who snatched her from the altar at the last moment, substituting a deer. Again, this variant legend could hardly become the basis of a *general* prohibition against human sacrifice, though it could certainly be used to strengthen the view that animal sacrifice could be an efficacious substitute. And such stories are evidence of a growing repugnance against the institution of human sacrifice, and a feeling that the gods, in their more merciful moods at any rate, were unwilling to accept such sacrifice.

Closer to the Abraham-Isaac story is a Hindu legend found in the Rigveda, and regarded by scholars as dating from the Vedism of about the fifteenth century BC. The legend is attached to a collection of seven hymns supposedly recited by Sunahshepa, when he was bound to a sacrificial post and was on the point of being sacrificed to the god Varuna. According to the story, a king called Harischandra made a vow to sacrifice his first-born son to the god. A son was born, called Rohita, but the king kept postponing the fulfilment of his vow until finally Rohita ran away. The king was therefore afflicted by the god with dropsy. The son Rohita, hearing of his father's affliction, determined to satisfy the god with a human sacrifice, without himself being the victim. Accordingly, he bought a youth called Sunahshepa for a hundred head of cattle from the youth's father, the Brahmin Ajigarta. He tied the youth to the sacrificial post and prepared to slaughter him. At this point a man called Vismvamitra, a member of the warrior caste (Kshatriya), came by and suggested to the victim that he should recite the seven hymns referred to. He did so, and such was the magical efficacy of the hymns that he was released, and a nearby goat was sacrificed as a substitute with which the god Varuna was satisfied.[4]

While this story is superficially similar to the Abraham-Isaac story (in the binding of the victim, the demand of the god and substitution of a providentially nearby animal), it is also significantly different. The father is not a willing sacrificer; there is no foundation motif; and the chief moral is the efficacy of the hymns. The story is thus not an epoch-making story, and the same must be said of the other stories cited from Greek legend. In none of them is the substitution of an animal associated with the most awesome possible occasion, the founding of the tribe; and in none of them is this substitution associated with a complete submission on the part of the sacrificing father (in the case of Agamemnon, the rescue of Iphigenia arises from conflict between the gods, and the rescuing goddess is not the deity to whom the sacrifice is being performed).

On the other hand, where we do find in Greek legend a complete devoted willingness on the part of the sacrificer, this is precisely where the sacrifice is actually performed and no substitute is allowed. For example, in Athens, the daughters of Leos were a byword for devotion to their country. Their story is as follows. There was a great famine in Athens in the days of Leos, son of Orpheus. The oracle of Delphi was consulted, and the answer was given that the famine would end only if a human sacrifice were offered. Upon this, Leos decided to offer up his three daughters, who agreed with great willingness to their death. After Leos had slain all three on the altar, the famine ended.[5] Another such story concerns Aristodemus of Messenia, who sacrificed his daughter in order to bring about the cessation of a plague.[6] This kind of daughter sacrifice has a parallel in the Bible in the story of Jephthah, who vowed to sacrifice the first creature to come out of his house to greet him after victory over the Ammonites.[7] This was his daughter, whom he then sacrificed with great sorrow. It is surprising that such explicit stories of human sacrifice were told with approval even when human sacrifice had been officially banned, both in Greece and Israel. Probably, daughter sacrifice was felt to be not so shocking as son sacrifice (after all, in Greece, daughters were expendable and were often exposed at birth). On the other hand, the story of Jephthah, with its cultic accompaniment (a four-day annual mourning rite for the fate of Jephthah's daughter), may be a survival from the early matriarchal age, when daughters were sacrificed by preference, as being superior to the male.[8]

The story of Abraham and Isaac, then, with its cancellation of a sacrifice of supreme importance to the tribe, must be regarded as unique in its implications. The other stories just considered are of much more local and restricted significance. Further, the doctrine of monotheism gave the Abraham-Isaac story a universality that could not be approached by a story in which one particular god or goddess showed mercy on a particular occasion, though admittedly the growth of such stories is an indication of a general trend towards disapproval of human sacrifice – a trend, however, which would have to be embodied in a story of truly focal importance before it could overcome the opposite tendency to slip back into human-sacrificial rites in times of panic. Such a story is the Abraham-Isaac story, which, placed

Abraham and Isaac

The familiar and poignant episode in the Bible whereby human sacrifice is at last expressly forbidden and animal sacrifice firmly substituted. (Abraham and Isaac: engraving by Rembrandt.)

Abraham and Isaac

where it is in the monotheistic Israelite record, must be accounted the human-sacrificial story to end all human-sacrificial rites. If the universal God was willing to accept an animal sacrifice on such a cosmic occasion (for the founding of the Israelite tribe was an event of cosmic importance, set as it is against the background of the Creation of the universe and the choice of Abraham from all the nations and families of the earth), then there was no need to require human sacrifice on any subsequent occasion whatever, and the institution of animal sacrifice can be relied on to do anything for which human sacrifice was previously held to be efficacious.

The Israelite authors of Genesis (shaping a mass of primitive material on which they worked during the seventh century BC) thus adapted a story which was originally about an actual human sacrifice, but instead of disguising the human-sacrificial content while retaining the actual slaying, as was done by the myth-adaptors of other tribes, they retained the plain human-sacrificial intention of the protagonist but changed the denouement to one of animal substitution, thus ensuring that no secret validation of human sacrifice could be read, consciously or unconsciously, from the adapted story. There was thus no need to import into the story the distancing devices by which the core of meaning is surrounded by 'secondary elaboration' (in Freud's phrase). Isaac is not killed by accident, for example by an arrow shot by a blind man. Nor is Isaac killed through the plotting of some malevolent agent, on whom the slaying can be blamed, so that we (the tribe) derive benefit from the providential death without making ourselves in any way responsible for it. To put the matter another way, the failure of the Bible to provide any accident or malevolence as ingredients in the story ensures that Isaac will be reprieved from death, because it is only such disguises that steel the resolve of the tribe to go through with the ritual execution; once all the excuses have been removed, there is no alternative to abolishing the sacrifice.

A malevolent element did actually creep into the Abraham-Isaac story in some of its post-Biblical developments in the Apocrypha and Midrash. Thus, in the Book of Jubilees, we find the figure of a dark angel, Mastema, who suggests to God that He should test Abraham by ordering him to sacrifice his son. When Abraham withstood the test, 'the prince Mastema was put to shame'.[9] The role of Mastema here is clearly derived from that of Satan in the Book of Job. He is not, however, blamed for the performance of the sacrifice and he has no independent power of action. Indeed, so far is he from being the dark power (Loki in the Norse myth) bringing about the death of the hero that his hope is that Abraham will fail in the test and *not* perform the sacrifice. In later Midrashic elaborations of the role of Satan (or Mastema), he is portrayed as putting obstacles in the way of

Abraham and Isaac

Abraham's attempts to sacrifice Isaac: 'Satan came and jogged Abraham's arm and the knife fell out of his hand. As he stretched out his hand to pick it up a Heavenly Voice cried out, "Lay not your hand upon the lad." But for that Isaac would already have been slain' (Tanhuma, Vayera, 23). Satan is here portrayed as saving Isaac's life in his efforts to prevent Abraham from obeying God's command. The angels, however, in another Midrash, are portrayed as doing the same thing, but out of pity for Isaac: their tears of pity, it is said, fell upon the knife wielded by Abraham and dissolved it.[10] In all these elaborations one thing is clear: that the responsibility for the sacrifice lies with God who commanded it and with Abraham who decided to obey the command. We see here a striking contrast with the role of Satan in the sacrifice of Jesus, where Satan, by entering into Judas, directs all his efforts to bring about the sacrifice, not knowing that the end result will be the breaking of his own power. The executioners, too, in the Jesus myth, are Satanized, with the result that God Himself is absolved of all responsibility for the deed, since the executioners are represented as working against Him, not in obedience to Him (though in the end, His wishes are fulfilled).

The responsibility of God Himself for the sacrifice is indeed a vitally important point. We have to note that one important element in the setting-up of a Sacred Executioner to take the blame for the execution is that the god to whom the sacrifice is made is thereby absolved of cruelty. Whatever distancing device is used (whether that of the Sacred Executioner, or the arrangement of an accident, or the plotting of a villain, or a combination of such devices) the effect is not only to clear the tribe from responsibility, but also to clear the god. The tribe, in effect, is saying, 'We are not cruel enough to perform a human sacrifice, and our god, who is merciful, does not demand one; yet if it should somehow come about, through accident or malevolence, it will be just as efficacious as if our god demanded it and we willingly obeyed.' To accuse the god of wanting a human sacrifice would be an insult, so this aspect must be carefully hidden from sight. How zealously, for example, in the Christian myth, the cruelty of the demand of God the Father is concealed from consciousness! His kindness and mercifulness, on the contrary, are stressed: it was because 'God so loved the world' that He sent His son to redeem it. That He required the son to be tortured to death (as a substitute for torturing all mankind for all eternity) is an aspect wholly swallowed up by the accounts of how wicked and cruel were the human and superhuman instruments (the Jews and Satan) through whom this requirement was fulfilled.

We now gain further insight into why the Sacred Executioner is so sacred, despite his accursed aspect which demands his expulsion into

Abraham and Isaac

the desert. For the Sacred Executioner is really a disguised form of the god himself. The hatred directed against the Sacred Executioner is really the hatred that the worshippers dare not direct against the god, whom they secretly hate because of his cruel demands. But along with the displacement of hatred goes a displacement of worship; so that the institution of the Sacred Executioner, whether he is conceived as human or superhuman, carries with it a powerful charge of devil-worship, and there is always the possibility that allegiance will be transferred from the sanitized figure of the god to his evil surrogate.

In the Biblical story of the sacrifice of Isaac these dualistic possibilities are completely banished. Even in the later elaborations, in which a demonic figure does appear, he is in no way a substitute for either the god or the executioner, but, on the contrary, represents the temptations and stumbling-blocks preventing man's fulfilment of the god's demand for sacrifice. In the Bible story we are brought face to face with this demand in its utmost nakedness. And just at this point, the demand is relaxed, never to be renewed.

It will be seen that the demand for sacrifice is basic to all religion, but that the history of a given religion turns on what mode of substitution it adopts. There are two principal modes of substitution: the first is to retain the sacrifice, but to provide substitutes or disguises for the victim (such as animals or criminals), and even for the sacrificer (such as malicious or unwitting persons), and to pretend that the god to whom the sacrifice is dedicated does not want the sacrifice – this is the method of disguise and secondary elaboration; the second method is to provide substitutes for the sacrifice ritual itself – this is the method of sublimation, which is capable of progressive refinement, starting with bodily substitutes (such as circumcision) and progressing to mental and spiritual substitutions (such as asceticism or prayer).

Mythology shows in abundance how attractive the first solution is: how easy it is to retain the sacrifice in its full goriness if only one is permitted to disguise the scene by all the tricks of inversion and permutation of which the mind is capable (it is these tricks that have been made the subject-matter of the 'structuralist' school of mythology, though without any effort to explain why such tricks comprise a defence-mechanism). The second method is hard: it goes against the grain of the psyche, which constantly tries to slip back to the real thing, despising all substitutes as inadequate.

It is in this light perhaps that we should regard the stories found in the Midrash which flagrantly contradict the plain meaning of the Bible account by saying that Isaac *was* sacrificed, either partially (by wounding or blood-letting) or wholly. These extraordinary stories have been studied particularly by Shalom Spiegel, who refutes the

Abraham and Isaac

view that they are post-Christian inventions, intended to provide a rival doctrine to that of the Crucifixion. On the contrary, these stories can be traced to a period before the advent of Christianity. They may even be a survival of the pre-Biblical story of an actual sacrifice of Isaac, since some Midrashic material, as we have seen, may well represent ancient folklore of a kind that was excluded deliberately from the Bible.[11]

These stories take various forms. In one variant, it is said that Abraham did make a mark or wound on Isaac's throat before the angel stopped the sacrifice.[12] Isaac was then taken by angels to the Garden of Eden for a period of two years in order to be healed of his wound (this accounts for the fact that only Abraham, not Isaac, is said by the Bible to have departed from Mount Moriah after the sacrifice (Genesis 22: 19). Yet another Midrash,[13] from a contrary tradition, stresses that Abraham made no mark on Isaac at all, deriving this from the verse that says, 'Do not raise your hand against the boy, and do not do anything to him.' 'Anything' in Hebrew is *me'umah* which this Midrash, by a pun, associates with the word *mum*, meaning 'wound', thus explicating 'do not produce a wound in him'. This Midrash may even have a polemical intent, combating the trend represented by the other Midrashic passages. It is even possible that the Bible itself, by stressing in such a particular fashion that Abraham was told not to do 'anything' to his son, was combating a folk tradition that Abraham at least wounded his son at the Akedah (Akedah, meaning 'binding', is the name given in tradition to the incident).

Other Midrashic passages go further, saying that Abraham drew 'the fourth part of a *log*' of blood from Isaac, this being a loss of blood regarded as dangerous to life.[14] Others go still further, saying that Isaac was actually killed by Abraham and reduced to ashes on the funeral pyre, but, by a miracle, he was brought back to life.[15] This kind of tradition was popular in the Middle Ages and was much cited by the poets who wrote dirges on the Jews massacred in the Christian persecutions. Isaac became the prototype of the martyr, and Abraham became the prototype of those Jewish fathers who killed their own children rather than let them fall into the hands of the Christian mobs.

There are other Midrashic passages (also found in the Talmud), which say that the willingness of Abraham to sacrifice his son, and the willingness of Isaac to be sacrificed (an aspect that receives no emphasis in the Bible but became increasingly stressed in the post-Biblical literature), counted in God's eyes as an actual sacrifice.[16] Thus, references in rabbinical literature to the 'blood of Isaac' or the 'ashes of Isaac' do not necessarily arise from the view that Isaac was actually sacrificed. They may equally well arise from the view that, as one Midrash expresses it, 'it was *as if* Isaac's ashes lay on the altar'. Some scholars, however, make the mistake of regarding such references as always deriving from the view that an actual sacrifice was performed.[17]

There can be no doubt that the Akedah story reflects a period when human sacrifice was believed to be the divine prerogative. Even in its fully developed form, as we have it in the Bible, the story expresses no abhorrence of human sacrifice as such, but instead stresses the mercy of God in waiving His right to such sacrifice. The law of the redemption of the first-born reflects the same attitude: by right, every first-born son should be sacrificed to God, but He, in His mercy, has allowed a ceremony of redemption instead. Very far from this are the later passages of the Hebrew Bible that express horror at the very idea of human sacrifice as being indistinguishable from murder.

There is an especially striking contrast between the story of the Akedah and the story of Abraham's argument with God, on the question of the proposed destruction of the Cities of the Plain. This argument is represented as having taken place before the Akedah, yet it expresses a posture towards God that seems to belong to a much later age. Here (Genesis 18), Abraham, far from acquiescing in God's stern decree to obliterate the guilty cities, pleads with Him in urgent style to spare them if only a handful of righteous people can be found among them. In one of the greatest verses of the Hebrew Bible, Abraham even adopts a peremptory tone with God: 'Far be it from thee to do this – to kill good and bad together; for then the good would suffer with the bad. Far be it from thee. Shall not the judge of all the earth do what is just?' (18: 25). God is called to account to adhere to His own rules and principles. Yet shortly afterwards, when Abraham receives the call from God to sacrifice his innocent son, he makes no protest whatever. Is this a glaring inconsistency on the part of the redactors of the Bible, who yoked together such apparently incompatible scenes? Should we not expect Abraham, on the basis of his courageous stand for justice even to the guilty, to repudiate God's demand for the blood of the innocent, and to say, 'If that is the kind of god you are, I want none of you'?

Using the insights of Kierkegaard[18] and Freud, we may arrive at a different view about this Biblical sequence. The Biblical ideal is one in which man has a covenantal relationship with God, but, though within this relationship he has rights on the basis of which he can make demands, the covenantal relationship itself is not a right but a gift of God's grace. Abraham has been admitted to a relationship ('walking with God') within which he is called 'God's friend' and may even call God to account. But when this Covenant itself is questioned and annulled, there is nothing he can do but revert to the pre-moral and pre-covenantal state of utter submission. The results of this submission is the renewal of the Covenant on a stronger basis than before; but while enjoying the Covenant, he and his descendants are never to forget its underpinning of grace, with those concomitants of grace, awe and horror, the *tremendum*, which God voluntarily lays aside when He enters into covenantal terms with man.

In patriarchal society, the image of the father-god is built up through the sacrifice, by individual men, of their own fatherhood, which is then given back to them in a conditional form. In this way, a tremendous father-image is created, by which men, collectively, are able to overcome their awe of the mother and subordinate her to the father. By sacrificing their own rebellious feelings towards the father, the men strengthen the father-image to the point where it is invincible. If there are any reservations about this sacrifice or surrender, the father-image is correspondingly weakened, and the power of the mother is restored. It is as if the men elect an all-powerful leader in their battle against the power of the women; the more they subordinate themselves to this leader, the more powerful they are in the battle. Loyalty to the leader expresses itself in a declaration of willingness to sacrifice their own lives, or, more important, their manhood (embodied in their generative powers and most sharply focused in the first-born son, especially an only son). Psychologically, every such sacrifice increases the vital force of the father; he is fed and sustained by such sacrifice, which acts as reparation and restitution for the aggressive desires of the sons against the fathers. But, by making the sacrifice (which may be made once and for all on their behalf by some mythical figure), the men now have the powerful father as their ally and friend; he expresses this friendship by restoring their manhood to them, requiring some token of submission, perhaps, such as circumcision, to remind them of what he could have exacted and of what power still remains behind his affability and reasonableness. Indeed, as the history of Judaism shows, the more secure and unquestioned the power of the father-god is, the more he is able to relax, show affability, and treat man as his partner in a covenantal relationship.

Accordingly, the tendency of distancing devices, blurring the responsibility for the sacrifice, is to leave room for aggressive inclinations of the sons towards the father, to weaken the bonds of patriarchal society, and to restore strength to the mother. Where, for example, the son is sacrificed through the machinations of an evil enemy, no true submission has been made to the father, and the death of the son may even serve as an aggressive move *against* the father, designed to dislodge him from his authority. The aggressive feelings, by being redirected against the evil power plotting against the son, have been given a new lease of life and are covertly directed against

Abraham and Isaac

the father himself (disguised in the surrogate figure of the Devil). The sacrifice can thus regain the character it had in matriarchal society of being an expression of rivalry between male aspirants to the favour of the mother (we saw an example of this matriarchal type of sacrifice in the myth underlying the conflict between Noah and Ham). This rebirth of matriarchal attitudes within a context of imperfect (because distanced) patriarchal sacrifice can be designated as *romanticism*, and will be discussed at more length in connection with Christianity, and especially in relation to the rise of the cult of the Virgin Mary in the Middle Ages.[19]

We turn now, however, to discussion of a topic closely related to the theme of sacrifice in the Israelite culture, namely the rite of circumcision.

Chapter Seven

Moses and circumcision

According to the Hebrew Bible, the rite of circumcision was instituted by a command of God to Abraham (Genesis 17). This rite marked a Covenant between God and Abraham, by which God would recompense the loyalty of Abraham and his descendants by making them a fruitful nation and by giving them the land of Canaan. Abraham was ninety-nine years old at the time of his circumcision, his son Ishmael was thirteen, and Isaac had not yet been born, but was circumcised eventually at the age of eight days, the correct time for the rite for future generations. No connection is made in this Genesis account between the rite of circumcision and the idea of human sacrifice. It is not suggested, for example, that there is any connection between the rite and the sparing of Isaac at the Akedah, so that circumcision might be regarded as the price paid for God's forgoing of his due of human sacrifice. As far as this account goes, the rite of circumcision seems to have no aura of fear or horror, but to be simply a way of marking on every male Israelite that the Covenant was in existence.

A difficulty is that an entirely different account is given of the actual inauguration of the Covenant between God and Abraham. This is the awe-inspiring episode known as the 'Covenant between the Pieces' (Genesis 15). In this account, the horror inherent in the motif of sacrifice is certainly present. Abraham (at this time still called Abram) is commanded by God to offer as a sacrifice three animals and two birds. He is to halve the carcasses of the animals, making a kind of corridor between the halves. He now keeps a day-long vigil, keeping off the birds of prey as they swoop down on the carcasses. As the night falls, he goes into a trance and is afflicted by a great fear. He hears the voice of God telling him that his descendants will suffer as slaves in Egypt, but that God will deliver them. In the dusk, he sees a fiery presence passing between the divided pieces; and the Covenant is thus sealed: 'To your descendants I give this land from the River of Egypt to the Great River, the River Euphrates, the territory of the Kenites, Kenizzites, Kadmonites, Hittites, Perizzites, Rephaim, Amorites, Canaanites, Girgashites, Hivites and Jebusites.' This scene, symbolic in multiple ways, is worthy of the greatness of the occasion;[1] after this, the institution of circumcision in Genesis 17 is presented as a mere confirmation or mark of the Covenant.

Moses and circumcision

We are led to suspect, then, that the prosaic and feebly charged account of the origin of circumcision in Genesis 17 is not the last Biblical word on the matter, and we should be inclined to look for an alternative account which would have some stronger connection with the theme of sacrifice. Such an account does exist, but it is told in relation not to Abraham but to Moses.

The passage, which is cryptic in the extreme and has given rise to voluminous commentary during the ages,[2] is as follows:

And it came to pass on the way at the lodging place, that the Lord met him, and sought to kill him. Then Zipporah took a flint, and cut off the foreskin of her son, and cast it at his feet; and she said, 'Surely a bridegroom of blood art thou to me.' So he let him alone. Then she said, 'A bridegroom of blood art thou, because of the circumcision.' (Exodus 4:24-6)

This strange and savage episode has been understood in many different ways, depending on the way in which the pronominal expressions 'him' and 'his' are understood. Did the Lord seek to kill Moses, or his son? Did Zipporah cast the foreskin of her son at the feet of Moses, or at the feet of the Lord, or of His angel? Whatever the answer, the episode induces the same sense of shock as that which we feel at the story of the Akedah, coming so suddenly out of what seemed a relationship of love between the protagonist and God. Abraham, after receiving loving promises, and after being consulted as a friend by God in the matter of the Cities of the Plain, is suddenly confronted by a demand for the life of his son. Moses, after receiving a vision of God's presence in the burning bush, and after being appointed as God's messenger to Pharaoh and as the deliverer and law-giver of Israel, and while actually travelling to Egypt to fulfil God's mission, suddenly meets a divine threat to his life or to that of his son.

The Midrashic comments on the passage, unlike some Midrashim we have considered on previously discussed Biblical topics, give us little help, since they are concerned with mere harmonizing and ad hoc rationalization.[3] They turn on the idea that Moses had incurred God's anger by delaying the duty of circumcising his son, incumbent on him as an Israelite under the Abrahamic Covenant. Some comments suggest that the son in question was Moses' first son Gershom, not, as one might think, his second son Eliezer, because Moses had made an agreement with Jethro his father-in-law at the time of his marriage that his first son would be brought up as an idolater. Later commentators, finding this too perplexing to believe of the virtuous Moses, suggest that the son in question was in fact the second, Eliezer, whose circumcision had been merely delayed, and with good reason because of the danger of taking a newly circumcised infant on a

Moses and circumcision

journey (which itself could *not* be delayed because of God's express command to Moses to go to Egypt); but Moses, on arriving at the inn for the night, had delayed some moments longer than necessary instead of immediately circumcising the child, which could then have been done with safety. Some comments substitute an angel for God, and there is even a tendency in some sources to substitute the dark angel, Satan or Mastema, as the assailant, and to absolve Moses from any offence against God whatever.[4]

All such comments are clearly remote from the drama and agony of the Biblical narrative, which has placed this incident at a juncture where it is both appalling and right. If Abraham had to undergo a tremendous ordeal just after being chosen as the founder of the people of God, it is not inappropriate that Moses too should have to undergo such an ordeal just after being chosen as the climactic figure who would bring God's promise to Abraham into effect. The analogy between Abraham's ordeal and that of Moses will help towards an understanding of the passage before us.

While commentators have differed, as we have seen, about the identity of the assailant (God, an angel, Satan), one possibility seems to have been overlooked by all commentators, whether ancient or modern. This is that the assailant was Moses himself. Yet such an interpretation is possible and even likely in the Hebrew of the passage. I suggest the following revised translation of the first part of the passage:

And it came to pass on the way at the lodging place, that the Lord afflicted[5] him (with divine madness), and he (Moses) sought to kill him (the child). And Zipporah took a flint, and cut off the foreskin of her son, and cast it at his (Moses') feet; and she said: 'Surely a bridegroom of blood art thou to me.' So He (God) withdrew from him (Moses – i.e. the fit of madness left him). Then she said, 'Bridegroom of blood for the circumcision.'

If the above translation is correct, what we have in this passage is an account of the origin of circumcision – one that would have to be regarded as earlier and more authentic than the account given in Genesis 17, where circumcision was said to have been instituted merely as a 'sign of the Covenant'. On the present view, circumcision was instituted as a substitute for child sacrifice. Its validating myth shows Moses, in the throes of a God-given frenzy, about to sacrifice his first-born son in order to inaugurate his mission as deliverer and, in a sense, founder of the Israelite nation. At the point of sacrifice, however, the equally God-given inspiration comes to his wife Zipporah to circumcise the child instead, upon which the frenzy leaves Moses, as a sign that God is satisfied with this substitution. The blood of the circumcision acts as a substitute for the blood of the

Moses and circumcision

sacrifice and is thus a kind of sacrifice itself, not merely a 'sign'. We thus have circumcision occupying a place in Israelite religion somewhat similar to that of animal sacrifice: both are sacrifices in themselves, substitutes for the great sacrifice; both are instituted at a historic moment, and involve an attempted human sacrifice of a child by his father. The difference is that while animal sacrifice is a substitute particularly for the slaying of the first-born, circumcision applies indiscriminately to all male children; and, while animal sacrifice is a sacrament that takes place only at the consecrated shrine and is performed only by priests, circumcision is a domestic rite, performed in the home, and therefore setting up a bond between every individual male and God. Just as the Levites were regarded as acting the role originally set apart for the first-born sons of Israel (who having been redeemed from ritual death should really have dedicated their lives to the service of God[6]), so the rank and file of Israelites, having been redeemed from ritual death by the rite of circumcision, became a 'nation of priests', with a priestly task on behalf of mankind as a whole, namely to serve God in a special way. The rite of circumcision thus became not just a redemption procedure, but an initiation rite by which an infant or even an adult (a 'proselyte') who decided to join the priestly nation achieved associate status.

Yet of course the first-born son was himself a substitute or rather representative of *all* the male children. To sacrifice the first-born son was to sacrifice all the male children existing at the time, and therefore to declare readiness, symbolically, to sacrifice any other male children that might be born. Thus the institution of circumcision is a return to the basic meaning of the first-born sacrifice. In the Moses story no emphasis is laid on whether the son redeemed by circumcision was the first-born or not – it is this doubt that gives rise to speculation by the rabbinic commentators. And yet even in the Moses story, the first-born son is not far away. Just before the story of what happened at the 'lodging place', we find this passage:

And thou shalt say unto Pharaoh: Thus saith the Lord: Israel is My son, My first-born. And I have said unto thee: Let My son go, that he may serve Me; and thou hast refused to let him go. Behold, I will slay thy son, thy first-born.

Then immediately follows the story of the narrowly averted slaying of Moses' own son. There is a strangely terrifying effect in this sequence: it is as if the talk about first-born sons – God threatening to take vengeance on Pharaoh's first-born son because of Pharaoh's ill-treatment of God's own first-born son, Israel – has released a ravenous appetite in God that seeks appeasement in the death of Moses' son. The theme of the dedication of the first-born is never far away, in the unconscious, from the theme of the sacrifice of the first-born. And here we see why circumcision, the origin of which is now described in mythic terms, applies not to the first-born alone but to every Israelite male – because 'Israel is My son, My first-born', and therefore, in relation to mankind as a whole, every Israelite is a first-born. The whole nation is dedicated to God, and is therefore in need of a dedication sacrifice, for dedication is a concept near to redemption.

It is necessary at this point to take account of an important theory put forward by the celebrated scholar, Julius Wellhausen.[7] Wellhausen builds on the fact that the Hebrew word for 'bridegroom', *hatan*, which appears twice in this passage, is derived from a Semitic root which means 'to circumcise', a meaning that still exists in Arabic today. The Hebrew for 'father-in-law' is *hoten*, from the same root and meant originally 'circumciser'. There is thus almost certainly some connection between the main theme of the passage, circumcision, and the use by Zipporah of this word *hatan*, or bridegroom. The solution given by Wellhausen is that the passage marks the transition among the Israelites from circumcision practised as a pre-marital rite at puberty to the circumcision of infants. 'Zipporah circumcises her son instead of her husband, makes the latter symbolically a blood-bridegroom, and thereby delivers him from the wrath of Jehovah to which he is exposed, because he has not submitted to circumcision before his marriage. In other words, the circumcision of male infants is here explained as a milder substitute for the original circumcision of young men before marriage.'

There is no doubt that circumcision was widely practised among Semitic tribes long before the Israelites appeared on the scene. Wellhausen is thus correct in seeing the Moses-Zipporah story as marking the transition between puberty circumcision and infancy circumcision. His explanation, however, of the reason for this transition is not so well considered. He sees the matter as one of humanitarianism; with the advance towards civilization, a 'milder' form of circumcision was instituted. This is to trivialize the matter. To the Israelites, infancy circumcision was not merely a milder form of a generally practised rite, but something of fundamental importance to their own culture. The meaning of the rite was profoundly changed by its transfer from puberty to infancy, and the change marked a new attitude towards society itself and the relationship between man and woman.

Some traces of puberty circumcision remain in the Bible itself. One such trace, probably, is the recording of the age of Ishmael at the time of his circumcision as thirteen (Genesis 17:24). This is represented as of no special significance, being merely the age Ishmael happened to be at the time when God gave the commandment of circumcision; but the coincidence with the known practice of pre-Islamic Arab tribes (supposed by the Biblical authors to be descended from Ishmael) is striking. Another possible reminiscence of pre-marital circumcision is the strange story of the inhabitants of Shechem (Genesis 34), who agreed to be circumcised as a preparation to intermarriage with the family of Jacob. A further possible reminiscence is the story of the circumcision by Joshua of the young men of Israel as a preparation for the invasion of Canaan (Joshua 5); there are symbolic connections between entry into marriage and invasion of a holy land. These stories are harmonized in the text with the doctrine of infancy circumcision, but they may be useful, as we shall see, in determining when that doctrine actually began.

The rite of circumcision, in its original pre-marital form, was most probably a matriarchal custom,[8] in which a young man entering marriage made a sacrifice of part of his penis to the goddess in order to propitiate her and forestall her possible anger at the invasion of her secret places – anger which might manifest itself in the complete destruction of the penis or of the man himself. Psychologists tell us of similar fears on the part of infants in the pre-Oedipal stage, when danger is apprehended from the mother. The rite was thus much bound up with the promotion of fertility, for which protection of the penis was required. Human fertility and that of the earth were always connected, so circumcision would be regarded as promoting successful agriculture; especially as the earth was regarded as the chief physical embodiment of the female principle and as consequently suffering a kind of rape when forcibly entered by the plough.

The rite of circumcision would thus take place in the presence of the bride (acting as representative of the goddess), and would be performed by the bride's father, acting as priest of the goddess. Circumcision of the bridegroom in the presence of the bride is practised in some primitive tribes even today, and in some cases this is also made into an ordeal testing the courage of the groom: if he shows any sign of pain, the bride rejects him as unfit.[9] This trial aspect is no doubt secondary, but it illustrates the subordinate position of the man to the woman in this kind of circumcision: to propitiate her anger or to win her favour by a display of manliness are aspects of the same thing.

The fear for the penis was certainly no idle one, for, as many myths and rites attest, it was at some time in matriarchal society the custom that the Sacred King, after mating with the Sacred Queen, was slain by having his genitals torn off, perhaps in imitation of the behaviour of the queen bee. The mythical figure of the castrated Attis represented this rite, and the priests of Cybele, who castrated themselves in a religious frenzy when dedicating themselves to the service of the goddess, re-enacted it.[10] The rite of circumcision acknowledged the due of the goddess in a milder form. At first it was confined to the priestly class (as in Egypt), but later spread to the whole male populace in most Semitic nations.[11]

When, however, the rite of circumcision was changed, among the Israelites alone, from puberty to infancy, this was a removal of the rite from the sphere of the goddess to the sphere of the father-god. All connection was thus severed between circumcision and marriage. Instead of being an act of deference to the goddess, who might be enraged by male invasion, it became an act of deference to the god, to whom the male first-born, and indeed every male child, ought by right to be sacrificed. Henceforward, marriage could take place without any special ceremony to ward off the power of the female; for the male god had been made so powerful (by the collective sacrifice to him of the masculine power of all his worshippers) that he was able to nullify completely the female threat. A new being appeared: patriarchal woman, subordinate to the male and disposable in marriage, to which she was assigned at the will of her father who acted in the marriage not as her priest, but as her master. The circumcised penis became not the symbol of man's awe of woman, but the symbol of man's domination over woman – the badge by which, through sacrifice, he shared in the power of the father-god.

This immensely important changeover was not accomplished without a struggle. We see particularly in Greek mythology the traces of a prolonged conflict, in which patriarchal religion, through a series of compromises, finally triumphed over matriarchal religion. Many instances of female resistance to the changeover are evident in Greek mythology, most obviously, of course, in the survival of goddesses in the pantheon in a subordinate, yet still strong, position.[12] In Israelite religion the triumph of patriarchy was much more complete, and a male god reigns supreme. In the basic patriarchal myths of Genesis, the female scarcely appears even as a subordinate factor.

When, therefore, some trace of female participation *does* appear in these myths, it is all the more interesting. We saw one such trace in the cryptic story of Lamech, in which Lamech addresses his song to his two wives, Adah and Zillah. If the interpretation given in a previous chapter is correct, this song was on the occasion of Lamech's sacrifice of his son Tubal-Cain, and the song itself was intended to appease his wives who were objecting to the sacrifice. The wives are thus portrayed as the natural defenders of the son, and as refusing to give their consent to the patriarchal sacrifice by which the male god is appeased. Later, in the story of Abraham's intended sacrifice of Isaac, the mother, Sarah, is conspicuous by her absence. Though Abraham is extolled for his obedience to the demand of God for Isaac's life, there is no suggestion that Sarah's acquiescence was sought or given. Indeed,

Moses and circumcision

the traditional commentary in the Midrash assumes that Sarah would never have given her consent, and that Abraham had to hide the whole matter from her. The Midrash even concludes from the close proximity of the announcement of Sarah's death that this was caused by the shock of the very news that Isaac had been exposed to such danger, even though she was informed that he had been spared.[13] Thus, while both Bible and tradition contain the concept of the patriarchal woman, consenting to domination by the man and acting as his helpmeet and supporter in his masculine aims, this ideal is never taken so far as to require assent by the woman to the fundamental male sacrifice. In matriarchal myth, there is always a threat from the woman to her consort, but never to her child, whom she frequently nurtures as the instrument of her violence against the father. Thus even what Freud took as the archetypal patriarchal myth, that of Oedipus, is capable of an earlier matriarchal interpretation, in which the mother actively plotted with the son against the father in order to install the son as her new lover. That such a meaning had to be exorcised is perhaps shown by the patriarchal proem to the story, in which Oedipus destroys the goddess in the shape of the female Sphinx.

In the story now before us, that of Moses and circumcision, the female element is much more prominent than in any other Biblical myth. Zipporah, Moses' wife, even plays the part of saviour, and also (given the aetiological character of the story) is portrayed as the true founder of the institution of circumcision as a patriarchal infancy rite. The story, therefore, ought to be regarded as a validation myth, investing the rite of infancy circumcision not only with male approval but with the consent of the female. Instances of female consent to patriarchal institutions are frequent in Greek myths, the most famous being Athene's endorsement of the father that is made the climax of Aeschylus' great trilogy, the *Oresteia*. That such endorsement was required shows a patriarchy not yet quite sure of itself, and still wishing to derive power from the authority of the female.

The institution of infancy circumcision can thus be seen as an important compromise, by which women were induced to accept the changeover to patriarchy. Zipporah prevents the male rite of infant sacrifice which Moses, in a frenzy, was about to perform; she saves the child, but only at the cost of transferring her own circumcision rite, the symbol of female dominance, to another setting, in which it serves a patriarchal purpose as a substitute for the sacrifice of the male child that would normally be required.

We may now turn back to the very compressed account of Zipporah's actions and words with the hope of understanding them better.

Moses and circumcision

Then Zipporah took a flint, and cut off the foreskin of her son, and cast it at his feet; and she said: 'Surely a bridegroom of blood art thou to me.' So he let him alone. Then she said: 'A bridegroom of blood art thou, because of the circumcision.'

Zipporah's use of a flint knife for the circumcision shows that we have to do with a very ancient rite, with its roots in the Stone Age. A similar knife was used by Cronus to castrate his father Uranus, acting on the instructions of his mother Ge (this myth embodies the ancient matriarchal rite for which marriage circumcision was a substitute, though at a stage when the castration was performed by the usurping king or suitor, rather than by the priestess of the goddess or her frenzied female acolytes or Maenads).

Zipporah then touches the feet of Moses with the foreskin of the child. This is a ceremony of submission, signifying that the circumcision stands symbolically for the sacrificial act that was basically required. Zipporah, at the same time, asserts the power which she herself has over Moses: she says, '(You must accept this offering) because (the real meaning of the Hebrew word *kiy*, usually translated in this passage as 'surely') you are my bridegroom of blood.' Zipporah is reminding Moses that he stands towards her in the relationship of 'bridegroom of blood', that is, when he married her, he was circumcised by her father, Jethro (always known by the sobriquet *hoten Mosheh* – literally, the 'circumciser of Moses'), as token of his submission to her. She thus has a claim on him which she is now invoking in rescue of her son. This appeal succeeds: Zipporah has played her card. But she now knows that she has played it at a cost. The wedding circumcision which she invoked to win her way with Moses has now been abrogated in favour of the infant circumcision with which she saved her son. The institution of 'blood-bridegroom' has now changed into the institution of infant circumcision, with all its attendant meanings.

Her realization and acceptance of this change is signaled by her next words She then said, '(I exchange) bridegroom-of-blood for circumcision.' (The attempted translation in this passage of the Hebrew preposition *la-*, normally meaning 'for', as 'because' or 'in regard of' or other similar phrases indicates great perplexity. Such a translation suggests either that the child has now somehow become a blood-bridegroom, or that Moses has become a less tragic figure of a bridegroom – though he is at this stage not a bridegroom but the father of two sons – by exchanging the blood of his son's circumcision for his own blood at the hands of God, who is enraged by Moses' failure to circumcise his son at the proper time. These meanings are forced in the extreme.) The word Zipporah uses here for 'circumcision' is derived from the root *mul*, which always refers to infant circumcision, as opposed to the root *hatan*, which refers to marriage circumcision. The latter meaning is in fact dropped altogether from the Hebrew language, though it remains in cognate languages; from now on *hatan* in Hebrew connotes only 'bridegroom' and related meanings, without any connotation of circumcision at all.

The story as a whole thus contains a complex process of bargaining by which a *modus vivendi* is achieved between men and women in the changed circumstances of patriarchal society. Men have won, but they have had to concede something to women. The special relationship of the mother to the son has been preserved, for the mother is pictured as the saviour of the son in the face of the aggression of the father. It should be noted that the previous rite, marriage circumcision, also represented such a compromise, since the men won it as a more merciful substitute for the death of the consort after mating, at least in the case of a king or priest. The war between the sexes is full of these compromises or arrangements. While a continuation of first-born sacrifice would never have won the women to support of patriarchy, the institution of infant circumcision was very successful in the Israelite culture: the preservation of the infant circumcision rite became a special concern of the mothers, who no doubt saw in it, unconsciously, the best safeguard of their infant's life. Thus Israelite and Jewish religious history is full of instances of Jewish mothers who, even at great personal danger to themselves, kept up the rite of infant circumcision at times when their husbands were helpless or even unwilling to preserve it.[14]

Yet the story of Zipporah did not retain the status which, I am suggesting, it originally had as the myth validating the institution of infant circumcision. The redactors of the Bible relegated it to a mere incident in the life of Moses, related in such a cryptic and abbreviated way that its significance almost disappeared, though its esoteric, primitive style (similar to that of the story of Lamech) has made it intriguing to all those who can sense a mystery. It has never been the official doctrine of Judaism that circumcision is a substitute for human sacrifice, or anything more than a 'sign of the Covenant'. The only institution regarded as a substitute for human sacrifice is that of animal sacrifice, validated by the myth of the Akedah, in which no female character has any part to play, except off the scenes in the Midrashic remarks about Sarah. The story of Zipporah, indeed, gives the female too great a part to be acknowledged in patriarchal Judaism as it eventually developed, a part as great as that of Athene in the acknowledgment of Zeus.

Chapter Eight

The sacrifice of Jesus

Much of the argument so far has turned on the idea that human sacrifice is particularly connected, historically, with a certain kind of great event, namely, the foundation of a new human grouping, whether a tribe, a city or a religion (categories that sometimes overlap). The stories in which the foundation is described we call 'foundation myths'. The recourse to human sacrifice at moments of great danger to the politico-religious entity is really only a variety of foundation sacrifice. When the very being and continued existence of the society is in doubt, to save it is to call it back from death, to resurrect it, and thus to found it anew.[1]

In the story of Abraham and Isaac, we find a foundation myth of quite unusual explicitness; as suggested above, the lack of any attempt to hide the nature of the sacrifice can be attributed to the fact that the sacrifice (in the myth as it developed) was called off – there was no need to disguise something that in fact did not happen. On the other hand, this very abrogation of the sacrifice is itself a disguise, or what I have called a distancing device. No society is willing to admit fully what happened at its birth; but the nature of a society is to some extent determined by the type of distancing devices it adopts; this is especially the case when distancing devices are employed as a way of shifting responsibility for the sacrifice, for this means that the shifting of moral responsibility is built into the moral ethos and fabric of the society in question.

The Abraham-Isaac foundation sacrifice is at the base not only of Judaism but also of two other great religious communities, Christianity and Islam. In the case of Christianity, the sacrifice of Jesus marks a new foundation, but this is to some extent supplementary to and modelled on the sacrifice of Isaac, though with some extremely significant variations and new distancing devices that alter very much the character of the sacrifice and its consequent effects on community ethos. In the case of Islam, it is the sacrifice undertaken by Abraham itself that serves as a foundation myth, but the victim is changed from Isaac to Ishmael, on the theory (derived by the Arab founder of Islam from Jewish sources) that Ishmael, the son of Abraham, was the founder of the Arab nation.[2] Thus a foundation

The sacrifice of Jesus

myth originally told to validate the foundation of the holy nation of the Israelites was adapted to validate the foundation of another holy nation, the Arabs, whose religious mission, modelled on that of the Israelites, was retrojected to a time about 2,500 years earlier than that of Muhammad, the actual founder of Islam.[3] Thus no sacrificial myth was required in relation to Muhammad himself, though the presence of a gap or psychological need here is no doubt signalized by the rise of Shiite Islam with its foundation sacrifice centred on the figure of Ali, whose death in a dynastic squabble was elevated into a mystical event.

We now turn to a fuller consideration of the extraordinary revival of human-sacrificial ideas in the concept of the sacrifice of Jesus, the foundation myth of Christianity. This concept is largely the work of Paul, who never knew Jesus personally, but became devoted to his person through a vision some years after Jesus's death. Jesus himself never regarded himself as a sacrificial figure. By declaring himself as the Messiah (at a rather late point in his career, which began with Jesus in the role of a prophet heralding the coming of the Messiah as John the Baptist had done), he announced his intention to overthrow the Roman invaders of Israel and to reign over the Jews in the manner of his ancestors David and Solomon, who also had the title 'Messiah'. Being an anti-militarist (though not a pacifist), he expected to defeat the Romans with the aid of a divine miracle, as prophesied by Zechariah, rather than by force of arms. The Gospels, written for the Paulinist Christian Church, are based on authentic traditions (which can be discerned by appropriate methods), but are slanted in such a way as to hide Jesus's anti-Roman intentions. Jesus's death on a Roman cross is interpreted as being due to Jewish, not Roman, hostility, and Jesus is portrayed as a rebel against Judaism, instead of as an opponent of the cruel occupation of the Holy Land by the Roman idolaters and militarists. By the rewriting of the Gospels, Jesus was detached from his Jewish background and cleared of the suspicion of having been anti-Roman, and was thus made a suitable object of worship for a Church now consisting mainly of non-Jews seeking official Roman recognition for their new cult.[4]

It is not, however, with the historical Jesus that we are concerned in this book, but with the mythical figure of Jesus and the way in which his death functioned as the foundation myth of the Christian Church. Yet the fact that this myth was grafted on to a historical incident that was in reality unsacrificial in character was important for the development of the myth and for its historical consequences.

The Christian version of the death of Jesus certainly comprises a foundation myth of a most grandiose type. It marked the beginning of a new tribe, Christendom, to whom the death of Jesus opened the way

The sacrifice of Jesus

to the favour of God who was regarded as angry with all mankind because of the sin of Adam. To belong to the new tribe was the only way to escape God's wrath, which would manifest itself by condemning all non-Christians to eternal torture.[5] It is of course true that every tribe ever founded has regarded itself as superior to the rest of mankind in some important respect. In polytheism, however, this intolerance was tempered by the view that each nation had its own god or gods, whose existence one's own god recognized and respected. Christianity, being a form of Jewish monotheism, did not have this option. It therefore condemned all forms of community except its own, and required all mankind to join Christendom. Judaism itself, though monotheistic, had not taken this path, having a pluralistic vision of many separate communities worshipping the one God in their own ways, with Israel, God's chosen people or 'firstborn', playing a priestlike role among the nations of the world. The foundation myth of Judaism was regarded as a preparation for this role, and did not therefore apply to all mankind, nor did it exclude non-Jews from God's grace (though those who wished to join the priest-nation as proselytes, such as Ruth, were accepted[6]).

Though the human-sacrificial myth of Christendom marked a new start, it was linked in many ways to the old dispensation of Judaism, and therefore to the foundation myth of Judaism, the Akedah, or attempted sacrifice of Isaac. As several scholars have pointed out, the language used by the New Testament in describing the sacrifice of Jesus frequently echoes the Old Testament description of the Akedah. For example, we find the following: 'For God so loved the world that He gave His only begotten son' (John 3:16). Elsewhere we find Jesus described as God's 'beloved' son, the same Greek word (*agapetos*) that is found in the Septuagint in reference to Isaac (Genesis 22:2). It is clear that a parallel is intended: just as Abraham was willing to sacrifice his beloved son, so God the Father was willing to sacrifice His son Jesus. The parallel, however, is strangely incomplete. For in the Akedah there were three *dramatis personae*, Abraham, Isaac and God who demanded the sacrifice. In the Christian myth, God the Father plays two roles at once: He is the sad, sacrificing father, and He is also the father-god who demands the sacrifice in appeasement of His anger at the Original Sin of mankind. God denies His fatherly feelings in order to bring about a sacrifice to Himself. As self-denying parent, God bows to some dark necessity beyond His control; but as father-god, He is Himself that necessity.

This double-faced role of the Christian father-god arises (as briefly pointed out on p. 81) from the chief difference between the Old Testament foundation sacrifice and that of the New Testament: the determination, in the latter, to shift responsibility for the sacrifice. In

The sacrifice of Jesus

the story of Abraham and Isaac there is no attempt to burke the full horror of the occasion: it is quite explicitly God who demands the sacrifice and it is quite explicitly Abraham who sets himself to perform it. In the story of the sacrifice of Jesus, however, so many distancing or responsibility-shifting devices are used that it can be regarded as a compendium of such devices. Other myths we have examined (for example, that of the death of Balder) were good examples of the art of shifting responsibility for a human sacrifice; but the Christian myth is the supreme example. And the compelling motive behind all these devices is the utter necessity that the sacrifice should actually take place; by hook or by crook, Jesus has to die. He cannot be reprieved as Isaac was, for there can be no substitute for his actual death, if even a fraction of mankind is to be saved from the eternal wrath.

In the myth of Balder, as we saw, one of the devices involved was the deification of the victim. That the victim of a human sacrifice should become divine at the point of death was demanded by many possible aspects of such a sacrifice. In the founding of a city, for example, the victim became the tutelary deity of the new city, his death having added him to the number of gods, among whom the city would now have its personal representative. In the sacrifices of the Aztecs, the victims became divine in the sense that their life-energy went to replenish that of the sun-god who would otherwise become weak; thus the victim attained an unindividuated immortality. Sometimes, however, the victims became divine even before their death; in such cases, the sacrifice was regarded as the enactment on earth of a cosmic process of death and rebirth that was continually taking place in the heavens. The myth of Balder took place in 'mythical time', which meant that it was always taking place; the death of a human victim on earth in the role of Balder ensured that the human community was not left out of the sweep of the cosmos.[7]

In the latter cases, however, there was another factor at work, namely that to kill a god, or to assist a cosmic process of death and rebirth, is something different from killing a fellow human being. It is therefore possible to disguise from oneself, in an ecstasy of cosmic participation, what one is actually doing. This particular kind of disguise has been very powerful in Christian worship. It is very rare indeed for Christian believers to regard the death of Jesus as belonging to the history of pagan human sacrifice (a notable exception was T. S. Eliot, one of the few adherents of Christianity who have understood fully its affinities with rites of pagan sacrifice[8]). While a Christian is accustomed to thinking of Jesus as both man and God, when he thinks of the atonement aspect of the Crucifixion, he attends to the divine aspect of Jesus; the thought that Jesus was a human

The sacrifice of Jesus

sacrifice thus never enters his mind, or, if it does, is fended off with the thought, 'But Jesus was not a man, he was God.' While thinking of the actual death of Jesus, however, he attends to the human aspects – his pitiable sufferings, and the wickedness of his human enemies; he becomes a man done to death by evil-doers, not a god suffering cosmically. Thus the thought that Jesus was a human sacrifice (or rather that his death functions as one in the mind of the worshipper) is overlooked, or, if momentarily evoked, dismissed as too barbaric to be relevant. We have therefore the phenomenon of a religion in which human sacrifice is more central than in any religion known to us (so much so that the Aztecs, who rivalled Christianity closely in this respect, found the doctrines of Christianity very familiar and unremarkable[9]), but which nevertheless repudiates human sacrifice as an alien an outdated notion.

It is necessary, therefore, to dwell somewhat on the place of sacrifice in Christianity and to bring out its full meaning. It must be stressed that the definition of a human death as a sacrifice depends on the use to which it is put religiously. It does *not* depend on historical proof that the worshippers or their ancestors actually participated in an openly acknowledged rite in which a human being was put to death for the purpose of founding a tribe or a religion, or to save the tribe from extinction or external torture after death, or to ensure the continuance of the agricultural cycle (all these possible reasons are really variations of each other, though which of the variations is selected as basic is a matter of taste). As we have seen, it is very rarely that the community that benefits, or thinks it benefits, from human sacrifice acknowledges reponsibility for performing it. It much prefers to ascribe the death to accident or malevolence beyond the control of the community. The means by which the death took place, whether human or even non-living, is in some way ostracised or repudiated. But, if the death is regarded as having saved the tribe, then we are in the presence of human sacrifice.

It may be objected that the above definition has left no room for a distinction between a human sacrifice and a *martyr*. The Christian religious history is full of martyrs, starting with Stephen, and it might be (and sometimes is) argued that Jesus was simply the first of this line of martyrs. But a martyr means a 'witness', and the reason for the death of martyrs is that they witness to some truth that they hold dearer than their lives. The truth for which the Christian martyrs died was the saving power of the Crucifixion of Jesus. It would be meaningless to say that this was the truth for which Jesus himself died. An act cannot witness to itself. Socrates can be called a martyr, for he died rather than renounce his philosophical beliefs. But, if he deliberately chose to die so that his death might shield the people of Athens from

The sacrifice of Jesus

the consequences of their sins, this would be an act of sacrifice, not of martyrdom. Of course, there can be some overlapping between the functions of sacrifice and of martyrdom. Martyrdom is quite commonly venerated as also having some of the quality of a sacrifice. It is believed that the martyr's suffering has a protective effect on believers, and (in Christianity) that he partakes in and renews the mystery of the Crucifixion.[10] The one case, however, in which this overlap does not and cannot occur is that of the original sacrifice itself, for without it, there would be no Crucifixion for the subsequent martyrs to participate in.

With the growth of modern liberalism, there have been Christians, even in the Roman Catholic Church, who have denied that the death of Jesus was a sacrifice, and who have insisted instead that it was a martyrdom. As one Roman Catholic theologian said to me, 'Jesus simply showed how a good man could die'.[11] To substantiate this view from the Gospels, one would have to demonstrate that there were some beliefs which Jesus advocated in the face of dangerous opposition and which he was prepared to die for rather than renounce.

What were these beliefs for which Jesus was prepared to die? If we say that it was his belief in his own divinity, then we are back in a vicious circle of reasoning. For the belief in Jesus's divinity, as expressed in the Gospels, is inextricably bound up with his sacrificial role. It was not simply as the Son of God that Jesus came into the world (imagine a Christianity in which Jesus declared himself to be the Son of God and lived on to a ripe old age!), but to enact the soteriological role of the Son of God who dies and is resurrected and acts as a 'ransom for many'. We cannot say, then, that Jesus was a martyr who died for his belief in the necessity of his own martyrdom. Such a death would be entirely empty of content. To 'give an example of how to die' when there was no reason why he should die would not be a good example at all, but a pointless suicide. Good men may certainly choose to die, very often by violent deaths; but only when there is something to die for.

What then shall we say (pursuing the idea of Jesus as a martyr) were the beliefs or principles for which Jesus gave his life? A commonly given answer is that he was a reformer, who lost his life in the struggle against reactionary authority. If this were so, Jesus could certainly be regarded as a martyr, like, say, Socrates, or Martin Luther King, in the cause of justice, freedom or progress. It is true that Jesus is portrayed in the Gospels as conflicting with the Pharisees on questions of Sabbath observance and as denouncing the Pharisees as oppressive authorities. When it comes to describing the circumstances of Jesus's death, however, these matters are forgotten. In the accounts of his

The sacrifice of Jesus

trial, it is nowhere said that the matter of Sabbath observance was brought up, or that the Pharisees denounced him for opposing their authority. Jesus's chief prosecutor was the High Priest, who was a Sadducee; and the charges against Jesus were all connected with his role as Messiah, or Son of God. The issue is represented to be entirely one of whether Jesus had committed blasphemy by claiming to be a divine figure. It is clear that if Jesus had been regarded as merely a reformer of the Jewish Law, he could not have become the centre of a new religion, but, at the most, the founder of a new sect of Judaism, such as Karaism. The essence of the charge against Jesus, as it was conceived by the Paulinist writers of the Gospels, was that he wished not to reform the Law, but to abolish it altogether, and to substitute for it a new form of religion, based on his own personality as divine saviour.[12] In order to fulfil this soteriological role, his death was a necessity. So we return to the point that Jesus, whatever his reforming activities, was not a martyr to reform or to anything else. His death was not that of a martyr but that of a saviour, as far as Christian doctrine is concerned. If he had succeedeed in getting the Pharisees to relax the Sabbath laws, he would not have fulfilled his mission at all.

It is possible of course that, as a matter of historical fact, Jesus *was* a reformer. This is irrelevant, however, to the question of what kind of Jesus-figure acted as the basis of Christianity as a religion distinct from Judaism. When we come to examine the historical facts about Jesus, as opposed to the history of the Christian Church, the most probable solution (as I argued in full in *Revolution in Judaea*) is that Jesus was a committed adherent of Judaism, who intended no reform of Judaism other than that for which the Pharisee movement was responsible; for Jesus's alleged Sabbath reforms all turn out, on examination, to be identical with those already instituted by the Pharisees.[13] Historically, Jesus's mission was neither to be a reformer nor to be the divine saviour, but to be a Messiah in the Jewish sense of the word, that is, a Davidic king, who would fulfil the prophecies of the Old Testament by driving out the foreign invaders, restoring Jewish independence, and inaugurating a worldwide era of peace. His alleged conflicts with the Pharisees can all be traced to two redactorial motives: to shift the blame for Jesus's death from the Romans to the Jews and thereby to depoliticize Jesus's aims; and to retroject into Jesus's lifetime the conflict of the early Church with the Pharisees in the period of the redaction of the Gospels (AD 70–120).

All such facts or theories are irrelevant to our present task, which is to examine the Christian myth, a myth that is not about the death of a reformer or religious patriot, but about a cosmic sacrifice. Some of the details of the myth would not be as they are were it not for historical circumstances, and it may be necessary to note such connections at

The sacrifice of Jesus

times, but the main theme is the myth itself. If there are Christians nowadays who prefer to jettison the myth and to regard Jesus as a reformer, they are of course entitled to do so, but their decision has nothing to do with Christianity as a historical movement, which came into existence only through belief in the myth.

The Christian myth being about a sacrifice, the relevant questions are: who was the sacrificer? who was the victim? for whose benefit was the sacrifice performed? to what divine being was the sacrifice offered? Having answered these questions, we shall have to consider what *type* of sacrifice this is: in particular, how is it related to pagan human sacrifice, to the mystery religions of the Hellenistic world and to Gnosticism? But, first of all, it is necessary to consider how it is related to Judaism itself, and to the sacrificial system of the Jerusalem Temple.

There is evidently a considerable desire, on the part of the New Testament writers, to relate the sacrifice of Jesus to the Jewish sacrificial system. Thus, Jesus is likened to the Paschal lamb by Paul: 'For indeed our Passover has begun; the sacrifice is offered – Christ himself' (I Corinthians 5:7). According to John, the fact that the Roman soldiers did not break Jesus's legs after his death, as was usual with crucified corpses, was in fulfilment of the law in Exodus about the Passover sacrifice: 'For these things were done that the scripture should be fulfilled, A bone of him shall not be broken' (John 19:36). The Epistle to the Hebrews particularly sees the death of Jesus as the culmination of the Jewish sacrificial system: 'Such a high priest does indeed fit our condition – devout, guileless, undefiled, separated from sinners, raised high above the heavens. He has no need to offer sacrifices daily, as the high priests do, first for his own sins and then for those of the people; for this he did once and for all when he offered up himself' (Hebrews 7:26-7). Jesus thus combines in himself the role of sacrificer (high priest) and sacrifice; and the function of atonement that was performed by the Jewish sacrifices imperfectly (since they had to be renewed daily) was performed perfectly and for ever by the sacrifice of Jesus.

The Passover sacrifice, as it happens, was not an atoning sacrifice in the practice of Judaism. It was rather an affirmation of thanks to God for the deliverance from Egypt and for the Covenant. It is true that the 'Passover sacrifice of Egypt' (as the original sacrifice described in Exodus was called) was a protective sacrifice by which the disaster decreed against the Egyptians was warded off from the Israelites. But the 'Passover sacrifice of the generations' had none of this aura of fear; it was carefully distinguished from the Egypt sacrifice and had different laws for its observance.[14] This is not a trivial point, for it applies to the Temple system of sacrifices as a whole. This system was not directed towards *salvation*. That had taken place long ago, at the time of the institution of the Covenant. All Jews lived within the Covenant, and did not have to worry about anything so basic as salvation. What they had to worry about was to fulfil the conditions of the Covenant, and even this was not really a great worry, as the existence of the Covenant did not depend on every single act performed. For individual sins could be wiped out by repentance, and atonement could then be ratified by the bringing of the appropriate sin-offering.[15]

As has been well argued by Professor J. Milgrom,[16] the sacrificial system of the Bible, in its finally redacted form, has eschewed the more primitive features of animal sacrifice as practised in other cultures of the Near East. The majority of the sacrifices have taken on the character of 'offerings' (as their Hebrew names attest), and are gifts to God rather than redeeming rites. Even the sin-offerings have lost all magical character, and are regarded as inefficacious without repentance on the part of the sinner. Most remarkable is the fact that the cleansing rites required before entry into the Temple precincts have been divested of all reference to evil spirits, and are therefore regarded as rules of etiquette rather than as substantive forms of exorcism, as in other cults. Even the rites of the Day of Atonement, which retain more of the awesome primitive quality than any others, are not a foundation ceremony in which the world is renewed, but merely a wiping-up of sins accumulated during the past year, a kind of annual spiritual reckoning which does not pretend to change the nature of the human lot, since another Day of Atonement will be required each year.

This piecemeal, rational approach was due to the conviction that the great sacrifice (the Akedah) had taken place long ago, that the Covenant had resulted from it, and that the worshipper thus lived in spiritual security within it. The Christian attitude to sacrifice, on the other hand, arose out of the shattering of this sense of security (or, more accurately, it arose from the standpoint of those who had never acquired it). To the author of the Epistle to the Hebrews, the fact that the Jewish sacrifices had to be continually repeated showed that they were 'imperfect' – that they left the problem of sin essentially unsolved. What was needed was a solution that would end the problem of sin once and for all. Christianity, in fact, was a return to the condition of primitive dread, in which the primary problem is not 'How shall I improve my deeds?' but 'How shall I be saved?'[17]

It is therefore quite mistaken to see the Christian concept of sacrifice as arising naturally out of the Jewish sacrificial system, or as providing the climax to which it tended. On the contrary, the natural tendency of Judaism was in Christianity catastrophically reversed. The whole tendency of the Jewish system was to *reduce* the importance of

The sacrifice of Jesus

sacrifice; the very term 'sacrifice' is a misnomer in relation to the majority of the offerings of the Jerusalem Temple, where in general the tone set was that of a communal meal with God, with the aim of thanksgiving rather than of redemption. In Christianity the age-long Jewish process of sublimation disappears as if in a sudden bout of psychosis. We are back at the primitive level at which the abyss opens and panic requires a victim. It is not surprising in these circumstances that the human victim reappears, after so many centuries of animal substitution. It is not surprising either that the theme of mass redemption reappears, so long after its replacement in Judaism by the theme of individual self-improvement.

But this air of sudden psychosis is really misleading, because Christianity is not an incident in the history of Judaism, but in the history of Hellenistic religion. Though Christian theorists set great store by the alleged continuity between Judaism and Christianity, and though this continuity has been claimed from the earliest days of the Christian Church (except by heretics such as Marcion, who vehemently denied it), it was never much more than an illusion, as far as the central foundation doctrines of Christianity are concerned (though this is not to deny the enormous influence of the Old Testament on Christian movements and individuals of a later age). In order to illuminate the Christian sacrificial myth, therefore, it is necessary to turn away from Judaism to the salvation cults of the Hellenistic world.

Chapter Nine

Christianity and Hellenistic religion

Christianity, with its concern with salvation, and its achievement of salvation through the death of a divine figure, shows a striking discontinuity with Judaism, which is concerned with neither of these motifs. In Judaism the word 'salvation' is used often enough, but it refers usually to physical or political deliverance. Moses, for example, was a 'saviour' (Hebrew – *moshiy'a*) becuase he delivered the Israelites from Egypt, and even the rather disreputable Samson was a 'saviour' because of his exploits against the Philistines. In Christianity 'salvation' means deliverance from eternal death, or hell; or, positively, it means the acquisition of eternal life for the soul. A doctrine of the 'resurrection of the dead' existed in Judaism at the time of Jesus, referring not the immortality of the soul but to the resurrection of the body in the time of the 'World to Come'; doctrines of the immortality of the soul have also existed in Judaism, but not with the full force of dogma.[1] In so far as the term 'salvation' was associated occasionally with these doctrines, it was God Himself who was the saviour, not any emissary or sacrificial figure; and nothing could be further removed from Judaism that the concept of God Himself suffering death.[2]

Yet the idea of a divine figure who dies and thereby 'saves' was very common in the ancient world. It therefore seems obvious that Christianity should be considered in relation to the other cults which had this concept. Such comparison, however, has been strongly opposed by most Christian scholars of the ancient and modern world.[3]

From the special standpoint of this book, we may begin by considering whether there were any devices in the mystery religions for shifting the blame for the death of the god. One of the best-known rites in the religions of Attis (Phrygia), Adonis (Syria) and Osiris (Egypt) was the rite of mourning the death of the god. This mourning rite was the special concern of the women, and has been described in many ancient sources.[4] How should we understand this rite? The god died in each of these religions only to rise again in glory, so why was it necessary to mourn his death with paroxysms of simulated grief as if entirely unaware of the happy outcome? There is of course a certain dramatic effect in this; the women are taking part in a kind of sacred play, in which the whole myth of the god and goddess is being enacted. It is in such simulations, regarded as having magical effects on a cosmic scale, that drama as an art form has its origin. Yet, at the same time, the mourning also has a motive of purgation of guilt. By mourning, the women, acting as representatives of the female principle or goddess, are disclaiming responsibility for the death. Yet we know that, in fact, the chief responsibility for the death lies with the goddess. For the death of Attis, or Adonis, or Osiris, is actually decreed by the goddess; the myths arise from a social reality in which the young king had to die at the end of his short reign in order to make way for a new consort for the queen.[5]

This social reality, of course, had long ceased to exist at the time of the Hellenistic mystery cults that were concerned with the worship of Attis, Adonis and Osiris. Though each was derived from a specific, non-Hellenistic region, each had adopted a universalistic colouring which would be helpful in spreading the cult throughout the Greco-Roman Empire. Moreover, the specifically agricultural connotation of these religions had been transcended in the mystery cults derived from them. It was no longer in the interests of a good harvest that the god died and came back to life, thus enacting the miracle of the revival of the fields in springtime. Nor was any earthly representative of the god actually done to death, as had been the case in the earlier history of these religions. Further, the 'mystery' aspect of the Greco-Roman cults was foreign to the religions into which it was grafted and which had originally been quite open and public systems of observance involving the total community, though containing some rites performed secretly, yet on behalf of the whole community, by a priestly caste. This priestly secrecy had now taken over the whole cult, which was for the benefit of an initiated minority, not of a whole national or tribal community.

The indigenous mystery cult of Greece was that of Eleusis, where secret initiation rites were performed in connection with the worship of Demeter, the goddess of agriculture. These ancient rites, however, should not be confused with the mystery cults of the Greco-Roman empire. The Eleusinian mysteries were carried on as a sort of adjunct to the public cult of the Olympian gods, not as a substitute for them. They were frankly for the privileged few, and carried with them a stamp of ultra-respectability, rather like the Masonic lodges of our own day. The majority, who were not initiates, were not thereby damned souls. The mysteries were held to give special insight into the hidden world and to equip the initiates with special qualifications for the next world, but they were not regarded as essential for salvation.[6] The less official Orphic mysteries, on the other hand, beginning in the sixth century BC, did have an evangelical tone, and can be regarded as

Christianity and Hellenistic religion

the precursors of the Greco-Roman mystery cults. In them also can be found the origins of the anti-world and anti-flesh orientation that became characteristic of the mystery cults.[7]

The Eleusinian mysteries, centring on the worship of a goddess of agriculture, may be regarded as an outlet for the matriarchal religion which had been supplanted by Greek patriarchalism, but practice of the cult was strictly limited and not allowed to interfere with the duties of citizenship in patriarchal society, which were regarded with great respect as the chief business of that society. It was when this respect began to break down, because of the decline of the city-states and the rise of great military empires in their place, that the mystery religions developed an aura of escape and ecstatic other-worldliness. The matriarchal elements in mystery cultism now acquired a new importance, because patriarchal society had become oppressive in a way it had not previously been; a man could no longer identify himself with his society, but felt tiny and powerless before the great patriarchal machine. The process of dying with the dying – and subsequently resurrected – god was a way of breaking down the patriarchal 'armour' (in Reich's term[8]) and achieving a new birth and a new identity, free of the crushing weight of a militarized and bureaucratic society.

Yet the matriarchal emphasis differed in the different mystery cults. In Mithraism, which, despite its origins in Persian religion, was the most artificial of the mystery cults, the matriarchal element was entirely suppressed, and the death and resurrection of the god, with the attendant initiation rites, were elaborated in purely masculine terms. This was a religion for the recovery of male pride rather than for escape into the maternal bosom.[9] In Osiris-worship, on the other hand, there was great emphasis on the figure of Isis, a mother-figure who anticipated the figure of the Virgin Mary in later Christianity, being portrayed as the mourner of the god and also as a mother with divine infant in the setting of a manger or cow-byre (with overtones of the ancient worship of the cow as a sacred animal symbolizing motherhood). The ecstatic sentimentality of Isis-worship was one reaction to the surrender of male supremacy, by which the death and emasculation of the male was diverted from the sphere of responsibility of the female.[10] In this type of religiosity, there was a proliferation of distancing devices that were important for the development of Christianity, especially the emergence of a dark male figure of evil as antagonist and slayer of the god; but there was no grim father-god demanding the sacrifice of the young god on patriarchal grounds, as there was in Christianity – which thus provides a unique amalgam of patriarchal and matriarchal motifs, with distancing devices derived from both.

Christianity and Hellenistic religion

On the other hand, in the Attis-worship of Phrygia, there was no attempt to disguise the cruelty of the goddess in demanding the death of the young god. The mother-goddess, Cybele, was worshipped in her full power. There was an ecstatic male masochism, evinced ritually by the orgiastic self-castration of devotees described so graphically by Catullus,[11] in which the devotees, often seized by an unforeseen impulse, enacted the role of the god Attis himself.[12] In Adonis-worship, however, the cruel aspects of the goddess Astarte (Venus) were muted; there were extended scenes of female mourning for the dead god; and the death was attributed to a malign male power in the form of a boar, sent by or incarnating a rival god. Yet Adonis-worship did not develop the sentimental divine mother-and-child motif found an Isis-worship, and its emphasis seems to have been on a more adult love-relationship between goddess and young lover, renewed continually through the death and resurrection of the young god.[13]

Each mystery religion thus had its own tone and character. They all had in common a turning-away from public to private religion, by which the cult no longer served to validate the tribal or national existence, but served the needs of the individual, alienated from the world around him and belonging to no earthly city. There was thus a paradoxical character about the mystery cults, in that they combined an atmosphere of secrecy and separatism with a tendency to universalism, whereas the national cults, such as Judaism or the Greek Olympian worship, were openly practised, but confined to a given culture and historical background (these cults had universalistic aspects too, though of a multi-cultural and pluralistic, rather than individualistic, nature).

Perhaps even more important than the mystery cults for the development of Christianity is the movement known as Gnosticism. This built largely on the mystery cults, but divested them entirely of their local affiliations. Gnosticism was a religion not about a god of Phrygia, or Syria, or Egypt, but about planet earth and its place in the universe as an outlying region occupied by the evil force struggling against the power of good (in describing Gnosticism, it is almost impossible to avoid the language of science-fiction, which indeed is partly given over to a modern form of Gnosticism).

To some extent Gnosticism arose also out of Judaism, from which it derived part of its cosmic scope, but here too it shed the local colouring and nationalist rootedness of Judaism, thus becoming the perfect expression of alienation in the Hellenistic world. From the mystery religions it took the idea of salvation through the death and resurrection of a god, but the sexual significances of salvation, still strongly retained in the mystery cults in male-female themes, were again made abstract. The entity to be saved (the soul) was regarded as sexless, and the aim of religion was to achieve this sexless state. As a consequence of this desexualization, the paranoia inherent in mystery religion became much sharper; the dualism of good and evil became central, and the discerning of evil forces, both on earth and in the heavens, became an urgent preoccupation. Where the mystery religions had vaguely adumbrated evil gods responsible for the death of the young god, Gnosticism focused its anguished attention on the cosmic evil which it became the main aim to escape or overcome. Zoroastrianism had previously regarded life as a struggle between cosmic good and evil, but not in terms that put the earth and its activities on the side of evil.[14]

There have been great fluctuations in the opinions of scholars on the history of Gnosticism. The traditional Christian view was that this movement was an offshoot of Christianity, and was in fact a Christian heresy, founded originally by Simon Magus. In the nineteenth and twentieth centuries scholars such as Reizenstein and, later, Bultmann took the view that Gnosticism actually began before Christianity, and that it had a strong influence on Christianity itself, especially in the formation of the view of Jesus found in the Epistles of Paul and in the Gospel of John. Then came a phase in which the view of Bultmann was discounted as without sufficient historical basis, and it became scholarly orthodoxy once more to regard Gnosticism as merely an eccentric variant of Christianity. Quite recently, however, new light has been thrown on Gnosticism by the discovery of a great library of Gnostic texts at Nag Hammadi, in Upper Egypt. These are Coptic translations of Greek originals, and are still being studied by an army of scholars. But one striking fact that has emerged is that some of these texts are Gnostic without being Christian. Consequently, it has become once more probable that Gnosticism preceded Christianity and was an important influence on it.[15]

Of the non-Christian Gnostic texts recently found at Nag Hammadi there are two main kinds: the pagan ones, without reference to either Judaism or Christianity, and the 'Jewish' ones, which contain much reference to Judaism, but none to Christianity. It would be more accurate, however, to call these latter texts 'anti-Jewish' rather than Jewish. Their wealth of references to Judaism has caused scholars to regard them as having been written by Jewish sectarians; but their uniformly hostile attitude towards Judaism as a limited or even evil religion makes it more likely that these texts were written by non-Jews who had come into contact with Judaism and were both fascinated and repelled by it; or perhaps an even more accurate description of their standpoint is that they wished to build their religious views on Judaism and at the same time repudiate it. Thus they selected from the Bible the figure of Seth for special reverence, because he was not a Jew

Christianity and Hellenistic religion

but a figure of the antediluvian period before Judaism began (in exactly the same way, and for the same reason, we find in the New Testament special reverence paid to the figure of Melchizedek). The sources of Judaism are used, with great ingenuity, to attack Judaism and develop a religious system transcending, yet in a way incorporating, the tenets of the Jewish Bible.

The peculiar combination of dependence on Jewish sources and hostility towards them is shown especially in the Gnostic attitude towards Jehovah, the God of Judaism. It was acknowledged by the Gnostics that there was such a God and that He was the author of the Old Testament, which He had transmitted to Moses. It was even admitted by some that He had created the earth. But it was denied that He was the supreme God, or that His handiwork was admirable, in either its literary form, the Torah, or its material form, the world. Far above Him was the true 'Highest God', to whom He failed to give due reverence, pretending to be the Highest God himself. But there had always been some, starting with Seth, who had seen through His pretensions, and had true knowledge (*gnosis*) of the Highest God. These people knew that one day the Highest God would intervene in the affairs of the lower world, so bungled by the jealousy and arrogance of the Jewish God, by sending down a son, who, by his death and resurrection, would overthrow the Jewish God, rescind the latter's imperfect Law, and rescue chosen souls for eternal life.

It is doubtful, however, whether Gnosticism itself contained the concept of sacrifice in the sense that is important for the present study. There was certainly in Gnosticism, even in its pre-Christian varieties, the figure of a saviour called the 'Son of God', who descended from the 'World of Light' and later ascended again.[16] But the accent was laid on the knowledge or esoteric information that he brought to the world, rather than on his suffering while on earth. If he was temporarily overwhelmed by evil powers, this was the inevitable result of his selfless descent rather than the main aim of his mission; it was not his death that brought salvation, but the knowledge, or *gnosis*, that he imparted to his disciples while on earth, and which they transmitted to further disciples. The Gnostics were thus the originators of the theory of the saviour as martyr, rather than as sacrifice, a theory that became popular in Christianity only at a very late stage, under the influence of modern liberalism, in which concepts of sacrifice had come to seem antiquated and irrational. In Gnosticism, the figure of the dying-and-resurrected god, derived from agricultural rites of sacrifice, became for the first time divorced from the idea of the beneficial, death-producing renewal. It is true that evil figures were concerned with the death of the saviour and these evil figures had their earthly incarnation, especially in the Jewish people, so that

Christianity and Hellenistic religion

Gnosticism was a seed-bed for anti-Semitism; but the particular equivocal aura of the Sacred Executioner, the guilty performer of the necessary sacrifice without which the rest of mankind could not be saved, was absent. The Jews were the villains of the story (even before the saviour was identified by some Gnostic sects as Jesus), but only in the sense that they were the special minions of the Demiurge who had created this evil world, and were therefore the enemies of *gnosis*.[17] It could even be said that Gnostics did not take *death* seriously enough to have a real concept of sacrifice, for death, to them, was merely a release from the material world and a highly desirable thing; on the other hand, the cosmic impact of death as the source of renewal of life is essential to sacrificial doctrine. Alternatively, one could say that Gnostics did not take the *world* and the *flesh* seriously enough to have a concept of sacrifice; for sacrifice implies that the world is worth redeeming and that the suffering of the flesh is of real significance. So it is not surprising that the heresy known as Docetism was characteristic of the Christian Gnostics: that is, that Jesus did not really suffer in the flesh, but only appeared to do so.

Christianity, therefore, was not identical either to the mystery religions or to Gnosticism, but built from them a new synthesis which at the same time reverted to the ancient prehistoric doctrines of sacrifice of which they were sophisticated developments. The fact that the sacrificial figure, Jesus, was a historical personage, who had actually lived and died on earth, gave an actuality to the sacrifice that was lacking in the mystery religions. There it had been a god who died and rose again, and no human representative of the god was killed as had once been the case in the remotely early times of the cults. But what Christianity did take from the mystery cults was the idea of the saving power of the death of the god and the conviction that it was not any *gnosis* imparted by the god that brought about salvation, but a mystic participation in his death. And from Gnosticism, Christianity took the cosmic framework, transcending all the local geographical reference of the mystery cults, and the concept of a battle between cosmic powers of good and evil (derived ultimately from Persian religion), as well as the concept of a saviour, or Son of God, descending from the World of Light. From Gnosticism too came the idea of a fallen world ruled by an evil power, Satan, though this power was not identified, as it was in Gnosticism, with the God of Judaism. From Gnosticism, it must also be said, came the anti-Semitic tone of Christianity, with the Jews cast in the role of antagonists of the Light, though in Christianity this role is sharper and more specific than in Gnosticism. From Judaism itself came the apocalyptic scheme of history, by which the saviour was identified with the Jewish figure of the Messiah, and the whole sacred history of the Old Testament was

Christianity and Hellenistic religion

pressed into service as prefiguring and leading up to the advent of Jesus, while the Christian Church took over the role assigned in Judaism to Israel, becoming the 'chosen people' of God and the bearer of His message to mankind.

The person in whose mind all these elements fused into unity was Paul, who was thus the true founder of Christianity. Jesus himself cannot be regarded as the founder of Christianity, since he was not, in fact, a Christian, but lived and died as a believing and practising Jew, to whom the Hebrew Bible alone was the Word of God. To him, the term 'Messiah' had no connotations connecting it with the Gnostic saviour or with the dying-and-rising gods of the mystery cults. It was simply the title (meaning, literally, the 'anointed one') of every Jewish king of the Davidic dynasty, and by claiming this title (at a rather late stage in his career, which he began in the role of a prophet) Jesus was claiming the Jewish throne and setting up a banner of revolt against the invading occupying power of Rome, which he identified with the invaders mentioned in the prophetic books of the Old Testament. Jesus thus had no intention of playing a sacrificial role, and his hope was to eject the Romans by means of a token resistance backed up by a mighty miracle from God, which was prophesied by Zechariah to take place on the Mount of Olives. When his revolt was crushed after some initial success and wide support from the Jewish people, Jesus was crucified by the Romans like many thousands of other Jews who took part in attempts to regain their liberty during this period. Jesus, like the other failed Messiahs, was quickly forgotten by the Jews,[18] except for a handful of his devoted followers who comforted themselves for his heroic failure by believing that he was still alive (like King Arthur in a later legend) and would come back soon to continue his mission of liberation. These loyal Jewish followers of Jesus (the Nazarenes), who continued to believe in him after his execution, did not regard him as a divine figure, but as a human Messiah whom God had brought back to life, like Lazarus, in advance of the general resurrection of the dead prophesied for all deserving human beings. The Nazarenes did not regard Jesus as an opponent of the Jewish Law or religion, and they themselves regarded themselves as Jews, observed Jewish laws, and attended the Jewish synagogues and Temple.

It was when Paul began to see the resurrection of Jesus in an entirely different light that Christianity was born. Paul was brought up not in Judaea or Galilee but in Tarsus, a great Hellenistic centre in Asia Minor. Here all the mystery cults were represented, and the conventicles of Gnostics were beginning to impart their secret knowledge. Later, Paul called himself a 'Pharisee of the Pharisees', and was careful not to mention in his Epistles that he was born not in Judaea but in Tarsus, which was certainly no centre of Pharisaism. It is probable that Paul was at some time briefly attached to the Pharisees, though he was certainly not a disciple of the great Gamaliel, as was claimed for him by Luke, though not by Paul himself. It seems, however, that he soon left the Pharisees and became attached to the Sadducees, for we find him carrying out a mission against the Nazarenes under the instructions of the High Priest, who was a Sadducee. The Pharisees had no quarrel with the Nazarenes, who were loyal adherents of Pharisaic Judaism and were protected by the Pharisees under Gamaliel from the persecution of the High Priest, who was a Roman appointee and regarded the Nazarenes as followers of a rebel against Rome.[19]

There is extant a report by the Nazarenes about the early life of Paul.[20] This is a valuable corrective to the picture of Paul as Pharisee that is given in Acts and in Paul's Epistles. In this account, Paul, so far from being a 'Pharisee of the Pharisees', and 'descended from the tribe of Benjamin', was the son of Gentile parents of Tarsus converted to Judaism. If this is true, Paul's background of Judaism was recent and superficial. He was brought up in near contact with Hellenistic religion, and would have been familiar with notions of dying-and-resurrected gods – concepts that were alien and unfamiliar to Jesus's Judaean and Galilean followers, the Nazarenes. Paul left Tarsus and came to Judaea, where he sought a Jewish identity, first with the Pharisees, then with the Sadducees, and perhaps with other Jewish groups too, such as the Essenes. He was a man seeking some way of reconciling and amalgamating the welter of influences to which he had been subjected, including the strange new sect which he had undertaken to harass on behalf of the quisling High Priest, but which evidently had a striking effect on him. The solution to his spiritual turmoil came to him on the road to Damascus, when all the religious influences that had impinged on him from his childhood onward suddenly coalesced into a new synthesis, ratified by a vision of Jesus as the culmination of the succession of dying-and-resurrected gods.

In Paul's Epistles we find expressed the synthesis that he created, which has remained characteristic of Christianity, despite efforts from time to time to suppress the Gnostic and mystery-religion elements in favour of Jewish concepts (as was done, for example, by Pelagius in his controversy with the Paulinist Augustine[21]), or to suppress the Jewish elements in favour of pure Gnosticism or mystery religion (as was attempted by Marcion[22]). Paul's debt to Gnosticism is shown in his vocabulary and basic framework of concepts: for example, in his distinction between 'spiritual' man (*pneumatikos*) and 'natural' man (*psychikos*); and in his terms for cosmic powers of evil, such as 'principality' (*arche*), 'power' (*exousia*) and 'might' (*dunamis*). It is seen also in his insistence that the Torah was given to Moses not by God, but by 'angels',[23] a strange idea for which there is no warrant in the Hebrew Bible or in later Jewish literature, but which is Paul's somewhat watered-down version of the Gnostic doctrine that the Torah was given by the Demiurge, or inferior power, who created the world and was identical with the Jewish God. For Paul, the God of the Old Testament was identical with the Highest God, and the role given by the Gnostics to the Demiurge was given by Paul, in a modified form, to Satan, a figure derived not from the Hebrew Bible (where he hardly appears, except as a being entirely subservient to God) but from the Apocryphal literature, which is regarded as authoritative only by a tiny minority of Jews. Satan was regarded by Paul not as the creator of this world, but as its 'prince' (in John's phrase), who had corrupted the world and thus gained power over it. The purpose of Jesus's descent to the world was to break the power of Satan, and return the world to its true owner, the Highest God, to whom Jesus had the relationship of son, and through whom he was lord and saviour. The terms 'lord' (*kurios*) and 'saviour' (*soter*) are used in a sense indistinguishable from their use in Gnosticism and quite different from the use of the corresponding terms in Hebrew. Paul even at times uses the expression *gnosis*, but for him the ' knowledge' which saves is that of faith and participation in Jesus's death, not the system of mystical exercises and passwords by which the Gnostics claimed to circumvent the powers of evil and pass through the 'Seven Heavens' to the domain of the Highest God.

Thus, though the outward limbs of Paul's system are those of Gnosticism, the heart of it is derived from the mystery religions, which preserved the ancient concept of the sacrificial death of a god. Whenever Paul writes about the sacrificial efficacy of the Crucifixion, he uses the language of the mystery religions. The interpretation of the Communion meal, for example, as a participation in the blood and body of Christ (for instance, in I Corinthians 10:16) is entirely alien to Judaism, and has no part in Gnosticism, but is a common theme in the mystery religions. Such communal meals, in which the food eaten was held to represent mystically the body and blood of the sacrificed god, are known to have featured in Mithraism and in the worship of Attis.[24] These communal meals are in fact sophisticated versions of a much older type of communal meal, found for example in the worship of Dionysus, in which an animal, often a bull, was torn apart and eaten raw as representative of the god. This ceremony itself is derived from an even earlier rite in which the animal was not regarded as representing a god (since the concept of personal deity had not yet arisen) but simply as the carrier of life-force which could be incorporated in the members of the tribe through a ceremonial meal. The Com-

Christianity and Hellenistic religion

munion, or Eucharist, indeed, goes back to the basic reason for the god sacrifice, which is simply to eat the god. It may be said that the Christian Communion meal has Jewish origins too, being based on the Kiddush ceremony, in which a festival or Sabbath meal is inaugurated by blessings on wine and bread. But the Kiddush ceremony has no sacrificial connotation whatever, being merely thanksgiving blessings to God for providing food, combined with a blessing for the festival day. It is true, however, that there is a historical connection between the Kiddush ceremony and the Eucharist, for it was the Kiddush ceremony performed by Jesus on the occasion of the Last Supper that was reinterpreted in mystery-religion style and thus transformed into a sacrificial rite. In the Gospels, Jesus is represented as giving this interpretation to the Last Supper himself, and the latest Gospel, John's, even represents Jesus as referring to the spiritual nutrition of his blood and flesh independently of the Last Supper: 'Verily, verily, I say unto you, Except ye eat of the flesh of the Son of man, and drink his blood, ye have no life in you. Whoso eateth my flesh, and drinketh my blood, hath eternal life; and I will raise him up at the last day . . . He that eateth my flesh, and drinketh my blood, dwelleth in me, and I in him' (John 6: 53-4). These expressions are good examples of the reworking of the historical traditions about Jesus in order to make them accord with Paul's mystery-religion interpretation of Jesus's life and death.

The Crucifixion: here the motif of participation in Jesus's sacrifice and the benefit which is thus gained are graphically represented. An angel collects the precious blood which is shed for mankind. (Detail of woodcut by Dürer.)

Christianity and Hellenistic religion

It is clear that the manner of Jesus's death, by hanging on a cross, was itself of great significance to Paul, since it was so evocative of the mystery religions, especially that of the Phrygian god, Attis. Here Paul has recourse to an interesting interpretation, or misinterpretation, of a verse in the Hebrew Bible (which Paul, incidentally, read in Greek, not in Hebrew, since it can be shown that his quotations are from the Septuagint, the Greek translation of the Old Testament[25]). Deuteronomy 21:22–3 reads (in the Authorized Version):

And if a man have committed a sin worthy of death, and he be to be put to death, and thou hang him on a tree: his body shall not remain all night upon the tree, but thou shalt in any wise bury him that day; for he that is hanged is accursed of God; that thy land be not defiled, which the Lord thy God giveth thee for an inheritance.

In Jewish exegesis, this was not held to mean that a hanged man was under a curse, for, on the contrary, it was held that an executed man was purged of all guilt by his execution. If his dead body, contrary to the law, was allowed to hang overnight, this could bring no curse upon the dead man, who had paid the penalty of his crime, but only upon those who contravened the law by exposing his body. Thus the relevant sentence is translated in the New English Bible, 'A hanged man is offensive in the sight of God', a translation very much in accord with Jewish traditional exegesis.[26]

Paul, however, understood the sentence very differently. His comment is, 'Christ hath redeemed us from the curse of the law, being made a curse for us: for it is written, Cursed is every one that hangeth on a tree' (Galatians 3:13). Many commentators have assumed that Paul was merely repeating here a current interpretation of the verse in Deuteronomy; some commentators have even given this as an example of Paul's 'rabbinical' mood. But the idea that a crucified man was under some kind of curse (presumably in the next world) would have been regarded by all Jewish authorities of the time as bizarre. After all, Jesus was only one of many thousands who were crucified by the Romans during this period. So far from being regarded as under a curse, these crucified people were regarded as martyrs and saints who had secured their place in the World to Come by their suffering.

How then did Paul arrive at his interpretation? The answer is that the theme of the hanged god was one that carried for him a charge of meaning from mystery religions. The god Attis, the lover of the goddess Cybele, was represented every spring by an effigy that was hung on a pine-tree. The actual myth of Attis does not tell that the god was hanged on a pine-tree, but that he met his death under a pine-tree by self-castration. But the annual rite points to an older version of the myth, in which he (or his human surrogate) was not only mutilated but hung alive on a tree so that his oozing blood might fertilize the fields. That such a story once existed is shown by the legend of Marsyas, also a devotee of Cybele, who was tied to a pine-tree and flayed and otherwise mutilated (allegedly as the result of his rivalry with the god Apollo). Norse religion too offers relevant evidence: human sacrifices to Odin were strung up on a tree or a gallows, wounded with a spear and left to die.[27]

To Paul, who came from the very area where the religion of Attis and Cybele was indigenous, the fact that Jesus died on the cross would have seemed especially significant – once he began to think of Jesus as a mystery god. Here was the very mystery of the hanged god, for which, as he would feel, mystery religion of the Phrygian variety had already prepared mankind. And he would very naturally look into the Septuagint to see whether Holy Writ contained any veiled prophecy of these things. He found such an allusion in the verse of Deuteronomy about the curse involved in leaving a corpse of a condemned man hanging overnight. This seemed to him to be much more than a strongly worded prohibition about the respectful treatment of corpses; it conjured up a dramatic picture of a hanged figure suffering from some cosmic curse. The sacrifice of Jesus, in Paul's eyes, was directed not towards the fertility of the fields but towards the removal of the curse of sin. Thus Jesus took the curse upon himself, and assumed the character of a condemned criminal bearing the weight of sin that mankind found intolerable. This is stated explicitly by Paul in another Epistle: 'For he hath made him to be sin for us, who knew no sin; that we might be made the righteousness of God in him' ((II Corinthians 5:21). (The New English Bible translation is 'Christ was innocent of sin, and yet for our sake God made him one with the sinfulness of men, so that in him we might be made one with the goodness of God himself'.)

That the innocent should take upon himself the sins of the guilty had always been essential to the purificatory kind of sacrifice, especially belonging to times of crisis such as famine or foreign invasion, but it was now being applied by Paul to the crisis of mankind as a whole faced with the wrath of God. Only the most innocent person could qualify as the sacrifice, not only because of the need in any sacrifice for perfection or lack of blemish, but because in a guilt-offering for the people any guilt in the sacrificial person himself would detract from his efficacy as a vicarious offering. There was thus an extraordinary paradox in the sacrificed person: a combination of total innocence with total depravity. It is this paradox that Paul read into the verse of Deuteronomy about the curse on the hanged man, and applied to the sacrifice (as he saw it) of Jesus.

It may even be that Paul saw further into the historical background of the Deuteronomic verse about the hanged criminal than did the rabbis. For it is very possible that the Deuteronomic curse on leaving the body of a criminal hanging overnight was based originally on a desire to stamp out any vestiges of the fertility-worship in which the prolonged hanging of a human victim was a central rite. There is evidence that in some periods capital punishment itself became a kind of religious sacrifice; a condemned criminal might be treated with the same kind of ceremony as an innocent sacrificial victim, in the hope that the execution might have the same effects as a sacrifice without the need for the crueller performance of sacrifice of the innocent. The same kind of shifting can be seen in the use of enemy prisoners as sacrificial victims. Crucifixion itself began as a sacrificial rite and only gradually became a form of civil execution, and probably never quite lost its religious overtones. Thus Paul, like a modern anthropologist, was disinterring traces of paganism in a post-pagan document. He was bringing back to life the pagan ways of thought against which the Hebrew Bible had carried out its long struggle and of which there remained only fossilized remnants in certain passages whose meaning had been forgotten in rabbinical Judaism.

Christianity, therefore, as it developed under the influence of Paul, was much indebted to the mystery religions for its central concept of a divine sacrifice. But whereas in the mystery religions the divine sacrifice took place in the mythological realm, Pauline Christianity located it on earth and identified the sacrificed god with a historical figure, Jesus, who died at a particular time and place, and was involved with historical communities, the Jews and the Romans. Thus the human-sacrificial aspects, which had become muted in the mystery religions when these became detached from their agricultural origins, were strongly revived in Christianity. Not only was the victim an actual person, but the other actors in the sacrificial drama, particularly the Jews, became mythologized while remaining a visible, actual body of people in the world. Given the strong Gnostic colouring of dualism and anti-Semitism which Christianity added to its mystery-religion central drama, this mythologization meant that it was the Jews who were given the role of Sacred Executioner, which in previous religion had never been attached to a whole people, but only to individuals or mythological personages.

It now becomes necessary to consider how the mechanisms which I have called 'distancing devices' operated in this revitalized atmosphere of a human-sacrificial cult: how, in this sharpened awareness of the actual death of a victim for the sake of the community, it became possible for that community to detach itself from the responsibility for the death whose value they prized to such a point that they regarded it as essential to their salvation.

Chapter Ten

Judas Iscariot

An important figure in the economy of the Gospel story is Judas Iscariot, who has become the archetypal betrayer in Western culture. He is the man who, while in a position of trust, betrayed the Son of God to his death. His motives are never explained in the Gospels, though certain explanations have become so current in exegetical works that many people are quite convinced that they have read these explanations in the New Testament. In fact, as we shall see, his *lack* of motive is an important element in his role.[1]

Judas is not exactly a Sacred Executioner, as no sanctity adheres to his act of betrayal, and indeed betrayal is not execution. To kill the divine sacrifice is an act that can never be quite divested of heroic quality, so the executioner himself is not usually made into a figure of pure malice. Alternatively, the slayer may be himself a victim, either of accident or of malicious plotting by which he is tricked into performing the execution. In the Norse myth of the death of Balder, it is Hother, the blind marksman, who performs the slaying; but the person really responsible for Balder's death is the evil plotter Loki who performs no deed of violence himself but arranges that it should occur. Yet Loki and Hother cannot be quite separated from each other. They represent two aspects of a single entity, the misfortune by which the victim fell. Misfortune can always be interpreted in two ways: as sheer bad luck, or as brought about by evil plotting. To the primitive mind, the two aspects are not entirely distinguishable, since evil powers are suspected behind every occurrence of bad luck. So, to obtain the right mixture of elements, a complexity in the *dramatis personae* has to be introduced: one person to stand for the bad luck, another for the malicious plotting. Indeed, in the Gospel story a third person is introduced, the evil spirit or demon, Satan, who 'entered into' Judas. This is the plotter on the mythological plane, who brings about the death of Jesus as a divine figure, just as Judas brings it about on the earthly plane. As both man and god, Jesus requires both a human and a superhuman antagonist.

Who then, in the Gospel story, corresponds to Hother, the innocent person who performs the actual slaying? The answer seems to be Pontius Pilate, who actually pronounces sentence of death on Jesus, and supervises his execution by crucifixion which is carried out by Roman soldiers. The Gospels entirely exonerate Pilate from blame, sealing his exoneration by the dramatic scene in which he washes his hands. Even the Roman soldiers who fix Jesus on the cross are in no way implicated in the guilt of his death and are totally neutral characters. It is a remarkable feat of sanitization, by which the actual executioners of Jesus are divested of all responsibility. In later interpretations, Pilate came to be represented as a feeble, vacillating character who failed to stand up to the pressure of the Jews, and therefore to that extent shared in the blame for Jesus's death. There is no hint of this interpretation, however, in the Gospels themselves; it was only certain contradictions in the narrative, easily explained on grounds of narrative exigency, that later gave ground to an anti-Pilate interpretation. So far, indeed, was Pilate from being blamed that the Ethiopian Church made him into a saint, and at one time it seemed probable that the rest of Christendom was about to endorse his canonization. It is clear that the aim of the Gospels is to make Pilate as blameless as Hother.

This being so, Pilate is not quite a Sacred Executioner. The essence of the Sacred Executioner is that he dares to take the responsibility for the sacrifice. In the Balder story, there is no Sacred Executioner, for the death is brought about entirely by a combination of bad luck and malice represented by Hother and Loki. There is no-one who can be pointed to as the man who killed the god, and was driven from the community into the desert, bearing the mark of identification proclaiming his deed, and exonerating the tribe by his continued existence and testimony, 'I did it'. To dissolve the sacrificial deed into an act of bad luck or malice or both is not finally satisfying, because the sacrificial character of the deed is liable to be lost, unless some of the trappings of the sacrificing priest adhere to the slayer, even if in an abhorred and exiled form. So, in addition to the men representing bad luck and malice, it is necessary to have a character in the *dramatis personae* who acknowledges the nature of the deed and is prepared to take the consequences. This is the Sacred Executioner, and in the Gospel story this role is played by the Jewish people as a whole, who call out, in the words of the Gospel of Matthew, 'His blood be on us and on our children.' The role is, of course, an ambivalent one that has to accommodate both negative and positive aspects; the purely evil figure of a Loki or a Judas cannot carry all the weight required; nor can the innocent, unlucky Hother or Pilate.

Nevertheless, the character of Judas contains, in a rudimentary form, some essential aspects of the Sacred Executioner such as are found more fully in the role of the Jewish people and, much later, in the Christian legend of the Wandering Jew. Indeed, it would be a

Judas Iscariot

mistake to look for the Sacred Executioner as a kind of institutionalized figure, with a recognized role in society. In some societies an approximation to such a functionary can be found, but there is always a reluctance to give official status to the slayer, as this would invest him with the approval of the community. It is thus always likely that an aura of the outlaw should hang about the slayer, not only after the performance of the deed, but before; this means that extraneous reasons (of malice or accident) must be attached to the deed and its doer. Something of the Judas and the Pilate (or the Loki and the Hother) are ingredients in the character (not, of course, necessarily a logically consistent one in the terms of the psychologist or the novelwriter) of the Sacred Executioner, together with the essential ingredient of willed action. Since it is hard to hold so many ingredients together (all tending towards the exoneration of the community for whose benefit the sacrifice is performed), it is to be expected that the role should sometimes disperse itself, as in the Christian myth, over several *dramatis personae*, each of them, so to speak, a separate attempt at the character required, though each attempt may successively incorporate more of the desired ingredients until finally a composite character is evolved satisfying the needs of the community so well that even glaring internal inconsistencies can be overlooked. We shall therefore look at a series of characters in the Christian myth each of which is an adumbration of the Sacred Executioner (Judas, Pilate, the Jewish people, the Wandering Jew); and in this series, a progress will be noted towards the full flowering of the required character.

In the character of Judas we may at once note an aspect that makes him much more than a mere Loki-type mischief-maker; an aspect that does put him, however imperfectly, into the role of the Sacred Executioner. This is the aura of fate that surrounds his act of betrayal. Jesus knows that someone will betray him; he even knows (in some versions of the story) who that someone will be. This may seem to deprive Judas of any free will in the matter, since he only does what he is fated to do; but this would be to apply a logic that is foreign to mythical thinking. Judas is fated, but he is also wicked; he is bound to betray Jesus, but he also wants to. This combination is essential to the Sacred Executioner; for, on the one hand, unless he voluntarily commits the act, he cannot be held responsible for it, and the responsibility reverts to the community that desperately desires the act to be done, since their salvation depends on it; but, on the other hand, if he commits the act on purely personal grounds, the act remains a trivial one, not the cosmic one that the community demands. He must therefore be impelled by fate, and be a figure of cosmic importance himself, one marked out from the beginning of time to commit just this act.

Judas Iscariot

It is interesting to examine the part of the Gospel myth in which this paradox of fate and free will comes to a point, that is, Jesus's designation of Judas as his betrayer. Here are the versions of this episode in all four Gospels, in their order of composition:

And as they sat and did eat, Jesus said, Verily I say unto you, One of you which eateth with me shall betray me.
And they began to be sorrowful, and to say unto him one by one, Is it I? and another said, Is it I?
And he answered and said unto them, It is one of the twelve, that dippeth with me in the dish.
The Son of man indeed goeth, as it is written of him: but woe to that man by whom the Son of man is betrayed! good were it for that man if he had never been born. (Mark 14:*18-21*)

And as they did eat, he said, Verily I say unto you, that one of you shall betray me.
And they were exceeding sorrowful, and began every one of them to say unto him, Lord, is it I?
And he answered and said, He that dippeth his hand with me in the dish, the same shall betray me.
The Son of man goeth as it is written of him: but woe unto that man by whom the Son of man is betrayed! it had been good for that man if he had not been born.
Then Judas, which betrayed him, answered and said, Master, is it I? He said unto him, Thou hast said. (Matthew 26:*21-5*)

And he took bread, and gave thanks, and brake it, and gave unto them, saying, This is my body which is given for you: this do in remembrance of me.
Likewise also the cup after supper, saying, This cup is the new testament in my blood, which is shed for you.
But behold, the hand of him that betrayeth me is with me on the table.
And truly the Son of man goeth, as it was determined: but woe unto that man by whom he is betrayed!
And they began to inquire among themselves, which of them it was that should do this thing. (Luke 22:*19-23*)

Jesus saith to him, He that is washed needeth not save to wash his feet, but is clean every whit: and ye are clean, but not all.
For he knew who should betray him: therefore said he, Ye are not all clean. . . .
I speak not of you all: I know whom I have chosen: but that the scripture may be fulfilled, He that eateth bread with me hath lifted up his heel against me.
Now I tell you before it come, that, when it is come to pass, ye may believe that I am he.
Verily, verily, I say unto you, He that receiveth whomsoever I send receiveth me; and he that receiveth me receiveth him that sent me.
When Jesus had thus said, he was troubled in spirit, and testified, and said, Verily, verily, I say unto you, that one of you shall betray me.
Then the disciples looked one on another, doubting of whom he spake.

Judas Iscariot

> Now there was leaning on Jesus' bosom one of his disciples, whom Jesus loved. Simon Peter therefore beckoned to him, that he should ask who it should be of whom he spake.
> He then lying on Jesus' breast saith unto him, Lord, who is it? Jesus answered, He it is, to whom I shall give a sop, when I have dipped it. And when he had dipped the sop, he gave it to Judas Iscariot, the son of Simon.
> And after the sop Satan entered into him. Then said Jesus unto him, That thou doest, do quickly.
> Now no man at the table knew for what intent he spake this unto him.
> For some thought, because Judas had the bag, that Jesus had said unto him, Buy those things that we have need of against the feast; or, that he should give something to the poor.
> He then having received the sop went immediately out: and it was night. (John 13:10, 18-30).

It is undoubtedly in the latest version, that of John, that we find the greatest stress on the mythological elements, and in particular on the fated nature of Judas's act, and on Jesus's designation of him as his own betrayer. In the earlier versions, Judas has already made contact with the 'chief priests' for the purpose of betraying Jesus *before* the Last Supper. In John's version, however, it is at the Last Supper itself that Judas receives the deciding impulse to betray Jesus. In the earlier versions, then, Jesus's foreknowledge of Judas's betrayal may only be a clairvoyant perception of what Judas had already plotted to do; in John's version, on the other hand, Jesus actually elects Judas for the role of betrayer. John thus boldly alters the previous story in order to emphasize the God-given, pre-ordained character of Judas's role. It is true that John (though he suppresses the meeting of Judas with the 'chief priests') does say (13:2) that the Devil had already put into the heart of Judas to betray Jesus; but he seems to forget this when he says later (13:27) that it was only when Jesus gave Judas the sop that 'Satan entered into him'. John even represents Jesus as telling Judas to get on with his task of betrayal. Thus, when Jesus says (v.18), 'I know whom I have chosen', a poignant ambiguity lies in these words. He may only mean that he knows whom he has chosen as his true disciples (i.e. all except Judas); but he may also mean (and the ambiguity seems deliberate) that he knows whom he has chosen as his betrayer.

All four Evangelists make a point of the commensality of Judas with Jesus, that he was one of those who 'dipped' together with Jesus in the dish. Only John connects this with a Biblical verse (Psalms 41:9), and only John actually makes the dipping the occasion for the sealing of Judas's lot as traitor. In Matthew's Gospel it is understood between Jesus and Judas that Judas is the betrayer, while in John's Gospel the Beloved Disciple too is let into the secret. (We cannot suppose that *all* the disciples heard Jesus explaining his sign, or they would not have been ignorant of the betrayer's identity, which, as is so carefully

Judas Iscariot

explained, they are; we may wonder, however, whether Peter, who incited the Beloved Disciple to interrogate Jesus, would have wanted to know the result of the interrogation.) The statement in John's version that 'no man at the table' understood Jesus's directive to Judas must surely not be intended to include the Beloved Disciple who heard and understood the whole transaction – indeed, since the Beloved Disciple is the pseudepigraphic author of the Gospel of John (i.e. John son of Zebedee) the intention here is to show that the author had privileged access to what went on between Jesus and Judas. [2]

The commensality of Judas with Jesus makes him one of Jesus's spiritual family. That Jesus should be betrayed by one so close to him, spiritually his brother, who ate out of the same dish (a strong bond in the East), makes his crime all the more horrifying. Viewed merely as a story of betrayal, this is just one more heightening of the drama, and is an instance of the 'wicked brother' motif so common in folk stories. But from the standpoint of myth, the close family relationship between the sacrificial victim and his betrayer or executioner (and the betrayer is just the executioner viewed from a particular aspect) is of thematic importance. We have already seen it several times: in the brother-relationship of Cain and Abel, of Romulus and Remus, of Osiris and Set, of Baal and Mot. There is here an ambivalence: on the one hand, it is desired that the sacrifice should come from the community and should therefore be performed by 'one of us' – that both the victim and the sacrificer should be firmly rooted in the community, which is viewed as a band of brothers. On the other hand, it is desired that the community should not be held responsible. Sometimes one of the two opposing desires holds sway, sometimes the other. As we have seen, the same ambivalence exists in relation to the victim: he ought to be an integral member of the community, a brother, but sometimes the guilt of killing a brother has the upper hand, and it is preferred to kill a stranger, usually a prisoner of war, but sometimes, as in the case of the Scythians, a passing traveller. More often, some mediating solution is found: the slayer is a brother, but his action is repudiated; his very brotherhood (actually regarded as a factor in making the sacrifice effectual) is made the ground of his repudiation. 'How could a brother do such a thing! (Yet how fortunate, for a stranger's sacrifice would be far less acceptable.)'

There are grounds for believing that the commensality of Judas and Jesus is a cover for an even deeper relationship – for believing that in an earlier version they were actually blood-brothers, like Cain and Abel. There are three people called Judas (Judah) in Jesus's story: Judas Iscariot; Judas the Apostle (known as Jude the Obscure and reputedly the author of the Epistle of Jude); and Judas, Jesus's brother, named in Matthew 13:55, together with two other brothers called Joses

Judas Iscariot

and Simon. Various pieces of evidence point to the conclusion that the second two Judases were in fact one person; and further evidence (such as the fact that Mark's and Matthew's lists of the Twelve Apostles give only one Judas) suggests that there was only one Judas altogether, who was Jesus's brother.[3] The split of this person into two figures, one the evil Judas Iscariot and the other the saintly but characterless Judas the Apostle, was due to the demands of myth, which required an evil brother-figure to perform the role of Cain or Set. That it was Judas who was chosen for this role rather than one of the other Apostles cannot be unconnected with the fact that his name functioned as the eponymous characterization of the Jewish people and is derived from the patriarch and tribe of Judah. The treachery of Judas Iscariot thus symbolized the treachery of the Jews (Judah) as a whole.

Why then did the myth develop in such a direction that the blood-brotherhood of Jesus and Judas was suppressed, and instead they became merely commensal spiritual brothers? The answer to this lies, no doubt, in the developing myth of Jesus's divine nature, combined with the developing myth of Mary's perpetual virginity. Jesus as a divine figure could not have any brothers, and Mary, as the 'bride' of God, could not be allowed to bear children after the birth of Jesus. In the Gospels themselves the suppression of Jesus's brothers is incomplete, but they are represented as hostile to him. In one revealing passage, however, this alleged hostility and ostracism is contradicted by an incident in which his brothers advise him about his career;[4] and the whole picture is contradicted by the prominence of Jesus's brothers in the Jerusalem Church after his death. Later Christianity has to invent implausible explanations to patch up these contradictions: Jesus's 'brothers' were half-brothers, sons of Joseph by a previous marriage (Joseph therefore has to be portrayed as an old man, though without Scriptural support); James, Jesus's brother, becomes converted only after the Resurrection (and yet is immediately appointed head of the Jerusalem Church!).[5]

We can thus trace three stages in the story of the relationship between Jesus and Judas: (i) Judas was Jesus's brother, was a member of his band of Apostles, did not betray him, and remained a prominent member of the Jerusalem Church after Jesus's death. This is the historical stage, before the development of the Pauline myth by which Jesus's death became a sacrifice, and a Sacred Executioner became a desideratum; (ii) Judas was Jesus's brother, but betrayed him, behaving as Set did to Osiris: this is the first mythical stage, at which Judas Iscariot the betrayer became separated from the innocuous Judas the Apostle; the betrayal by Judas became symbolic of the betrayal by the Jewish people, Jesus's blood-brothers (who, in historical fact, did not betray him, but hailed him as Messiah on Palm

Judas Iscariot

Sunday, called for his release from prison,[6] and mourned him when Pilate executed him); (iii) Judas was not Jesus's brother (since his brothers, if he really had any, were all hostile to his mission and could not have been among the Twelve Apostles), but, as an Apostle, was his commensal spiritual brother, and thus by betraying him, he fulfilled the role of Set: this is the final mythical stage, in which the mythological need for a brother-figure is somewhat at odds with the need to divest Jesus, as a divine personage born of a virgin, of human brothers.

The need for an evil brother-figure on the mythological level is to some extent also met, however, by the figure of Satan, who, as fallen angel and former member of the assembly known as the 'sons of God', counts as Jesus's evil brother in the supernatural sphere. True, Satan is also a father-figure, and as such is brother to God Himself – and thus the first of all the 'wicked uncles' of folklore and literature. As brother, or twin, of God, Satan is a surrogate-figure for God Himself, drawing away the hatred that might have been directed at the father-god for demanding the death of the son. But as rival son or Jesus's evil brother, Satan is also the other side of Jesus too; he is the picture of how the innocent sacrifice takes upon himself the sins of the whole community, thus becoming loathsome and wicked. From this standpoint, the Sacred Executioner is simply another aspect of the sacrificed victim. After taking upon himself all the community's sins, he assumes in addition the sin of performing the sacrifice, and is therefore justly banished to a life of wandering in the desert. The brotherhood, or twinship, of the sacrificer and victim may thus express not merely the kinship of the community with the victim, but the identity of victim and sacrificer. In the last resort, the victim has sacrificed himself, so no-one but he is to blame. Moreover, not only does he lie dead on the altar, atoning for the community's sins, but he remains alive, perpetually bearing the sins of the community where they can do no harm – in the desert.[7]

It should be noted, by the way, that there are grounds for the view that Judas was not only Jesus's brother, but his twin brother, if not in fact then at one stage of the development of the myth. For the Apostle known as Thomas is called in some sources Judas Thomas, and the name Thomas simply means 'twin'. That Thomas was the twin of Jesus himself is by no means a new notion, for this was held as a fact by the Mesopotamian Church, and has been taken seriously by several modern scholars.[8] If, on the other hand, Judas Thomas is a separate person from Judas Iscariot, and if all the other persons named Judas are regarded as separate persons, we arrive at a figure of no less than four people called Judas all closely connected with Jesus. This proliferation seems best explained in the light of mythological needs and the contradictions generated by the choice of Judas, Jesus's brother and Apostle, as traitor.

The basic contradiction, however, from which all the other contradictions arise is that of the sacrifice itself: in any expiatory human sacrifice the community wants the victim to die, but also wants to be free of all responsibility for his death. From this contradiction arise the internal contradictions of the Sacred Executioner, who slays by accident, and yet on purpose; through malice, and yet in fulfilment of a beneficent will; as an outcast from the community, yet representing it. The basic contradiction, profoundly appealing and profoundly immoral at the same time, has never been so well expressed as in the formulation that appears in the three Synoptic Gospels, with slight variations: 'The Son of man indeed goeth, as it is written of him: but woe to that man by whom the Son of man is betrayed! good were it for that man if he had never been born.'

This sentence deserves to stand as the motto of all rites of human sacrifice, combining as it does profound thankfulness that the sacrifice has been brought about with indignation and loathing of the human agent through whom this is done. The more the agent is loathed, the more the true believer, whose soul benefits from the sacrifice, can repudiate the thought that he himself, and his community as a whole, desired and were responsible for the death of the victim. The figure of Pilate, by whose command the Crucifixion of Jesus actually took place yet who publicly washed his hands of all responsibility for the deed, thus symbolizes perfectly the role of the community in washing its hands and shifting all blame to Judas and the Jews.

It is necessary to distinguish carefully between the Judas-type and the concept of the 'scourge of God', with which it might be superficially equated. We find in the Old Testament and in other literature the idea of a person or nation that fulfils the purposes of God in punishing His people or Church for its shortcomings, without, however, doing so intentionally, but rather in pursuit of their own base or limited purposes. Nebuchadnezzar and later Attila were regarded in this light: unknowingly their cruel persecutions carried out the will of God in purging His people of their sins.[9] The difference here is that the victim deserves his sufferings. The 'scourge' may be despised as the uncomprehending and crude vehicle of God's higher purposes; but he is essentially an external device, not an integral actor in the communal drama. No special ritualized loathing attaches to him; he is a passing incident, not a cosmic force; his transitory, unintended mission done, he disappears from history. His mission is to punish the guilty, while the mission of Judas, or of the Sacred Executioner generally, is precisely to slay the innocent so that the guilty shall not suffer. For this he

Judas Iscariot

himself must belong to the community; and, even after his banishment, he must remain a permanent presence in the community's consciousness, perpetually bearing the mark of his deed. Historically, he is as immortal as the community itself.

This brings us to the question of Judas's motive in betraying Jesus. In view of the fact that he is the vehicle of a cosmic purpose, a necessary actor in a drama of sacrifice, we should expect to find that any personal motives ascribed to him are flimsy, ad hoc, or contradictory; and this is just what we do find. The only motive suggested in the Gospels is desire for money (in Matthew 26:14-16, for example: 'What will you give me to betray him to you?'). John develops the theme of Judas's avariciousness by accusing him of pilfering the money put into the common purse, of which he had charge (John 12:4-6 and 13:29). This idea no doubt contributed to the medieval and modern anti-Semitic picture of the Jew as a grasping miser. At the same time, John (6:70) stresses more than the others the demonic nature of Judas's role: 'Have I not chosen you, all twelve? Yet one of you is a devil' – a speech that emphasizes Jesus's designation of Judas as his fated betrayer. The money involved seems paltry, and the motive of greed is so casually introduced that it seems makeshift. Far more to the point is John's assertion that Satan entered into Judas (13:27).

Commentators through the ages have been dissatisfied with Judas's motiveless evil, and have ascribed conjectural motives to him of various kinds. On the basis of a highly speculative etymology of the name Iscariot, a picture has been built up of Judas as the only Judaean among a band of Galileans, and thus as a strong adherent of the Law, and an opponent of Jesus's alleged flouting of Sabbath laws and purity laws.[10] This is sheer fantasy, as are the other speculations that Judas disapproved of Jesus's allegedly new concept of the Messiah, or that he came to the conclusion that Jesus was a false Messiah. None of these theories has any support in the text.

Vladimir Propp, in his analysis of Russian folk-tales,[11] concluded that the figure of the 'Antagonist' was a necessary ingredient in them, and that any motives assigned to the Antagonist were secondary to the narrative requirement for such a figure. Frank Kermode,[12] applying this theory to the Gospel figure of Judas, shows that Judas starts off as a bare figure of an Antagonist and is only gradually fleshed out, in later versions of the story, as a person of psychological motivation: the outline of the story is primary, and novelistic elaborations of 'characterization' are secondary. Kermode's analysis is convincing, but it stays entirely on the level of narrational theory or literary criticism. It needs to be supplemented by understanding of the special type of Antagonist here required, namely, he who brings about the sacrificial death of a divine figure.[13]

Judas Iscariot

In so far as Judas is the human representative of Satan, he requires no motive except the natural antagonism between evil and good. Satan, as perceived in Christian dualism, is on the lookout to attack God's entourage at all times, and indeed an early Christian theory saw Satan tricked by God into performing the saving sacrifice of Jesus through his own blind antagonism.[14] Satan thus plays the part of Loki in the Scandinavian myth, acting through sheer malice, and Judas, as Satan's earthly representative or possessed devotee, requires no more motive than Satan himself. This role is echoed in Christian literature: for example, the motiveless malice of Iago against Othello owes much to the New Testament portrayal of Judas, and the hatred of Shylock for Antonio is similarly motiveless, being summed up in the phrase, 'I hate him for he is a Christian.' (In both cases, some motives are imputed, but they are so flimsy and contradictory that they carry no conviction.)[15]

The death of Judas, however, carries him outside the role of the Sacred Executioner, who is characteristically driven out to long wanderings rather than visited with summary punishment. According to Matthew, Judas was seized with remorse, tried to give the thirty pieces of silver back, was refused, and then threw down the silver before the priests and went and hanged himself (Matthew 27:3-5). The thirty pieces of silver were then used to buy the 'potter's field, to bury strangers in', an incident alleged by Matthew to be a fulfilment of a prophecy pronounced by Zechariah (though Matthew wrongly attributes it to Jeremiah). In Acts, however, an entirely different story of the death of Judas is given. Here it is said (Acts 1:*18-19*) that Judas bought a field with his ill-gotten gains, but fell down in the field and died, his bowels having burst. Both accounts agree, however, that the field was subsequently called the Field of Blood. The accounts agree, then, that the field was bought with the 'thirty pieces of silver', in the first case by the priests, and in the second by Judas himself. In the second account, unlike that given in Matthew, Judas does not repent.

It is Matthew's story of the death of Judas that provides the greater human interest, for the figure of the repentant betrayer is one of great pathos (for example, Shakespeare's Enobarbus, who owes something to the Matthean Judas, as well as to Plutarch). The unrepentant Judas of Acts, struck down horribly by God while attempting to enjoy the fruits of his treachery, is a mere footnote to the story, not a development of it. Even Matthew's version, however, reduces the status of Judas from the mythic to the folkloric. The impression given is that Judas, having been possessed by Satan, and having performed a mythic role while in this state of possession, suddenly found himself back in his normal senses. Satan had used him as an instrument and had then discarded him, and Judas found with horror what he had done and sought vainly to undo it. All that was left for him then was suicide. The role of the continuing mythic figure, bearing during prolonged wanderings the mark of God, was transferred from Judas to the Jewish people. Judas, in a sense, was released from his burden, and allowed to die. The next chapter, therefore, will deal with the role given in the Christian myth to the Jewish people, as a fuller development of the role of Sacred Executioner.[16]

But before turning away from Judas, we may ask whether there is not something mythic in the *mode* of Judas's death, especially in its location in a 'field of blood'. In Matthew's account, Judas does not actually die in the field. He hangs himself elsewhere, and the field is named the Field of Blood for another reason – that it was bought (by the priests) with blood-money, the money paid for the betrayal of Jesus. In the Acts account, however, it is Judas's blood, gushing from his burst bowels over the field, that gives it the name Field of Blood. Nothing is said here about it being the 'potter's field', a detail evidently introduced to relate the incident to an Old Testament prophecy.

If we collate the salient features of both accounts we arrive at this: Judas hanged himself (presumably from a tree) in a field. His bowels burst open on to the ground, and the field was subsequently known as the Field of Blood.

This account immediately relates Judas's death to the human sacrifices performed in agricultural religions. In Attis-worship, for example, the victim was hanged on a tree and also flayed, so that his blood ran down to fertilize the field. The disembowelling of the victim was also common in this type of rite, the entrails being spread over the fields.

In the story of Cain and Abel in Genesis, we may note a vestige of this aspect of human sacrifice, when God says to Cain:

What hast thou done? the voice of thy brother's blood crieth unto Me from the ground. And now cursed art thou from the ground, which hath opened her mouth to receive thy brother's blood from thy hand. When thou tillest the ground, she will not henceforth yield unto thee her strength. (Genesis 4:*10*)

Here, the earth rejects with disgust the infusion of blood from the slaying of Abel. There could be no greater repudiation of the ethos of human sacrifice, by which the mother-goddess, the earth, receives the blood gladly and produces in return a good harvest. Yet even in the repudiation, the outlines of the previous doctrine can be discerned: the earth is vividly personified as a female personality, drinking the blood through her mouth, and reacting (though negatively) in her production of crops.

Why, then, does Judas, the agent of death, the betrayer of the

Judas Iscariot

sacrificed Jesus, display in his own death the features of a sacrificial victim? Clearly this is not the conscious intention of the Gospel writers, who wish only to portray Judas as suffering due punishment for his sin. Moreover, the punishment of Judas is functional in that it draws attention away from the complicity of all Christians in the death of Jesus, by whose sacrifice their souls are saved. Though Judas, in his death, does not enact the role of the Sacred Executioner, condemned like Cain to stay alive, he does enact the death that the Sacred Executioner *deserves* to have, the death from which he is released in order to become a permanent, long-lived outcast. Judas thus fills in one aspect of the fantasy.

But it is interesting that, in suffering his punishment, Judas is unwittingly assimilated to the sacrificial victim himself. This bears out what was said above about the frequently found twin-relationship between sacrificer and victim. In the last resort, the sacrificer and victim are one. This unity derives from a time when the sacrifice did not produce such guilt in the community as to require the banishment or repudiation of the sacrificer. Instead, the sacrificer actually took the place of the victim, and reigned as king in his stead, and was regarded as being himself the resurrected incarnation of the victim whom he had slain. A myth that embodies this relationship is that of the twins Castor and Pollux, who had a pact to spend alternate half-years in Hades and in the land of the living.[17]

So, curiously enough, Judas in his death is in some ways a more authentic sacrificial victim than Jesus himself. He recovers the agricultural ambience ('field of blood') which the mystery religions, culminating in Christianity, had lost in the urbanized setting of the Greco-Roman Empire. His blood, like that of Abel, does not nourish the earth, but rather sickens her (for 'field of blood' has become an epithet of horror instead of what it originally was, an epithet of honour). Yet underneath the surface picture of an evil death, we may discern the original mystery of which Jesus's death was a 'spiritualized' development.

Chapter Eleven

The role of the Jews in the New Testament

The Christian myth, in so far as it concerns the Jews, runs as follows. The Jews were originally the people of God, but God has now rejected them, because of their betrayal of Jesus. They refused to believe in Jesus's divinity and betrayed him to his death at the hands of the Romans. In consequence, they became an accursed people. Their Temple was destroyed, as Jesus had prophesied, and they were driven into exile and became wanderers over the face of the earth.[1]

On the face of it, this is simply a dispossession myth, by which the Christian Church justified its appropriation of all the desirable props and appurtenances of Judaism. The Christian Church wished to regard itself as the true Israel – in other words, as the true Jews. Accordingly, it applied to itself the 'promises' made to Abraham, and the whole Jewish concept of election. All the Jewish prophets were made up into Christian saints. All the blessings of the Old Testament were regarded as applying to the Christian Church, while all the curses were allotted exclusively to the Jews: a neat division. This strategy was in many ways similar to that by which the Israelites had allotted a 'curse' to Canaan, in order to justify their taking over the land of the Canaanites. The Israelites, however, only took over the Canaanites' land; they did not appropriate also their religious identity, but on the contrary repudiated it. More similar was the strategy of Islam, in taking over the 'promises' of both Judaism and Christianity, and turning all the chief figures of both religions into Muslim saints. Islam, of course, had the successful model of Christianity to work from in carrying through this process of appropriation.

The Christian myth remains unique, however, in its ingenious combination of its dispossession myth with other mythical requirements. Not only are the Jews dispossessed, but they are given a new continuing role within the landscape of the Christian myth. The reason for this is that Christianity, unlike Judaism or Islam, has a human sacrifice, unacknowledged as such, as its central sacramental feature. The Israelites dispossessed the Canaanites, but they did not require them for any sacrificial purpose, since their religion began with a sacrifice that never happened, or (if in some earlier version it

The role of the Jews in the New Testament

did happen) was performed by their own ancestor at the command of God, without the need for a scapegoat. Islam did not regard Muhammad, its founder, as a sacrificial figure. In so far as a foundation sacrifice was required for Islam, the need was met by making over the Jewish foundation sacrifice, the Akedah, into a Muslim event where Ishmael (the alleged ancestor of the Arabs) was substituted for Isaac of the Bible story. (The supplementary fiction was that the Jews had falsified the Bible story, substituting Isaac for Ishmael.)

The Jews are thus indispensable, integral figures in the Christian myth. Not only are they dispossessed of their treasure, of the promises given to Abraham and of their position as the people of God, but the reason given for this dispossession, that they had hounded Jesus to death, neatly absolves Christians from responsibility for the sacrifice that brings about their salvation, and even from the thought that such a means of salvation is human-sacrificial. The bringing about of Jesus's death can thus be thought of both as a terrible crime (for which the Jews were responsible) and as a fortunate, saving event (by which all Christians can profit).

The way in which this conception evolved can be traced in the New Testament. Some historical considerations are here relevant. It was not, on the face of it, necessary that the Jews should have been held primarily responsible for the death of Jesus, and thus elevated to mythical status as the human instruments of Satan. More obvious candidates for this role were the Romans, who carried out the execution of Jesus by the Roman punishment of crucifixion, a penalty reserved for rebels against Roman rule. In the Dead Sea Scrolls the Romans are actually given a Satanic role as the earthly representatives of the evil angels in an apocalyptic cosmic struggle.[2] There is some evidence in the New Testament itself, in the Book of Revelation, that in the earliest days of Christianity the anti-Roman option was an active possibility, instead of the anti-Jewish option. The few Jews who were involved in the arrest of Jesus were so untypical of the Jews as a whole that their participation should have added to the guilt of the Romans rather than to that of the Jews: for it was the High Priest, a tool of the Romans, who acted with his entourage in the matter of denouncing Jesus to Pontius Pilate as a danger to the Roman occupying power.[3] Yet the anti-Roman option was eventually rejected so decisively that the main Roman figure responsible for Jesus's death, Pontius Pilate himself, was made to absolve himself in the hand-washing scene, which symbolized the refusal to implicate the Roman Empire in the guilt of Jesus's slaying. All anti-Roman aspects were carefully expunged from those Gospels that became the canon of Christian Scripture,[4] and scenes (such as the unhistorical Sanhedrin trial scene, and the equally unhistorical crowd scene in

The role of the Jews in the New Testament

which the Jews called for Jesus's crucifixion) were inserted that shifted the blame to the Jews as a whole or to their central representatives.

This shift can be ascribed primarily to Paul, who realized, with characteristic shrewdness, that there was little future for a non-localized cult in the Greco-Roman Empire if it adopted an anti-Roman stance. It was Paul who detached the figure of Jesus from his Jewish background and made him the centre of a salvation cult on the model of the mystery cults of Attis, Adonis and Osiris. Accordingly, Paul laid down a new principle, that 'the powers that be are ordained of God',[5] thus cleansing the Roman Empire of its identification with the power of Satan and leaving the position of Satanic acolyte vacant, to be filled by the chief anti-Roman force in existence, the fervently nationalistic and continually rebellious Jews. Paul also made use of the mystical anti-Semitism associated with Gnosticism, which, while it identified the Jews with the powers of evil who supposedly had this world in their grip, at the same time used the Jewish Scriptures as the source for an anti-Jewish ideology (e.g. the Sethian Gnostics used the early chapters of Genesis to show that the Jewish God was an inferior deity, responsible for the flaws of this world and of the Torah). This strategy had the further advantage of singling out as chief representatives of evil a weak and defeated people rather than the strongest power on earth, the Romans, opposition to whom might have been attended with serious inconveniences.

Paul's outline of the position to be held by the Jews in the new mythology is filled out in detail in the Gospels, which were composed by Paulinist writers in the period AD 70-110, on the basis of earlier, more authentic writings and traditions, which were slanted and emended to accommodate Paul's view of the Jews as a God-rejected people.

The diabolization of the Jews undoubtedly begins with Paul, in his diatribe against them in Thessalonians: ' . . . the Jews, who killed the Lord Jesus and the prophets and drove us out, the Jews who are heedless of God's will and enemies of their fellow-men, hindering us from speaking to the Gentiles to lead them to salvation. All this time they have been making up the full measure of their guilt, and now retribution has overtaken them for good and all' (I Thessalonians 2:15-16). The expression 'enemies of their fellow-men' was a commonplace of Greco-Roman anti-Semitism, and the expression 'they have been making up the full measure of their guilt' assimilates the Jews to the Canaanites, to whom a similar expression is applied in the Old Testament (Genesis 15:16): 'for the iniquity of the Amorite is not yet full'. Thus the passage contains a full dispossession myth, in which the Jews are displayed as rejected by God because of a long record of disobedience and violence against God's messengers

The role of the Jews in the New Testament

culminating in the murder of His son Jesus. But there is also more than a hint of what might be called the 'negative-election myth', by which the Jews are God's instrument for the sacrifice of the Son of God; for only by being born in the midst of a nation with such a proven record of murder could God's son be sure that his necessary violent death would occur. Note that there is no mention of the Romans as being involved in his death; it is the Jews who 'killed the Lord Jesus'. Paul thus initiates the pro-Roman, anti-Jewish version of the Crucifixion, in a form even more extreme than that found in the Gospels.

So vicious is this attack that many scholars argue that it must be a later interpolation.[6] This is probably true of the second clause of the last sentence, 'and now retribution has overtaken them for good and all', which probably refers to the destruction of the Temple; but the rest of the passage cannot be detached from Paul. More temperate expressions about the Jews can of course be found in the Epistles, especially the celebrated passage in Romans, where Paul speaks sorrowfully of the Jews's rejection of Jesus and reveals that this 'blindness' has come about through God's will, so that the Gentiles may have their opportunity for salvation. Once the Gentiles have accepted this opportunity, the 'blindness' of the Jews will be removed and 'the whole of Israel will be saved'. Meanwhile, Paul tells the Gentiles, the Jews 'are treated as God's enemies for your sake' (Romans 11:25-32). This strange passage (which sometimes saved the Jews from complete extermination in the massacres of the Middle Ages) is often quoted to show Paul's friendly feelings towards the Jews. But it is overlooked that the passage is made tolerable only by its careful omission to spell out the implications of its stance. That the Jews were made 'blind' to Jesus's divine identity by the plan of God the Father means that God engineered the death of Jesus through these same blinded Jews. This aspect, however, Paul omits to explain openly. Yet the inference is plain. The Jews were the elected Sacred Executioner, blinded by God for one aspect of this role, just as it was the blind Hother who unwittingly killed the god Balder and the blind Lamech who killed Cain. The device of a blind, unwitting executioner alternates throughout the mythology of human sacrifice with the notion of a wicked executioner fulfilling God's purposes for the wrong reasons. Sometimes the two figures feature in the same myth, as when Loki, the evil one, collaborates with the dupe Hother to bring about the necessary death. But sometimes, as in the Gospel myth, both notions (incompatible as they may appear) are combined in the same person, regarded alternately as a criminal and as a dupe. This strategy of alternation was initiated, like so much else in Christianity, by Paul.

An interesting example of this double mechanism is found in the treatment in two Gospels, those of Mark and Matthew, of Jesus's

The role of the Jews in the New Testament

explanation to his disciples of his use of parables. The incident itself cannot be regarded as historically authentic, since it purports to show that Jesus regarded his fellow-Jews as beyond salvation and as unworthy of enlightenment from him. Jesus is represented as saying that he uses parables, not to illuminate his message, but to *hide* his meaning from the Jewish masses. The version found in the earlier Gospel, Mark, is as follows:

When he was alone, the Twelve and others who were round him questioned him about the parables. He replied, 'To you the secret of the kingdom of God has been given; but to those who are outside everything comes by way of parables, so that [Greek – *hina*], as Scripture says, they may look and look, but see nothing; they may hear and hear, but understand nothing; otherwise they might turn to God and be forgiven.' (Mark 4:*11-12*).

The version found in Matthew is somewhat different:

The disciples went up to him and asked, 'Why do you speak to them in parables?' He replied, 'It has been granted to you to know the secrets of the kingdom of Heaven; but to those others it has not been granted. For the man who has will be given more, till he has enough and to spare; and the man who has not will forfeit even what he has. That is why I speak to them in parables; for [Greek – *hoti*] they look without seeing, and listen without hearing or understanding. There is a prophecy of Isaiah which is being fulfilled for them: "You may hear and hear, but you will never understand; you may look and look, but you will never see. For this people's mind has become gross; their ears are dulled, and their eyes are closed. Otherwise, their eyes might see, their ears hear, and their mind understand, and then they might turn again, and I would heal them."' (Matthew 13:*10-15*)

The great difference between these two passages lies in the difference between two Greek particles, *hina* and *hoti*. Mark says that Jesus withheld information from the Jews *so that* (*hina*) they would not understand. Matthew says that he withheld it *because* (*hoti*) they were unable to understand. The difference is that Mark conceives the Jews as fated to be the rejecters and betrayers of Jesus, while Matthew ascribes this role to their wilful refusal to listen and understand. In Mark, Jesus deliberately prevents the Jews from being informed (by talking to them in riddles), and thereby he designates the Jews for the role of Christ-deniers (just as in some passages Jesus deliberately designates Judas as his betrayer). In Matthew, Jesus also deliberately talks to the Jews in riddles, but not to prevent them from understanding, but because he has despaired of their ever making an effort to understand, so wilfully obtuse have they made themselves. Many Christian commentators have felt shocked by Mark's *hina* (how could Jesus deliberately confuse his audience?), but have felt that Matthew's account is the more acceptable. Actually, I suggest that Mark's version is marginally less anti-Jewish, since it attributes the baleful role of the

The role of the Jews in the New Testament

Jews to fate rather than to obdurate, wilful refusal to listen. Mark actually represents Jesus as refraining from enlightening the Jews for the very reason that they might thereby repent and their destined role as slayers of the divine sacrifice would be unfulfilled.

This whole conception, of course, is late and Hellenistic, because parables are not riddles. The parable was the typical art-form of the Pharisee rabbis (of whom Jesus was one) and is found in abundance in the rabbinical writings.[7] It is invariably aimed at making the message *easier* to understand by putting it into graphic anecdotal form. It is precisely for the better understanding of the common people that this art-form was developed. On the other hand, the obscure, riddling allegory was a Greek religious art-form, and the late redactors of the Gospels (as C. H. Dodd has pointed out[8]) attempted to present Jesus's simple Jewish parables as if they were Gnostic allegories, though most of the parables have still retained their Jewish features, and by their direct illumination give the lie to the above-quoted passages which attempt to turn them into riddles, aimed at hiding an esoteric message from a populace doomed to damnation.

Yet the version of Mark is not really inconsistent with that of Matthew, except in the formal, logical sense, since, in myth, the wicked betrayer alternates with the destined betrayer, and both ideas are felt to be necessary. In the Gospels, a set of texts could be collected to show that the Jews were the destined betrayers of Jesus; and another set of texts could be collected to show that the Jews were the wicked enemies of the Light and thus chose deliberately to be betrayers. An interesting demonstration of this occurred in a fairly recent court case in France. Jacques Isorni, a well-known advocate, sued Abbé Georges de Nantes for libelling him in an article which attacked his book *Le Vrai Procès de Jesus*. The contest was represented in the world press as one between a 'liberal' and a 'reactionary' view of Jewish responsibility for the death of Jesus. Isorni's defence of the Jews (for which de Nantes had attacked him as a falsifier of the Gospels) was that they had brought about Jesus's death in genuine and excusable error because they did not realize that Jesus was God. De Nantes's case, on the other hand, was that the Gospels represent the Jews as deliberately bringing about Jesus's death *fully knowing him to be God*. Both sides confined themselves to what the Gospels say, so the question of whether the Gospels have falsified any of the events and blamed the Jews for a crime that they did not commit did not enter the discussion. Also, both sides also assumed that Jesus *was* God, so that the crime discussed was deicide, unwitting or deliberate, not judicial murder or manslaughter.[9]

The discussion was thus whether the Jews were to be regarded as a Hother (killing the god unwittingly) or a Loki (killing the god, or

The role of the Jews in the New Testament

sneakily bringing about his death, out of deliberate malice and hatred of the Light). The important point, however, is that both contestants were able to cite texts convincingly supporting their respective positions. The Gospels present the Jews both as Hother and as Loki. These are the two main alternatives; but there are also some intermediate positions which are also adumbrated in the Gospels: (i) The Jews did not know that they were killing God, but thought that they were killing just another of their prophets (the New Testament accuses the Jews of killing nearly all their prophets, though it is hard to find in the Old Testament any evidence of their killing even one prophet[10]). (ii) The information that Jesus was God was purposely withheld from the Jews, because they did not deserve to be saved, in view of their wicked past history. Their unwittingness, therefore, cannot be used to excuse them, as it was part of their punishment to be chosen as deicides, and not be given the opportunity to withdraw from this role. (iii) The Jews really knew that Jesus was God, but deliberately blinded themselves to this truth, so that their unwittingness was an act of will, not a palliating circumstance.

Thus there are various grey areas, mediating between the two extreme positions of complete guilt and complete unwittingness. Strictly speaking, all these positions are incompatible with each other, but they are all necessary to the total myth, since they represent all possible ways in which the Jews may be held responsible for the death of Jesus, and thus act as scapegoats for the Christian community. It is thus quite inadequate to point to a single saying, such as 'Father, forgive them; for they know not what they do' (Luke 23:34) as representing *the* attitude of the Gospels. (Even taken in isolation, this saying increases rather than diminishes the guilt of the Jews, contrasting the all-forgiving, inoffensive Jesus with the merciless Jews. The artistic effect is to make the reader hate the Jews more than ever: 'Look what kind of person the Jews have done such things to!')

The text in which the alleged preternatural wickedness of the Jews is utilized to combine the dispossession myth with the sacrificial myth is pre-eminently the twenty-third chapter of Matthew. Even the fulminations of John against the Jews hardly come up to this level of vituperation:

Woe to you, scribes and Pharisees, hypocrites! for you build the tombs of the prophets and adorn the monuments of the righteous, saying, 'If we had lived in the days of our fathers, we would not have taken part with them in shedding the blood of the prophets.' Thus you witness against yourselves, that you are sons of those who murdered the prophets. Fill up, then, the measure of your fathers. You serpents, you brood of vipers, how are you to escape being sentenced to hell? Therefore I send you prophets and wise men and scribes, some of whom you will kill and crucify, and some you will scourge in your

The role of the Jews in the New Testament

synagogues and persecute from town to town, that upon you may come all the righteous blood shed on earth, from the blood of the innocent Abel to the blood of Zechariah the son of Barachiah, whom you murdered between the sanctuary and the altar. (Matthew 23:29-35)

Though this imprecation is pronounced against the 'scribes and Pharisees', the sequel, promising the punishment that the Temple will be destroyed, shows that the Pharisees are here regarded as representative (as indeed they were) of Jews and their religious tradition as a whole. The continually repeated allegation that the Pharisees are 'hypocrites' is intended to counter the fact that the Pharisees, in appearance, are virtuous, God-fearing people, who therefore hardly bear out the role assigned to them, namely, that of earthly representatives of Satan, and the people marked out for the loathly task of slaying the divine sacrifice. Their ancestors have all killed prophets, and they too, despite their misleading appearance of virtue, will also kill prophets (thus continually repeating their primary sin, the killing of the divine sacrifice, for which their whole previous and future history befits them). By fulfilling this role, the Jews will become responsible for 'all the righteous blood shed on earth', and especially for the righteous blood of Jesus himself, which might otherwise be blamed on others such as the Romans – or the Christians themselves who benefit by this bloodshed of the righteous, since through it they attain salvation and might therefore be held responsible in that they wanted it to happen. The outpouring of venomous anger against the Jews in this passage fulfils a real psychological need – the need to find an outlet for the guilt of bloodshed, felt consciously or unconsciously by all those who depend on bloodshed, or the idea of bloodshed, for their psychological balance. The litany of bloodshed in the passage, listing, in intention, *all* the cases of bloodshed of the innocent in history, starts with Abel (a significant name) and ends with 'Zechariah the son of Barachiah' (this name is misquoted from II Chronicles 24:30). The list could not, however, be longer because in fact very few instances of the killing of prophets can be found in the Old Testament. Abel, indeed, was not killed by the Jews at all, since his death took place before the Jewish people came into existence; but this is no bar to the imprecation of the Jews – they are made responsible for the death of Abel too, because their role of god-killers makes them a convenient repository for all the guilt in history, leaving the Christian community serenely innocent.

The reference to the destruction of the Temple (Matthew 24:2), with which the imprecation culminates, shows, of course, that this unsavoury passage was composed much later than the time of Jesus, some time after AD 40, and inserted into the mouth of Jesus in order to represent him as the implacable opponent of the Jewish people, for whom, in historical fact, he gave his life. The passage played an important part in the process of diabolization of the Jews and their consequent sufferings in Europe. [11]

The mention of Abel puts the Jews into the role of Cain, and this identification is found frequently in the writings of the Church Fathers and later Christian authors.[12] The identification is more than a mere accusation of murder, for, as we have seen, the slaying of Abel was originally a human sacrifice, and was undoubtedly felt unconsciously to be so by the authors of this passage, who thus impose upon the Jews the fate of Cain – to wander through the world, hated and persecuted yet protected from complete extinction because of the awe surrounding their ambiguous and mysterious crime.

Even more influential in building up the picture of the Jews as a collective Sacred Executioner is the crowd scene in Matthew 27, in which the Jews call, in a mass, for the execution of Jesus. It is Matthew, alone of the Evangelists, who adds the baleful detail that the Jews called a curse upon themselves: 'His blood be on us and on our children' (Matthew 27:25). This sentence perfects the role of the Jews in the Christian myth. The prolongation of a miserable life is always felt to be necessary for the Sacred Executioner, for his expiatory role would be diminished by an early death. Thus Cain was promised immunity, and other great sinners who sinned on behalf of mankind (such as Oedipus and Teiresias) were given the gift of long life. But an individual's life must eventually come to an end. Better, from this point of view, is the election of a whole nation to the role of expiatory sinner; for, on the one hand, a nation can live for ever, and, on the other, it becomes possible to kill and persecute the nation as individuals with the only provision that enough of them are spared to continue their function. Thus the invention of the concept of a whole guilty nation as slayers of the god must be regarded as one of the great contributions of Christianity to the development of expiation by human sacrifice. The eternal Jew ('*der ewige Jude*') becomes a guarantee of the permanence of the salvation afforded by the Crucifixion; as long as the Jew continues his mysteriously prolonged existence in suffering, the Christian can feel assured of salvation. Any sign that this suffering may come to an end, however, arouses intolerable anxiety in Christendom.

I have discussed elsewhere the Barabbas episode from a historical standpoint, showing how many of its most effective ingredients can be shown to be unhistorical.[13] The picture of Pilate as a mild, conscience-ridden person is entirely contradicted by accounts in Tacitus, Philo and Josephus that show Pilate to have been a coarse and venal butcher. The *privilegium paschale*, by which the Jews are alleged to have had the right to free a prisoner, never existed. Even if it

The most haunting image in the Christian myth, and the most forceful piece of propaganda: the trial of Jesus. Pilate stands by, helpless; Jesus is at the mercy of the howling Jewish mob. (Detail of 'Ecce Homo': engraving after Rubens.)

had existed, that could not have prevented Pilate from freeing another prisoner, or many other prisoners, in addition, if he had wanted to. The Roman Procurator's alleged fear of the Jewish crowd is a figment, as is the supposition that a Roman governor would see nothing wrong in a prisoner claiming to be king of the Jews, at a time when such a claim was sedition punishable by death – and so on.

Here, we are more concerned with the mythical aspects of the Barabbas incident than with its relation, or rather non-relation, to historical fact. Its imaginative impact has been incalculable. In one vivid scene, the whole anti-Semitic myth of the Gospels is unforgettably displayed: the inoffensive Jesus, resigned to his sacrificial death, standing meekly before the howling Jewish mob, in which all the elements of the Jewish people are represented – priests, Sadducees, Pharisees, Sanhedrin and common people – united in the cry, 'Crucify him!' Pilate, the Roman governor, stands by in helpless sorrow; the Romans are not to blame. The scene stands in ironic contrast to that other scene of mythology, the death of Balder. There, all the devices of displacement are employed to *exonerate* the crowd. The manifest content of the scene is that the crowd is pelting Balder with stones and missiles, doing him to death. But the 'secondary elaboration' tells us that this manifest content is erroneous, that the crowd is not killing Balder at all, but innocently testing his supposed invulnerability; the real culprit is the lone figure of Loki, apparently taking no part in the stoning. In the Gospel scene, on the other hand, the manifest content is that of a crowd shouting or pleading for Jesus's release; a Roman governor, appointee of a pitiless power, stands before them frustrating their desire. But the 'secondary elaboration' tells us that this is all wrong. The Roman governor is full of pity; the Jewish crowd is pleading for the release of the wrong man, Barabbas; the Roman governor is only too willing to release the right man, Jesus, but the crowd will not let him; when the execution eventually takes place, it is not the Roman governor who is responsible, but the crowd.[14] The Balder scene and the Barabbas scene are neat inversions of each other, showing in contrasted ways the power of secondary elaboration to reverse the meaning of a dreamed or imagined scene, so that the dreamer or imaginer can evade the acknowledgment of his own desires.

The much-praised resolution of Vatican Council II that purported to release the Jews from the Christian charge of deicide concentrated on this very scene, and pronounced that the *whole* Jewish people was not involved, since a crowd gathered in Jerusalem could comprise only a small proportion of the Jewish nation. Moreover, the Jews of that particular time comprised only a very small proportion of the total of Jews of all generations. The Jews as a whole, therefore, could not be convicted of deicide because of the guilt of such a tiny minority. This argument, though formally correct, is really beside the point. The nub of the question is not whether all Jews, past, present and future, were literally present in the Barabbas scene, calling for the crucifixion of Jesus, but that this is the *imaginative intention* of the scene and its mythological effect, as can be seen amply in Christian reaction to it throughout the ages. To deny that the charge of deicide is correct is an excellent move; but to deny that such a charge was ever intended in the Gospel scene is either deliberate whitewashing of a horrific aspect of the Gospels, or insensitivity to a potent and unmistakeable artistic effect. It also shows ignorance of ancient ways of thinking. That a whole nation should take upon itself an eternal and unrescindible mission was one of the accepted imaginative possibilities of antiquity. It is especially associated with the Jewish people, who took upon themselves at Sinai a mission that was binding on themselves and their descendants for all time. It is indeed in a kind of devilish parody of that occasion that the Jews are portrayed by Matthew as swearing to accept a curse upon themselves to the end of all generations: 'His blood be on us and on our children.'

The role of the Jews in the New Testament

In any case, the abrogation of the charge of deicide by Vatican II is of little significance when one considers its accompanying clause that Jews can be cleared of this charge only if they do not associate themselves with the 'wicked generation' of the time of Jesus. That so-called 'wicked generation' was in fact one of the greatest generations in Jewish religious history: the age of the Tannaim, of Hillel and Shammai, Johanan ben Zakkai and Gamaliel was an age corresponding in Jewish development to that of the Church Fathers in Christianity. To dissociate themselves from this generation would be, for Jews, to dissociate themselves from Judaism. This particular approach to emendation of the charge of deicide must therefore be regarded as totally inadequate (though is to be welcomed as at least a move, however feeble, in the direction of acknowledgment of Christian responsibility for anti-Semitism[15]). Some real progress will be made when it is realized by Christian authorities that the charge of deicide is a primitive fantasy, deriving from pagan ideas of divine sacrifice; and, at the level of historical reality, that the death of Jesus was the responsibility of those who saw him as a menace, i.e. the Romans, not the Jews – to whom he was a would-be rescuer from foreign domination and religious persecution, a fellow-Jew, and a person regarded without animosity by all Jews except the tiny minority of Sadducees and Herodians who had become paid collaborators with the Romans.

The Barabbas incident is the central set-piece in which Jesus is portrayed as a lone figure hated by all significant sections of the Jewish people. As such, this episode has made an enormous contribution to the image of the Jew in the Christian imagination. Even more effective in this regard, however, because more pervasive and insistent, is the picture given throughout the Gospel of John. In this Gospel, 'the Jews' (the phrase is constantly repeated in a litany of hate) are portrayed as an evil, unitary entity, continually desiring one thing: the death of Jesus. The Catholic theologian Rosemary Ruether has put the matter in this way:

'The Jews', for John, are the very incarnation of the false, apostate principle of the fallen world, alienated from its true being in God. They are the type of the carnal man, who knows nothing spiritually. They are the type of the perishing man who belongs to the 'time' of the world, but, unlike the spiritual brethren of Jesus, can never recognize the *kairos* of the eternal event (7:6). Because they belong essentially to the world and its hostile, alienated principle of existence, their instinctive reaction to the revelation of the spiritual Son of God is murderousness. What they do recognize is that in Christ their false principle of existence has been unmasked and comes to an end. So whenever the light breaks through in their presence, they immediately seek to 'kill him'. In this murderousness they manifest their true principle of existence. They show that they are 'not of God', but 'of the Devil', who was a liar and a murderer from the beginning (8:43-7).[16]

This characterization of John, drawn by a Christian writer with great embarrassment and pain, is by no means exaggerated. More than the other Evangelists, John has set up the Jews as a *collective* Sacred Executioner. They are the embodiment on earth of those cosmic powers of evil that have only to encounter the Light in order to strive to annihilate it. John, the latest of the Gospels, is the 'Gospel of the Church', and is furthest removed from the historical reality of Jesus as a Jewish teacher and political figure. Jesus has become a visitant from outer space, who has nothing in common with 'the Jews' among whom he has landed. This is the furthest possible development of a particular type of distancing device by which the saved community removes itself from all responsibility for the death of the divine sacrifice. This is the device of regarding the sacrificer as evil. In a less guilt-ridden human-sacrificial community, the sacrificer can be regarded with honour, as among the Aztecs; but, where the killing of the sacrifice is regarded with horror, the sacrificer must be rejected with all the force of which the community is capable. The profound dualism of this scheme arises from an agonizing psychological dilemma: salvation can be achieved only by an act that the conscience repudiates. There is a deeply ashamed atavism about the whole religious configuration: here is a people that has reached a high stage of civilization, but which nevertheless can achieve peace only by reverting to a primitive form of expiation. The split in the personality is symbolized by a split in the universe: the powers of atavism become evil cosmic powers which can be relied upon to carry out the necessary extinguishing of the Light, which is only a prelude to its rebirth. The community has achieved its aim by outlawing the means by which it achieves it.

The diabolization of the Jews is accomplished in the Gospel of John. In the other Gospels other means are developed to the same end: the story of Judas, the story of Barabbas, the vilification of the Pharisees. In the subsequent development of the Christian Church, the fantasy of the Jews as collective Sacred Executioner and people of the Devil receives further elaboration and issues in tragic consequences, from the persecutions of the Middle Ages to the Holocaust of our own day.

Chapter Twelve

The Church and the Jews

John's picture of the Jews as hungry for the death of Jesus for no reason other than that the Darkness naturally hates the Light is continued within the Church's mythology, with the idea that the Jews are continually hungry for the death of Christians. The Church myth runs as follows: Jews see in every Christian the lineaments of Jesus himself; they therefore wish to repeat their crime of Christ-murder whenever opportunity occurs. This myth took its most horrific form in the blood-libel of the Middle Ages, when Jews were accused of capturing Christian children in order to crucify them and drink their blood. But this climactic fantasy was foreshadowed in many previous fantasies that proliferated in Christendom.

The beginnings of these fantasies occur in the New Testament itself, in the Acts of the Apostles, which recounts the earliest years of the Church after the death of Jesus. Here again the Jews are portrayed as vicious murderers who bring about the death of Christian martyrs. And these martyrs atone by their death for the sins of the world – i.e. of the Christian world, for those outside this world are condemned to hell. Thus the sufferings and bloodshed of Jesus are continually renewed, and the natural agents of this renewal are the destined Sacred Executioners, the Jews, whose role is thus a never-ending story. When one examines more closely, however, these stories of the Jewish persecution of the early Church, the air of verisimilitude that surrounds them tends to evaporate, and their mythical quality is revealed.[1]

The earliest persecution recorded is that carried out by Saul, later Paul. This counts as a Pharisee persecution, since Paul was allegedly a Pharisee at this time. It is puzzling, however, that Paul is plainly stated to have acted under orders from the High Priest, who was a Sadducee (Acts 9:2). The High Priest would naturally oppose the followers of Jesus, just as he had opposed Jesus himself, and for the same reasons: that, as an appointee of the Romans, and a quisling, he, the High Priest, was bound to pursue all movements that constituted a threat to Roman power in Palestine. Thus Saul persecuted the Jerusalem Church (the Nazarenes) not in pursuit of Pharisee aims, but for *political* reasons, as an agent of the quisling High Priest. It is part of

The Church and the Jews

the policy of blackening the Jewish mainstream religious party, the Pharisees, that this activity of Paul's is attributed to his alleged attachment to the Pharisee party. That this is not so is inadvertently revealed in Acts in the scene in which the Pharisees, under their great leader Gamaliel, actually rescue the Nazarene leader, Peter, from indictment by the High Priest (Acts 5), an episode that contradicts the whole picture found elsewhere in Acts of the Pharisees as enemies of the Nazarenes.

The alleged martyrdom of Stephen is laid to the account of the Jews as a whole, and has played a great part in the picture of the Jews as carrying on a murderous persecution of the early Christians. The evidence, however, as shown by Hare and other authors, is that Stephen was killed in some obscure riot, and that his death was worked up into a full martyrdom by the invention of a trial before the Sanhedrin that was no more historical than the 'trial' of Jesus himself.[2] An elaborate speech is put into Stephen's mouth, full of Pauline ideas that did not exist in these early years, and firmly setting his death in the context of Jewish murderousness throughout the ages: 'Was there ever a prophet whom your fathers did not persecute? They killed those who foretold the coming of the Righteous One; and now you have betrayed him and murdered him, you who received the Law as God's angels gave it to you, and yet have not kept it' (Acts 7:52-3). Paul's curious idea that the Law was given to the Israelites by angels, not by God, is put into the mouth of Stephen. This idea does not come from any Jewish source, but from Gnosticism, which regarded the Torah as the work of an inferior Power, not of the Highest God.

Even though the Pharisees rescued Peter from the High Priest, Acts portrays 'the Jews' (the expression appears almost as many times as in the Gospel of John) as constantly plotting to bring about Peter's death. Similarly, 'the Jews' are blamed for the arrest of Paul, though again it is admitted that the Pharisees voted in his favour. As Rosemary Ruether says, 'The actual arrest of Paul in Jerusalem and his transfer to a prison in Caesarea is elaborately excused to make the Jews look reponsible, while the Romans who constantly recognize Paul's innocence and want to release him, appear as innocent victims of Jewish malice.'[3]

All in all, the picture of malevolent Jews plotting the deaths of early Christians is, as Hare argues, theologically motivated, rather than historical.[4] But this is not, as Hare and Rosemary Ruether think, purely a matter of supplanting the Jews as the people of God and transferring the favour of God to the Christian Church. It is also a matter of completing the picture of the Jews as collective Sacred Executioner. This role does not end with the death of Jesus but has to be continued throughout the story of the Church, kept alive by the concept of

The Church and the Jews

martyrdoms renewing the sufferings of Jesus, and therefore requiring a Judas in every generation.

Contrary to the Christian idea that the minds of Jews were full of hate against Jesus and Christians generally, the remarkable fact is that Jewish sources show very little reference to the whole phenomenon of Christianity, which does not seem to have been a matter of even moderate interest on the part of Jews. The voluminous Talmudic literature contains only a few passing references to Jesus and Christianity; there is certainly no evidence of any strong interest in the subject, let alone a consuming obsession of hatred such as the Christian writers of the period allege. On the other hand, Christian literature *does* contain an obsession – an obsession with the Jews, who are vilified and abused in a startling fashion.[5] The alleged hatred of Jews for Christians is thus partly a projection of the actual hatred felt by Christians towards Jews and partly a theological necessity arising from the role assigned to the Jews in the Christian mythology. There is also the fact that while Judaism could be expounded without any reference to Christianity, it was impossible to expound Christianity without explaining why it involved the rejection of Judaism. The Christian claims could not be established without first demolishing the Jewish claims on the basis of which they lay and which they were intended to supersede. The vilification of the Jews was thus essential to the very fabric of Christianity, while the belief and practice of Judaism did not require that Christianity should even be mentioned. This situation, of course, could not be acknowledged by Christians, to whom mere lack of interest on the part of the Jews was far harder to bear than active opposition, which would indeed have been welcomed as confirmation of the Christian configuration. The Jews were therefore fantasized as actually *believing* in Christianity, but refusing to succumb to their belief. The continuing development of Judaism was ignored by Christians, who thought of Jews as stubbornly perpetuating a fossilized, exploded religion out of sheer malice and chagrin for the sole purpose of thwarting Christianity, and with minds filled with hostile thoughts towards Christianity. Nothing, in fact, was further from the case, as this period was one of great creative activity, when the great rabbinical literature was in the process of composition: the Mishnah, Tosefta, Midrashim and Talmudim; and any slight interest shown by Jews in Christianity was peripheral to their greater concerns.

Nevertheless, the writings of the Church Fathers are full of allegations expressed in general terms, of Jewish malice towards Christians and Christianity and of active persecution of Christians by Jews. Thus Origen (c.185-c.254) writes, 'The Jews do not vent their wrath on the Gentiles who worship idols and blaspheme God, and they neither

The Church and the Jews

hate them nor rage against them. But against the Christians they rage with an insatiable fury.'[6] Yet Origen is known to have been on personally friendly terms with many Jews, from whom he learnt much that he incorporated into his writings. The assertion of the Jews' inveterate hatred of Christianity is not an empirical observation at all, but a theological idea, based on a passage in the Psalms, which he interprets as referring to the relations between Jews and Christians (though, in fact, of course, it has nothing to do with this topic).[7]

Origen's remark may be regarded as a conventional gesture (though, of course, the average churchgoer, reading his works, would take it much more seriously), but Chrysostom (347–407) combines the same generalizing manner and Old Testament pseudocommentary with a very real venom against the Jews of his day. The diatribes of this canonized saint and venerated teacher are rivalled only by those of Hitler. He accuses the Jews of every possible crime, even killing and eating their own children (a charge that again turns out to be based on an interpretation of a verse in the Psalms). Later he half-admits that the Jews no longer eat their own children, but asserts that they murdered Christ, which was worse. He urges Christians to hate Jews: 'If someone had killed your son, could you stand the sight of him or the sound of his greeting? Would you not try to get away from him as if he were an evil demon, as if he were the Devil himself? The Jews killed the Son of your Master . . . Will you so dishonour Him as to respect and cultivate His murderers, the men who crucified Him? (*Or. C. Jud.* I, 7). Among Chrysostom's other choice remarks are that the Jews worship demons; that God has always hated them; that God does not allow them to repent for the murder of Jesus. The occasion for these diatribes was that the Christians of Antioch were too friendly with the Jews, and Chrysostom therefore thought it his duty to put an end to such friendship. Here he took part in an activity that was characteristic of the Christian clergy for over a thousand years, until it finally succeeded in its aim: to turn all feelings of friendliness towards Jews that arose from the natural human fellow-feelings of rank-and-file Christians into an ingrained attitude of loathing and horror. This was the greatest brain-washing operation in history, and it was not easily accomplished, for there is much evidence that for centuries the ordinary Christian resisted the process. Eventually, it succeeded only too well, as was shown by the passive and active support given to the Nazi Holocaust by the populace, whose anti-Jewish reactions had become so profound, after many centuries of Christian indoctrination, that they could be regarded as instinctive and could be absolutely depended upon as such.

Another great doctor and saint of the Church who devoted much energy to promoting hatred of the Jews was Augustine (354–430). In

The Church and the Jews

his work *Contra Judaeos* he argues that the Jews were never the people of God, but were always a preternaturally wicked people (figures such as Moses, David, Elijah or Isaiah are not exceptions, since they were all Christians, not Jews!). The Jews, in a career of continual murder, were preparing for their greatest crime, the murder of Jesus. Augustine sees in the various contrasting pairs of the Old Testament – Cain and Abel, Ishmael and Isaac, Esau and Jacob, Hagar and Sarah – a prefiguring of the rejection of the Jews and the election of the Church, the Jews being symbolized by Cain (a favourite idea of Augustine's), Hagar, Ishmael and Esau.

This is, of course, a favourite identification with the Church Fathers, and can be found, for example, in the writings of Tertullian, Chrysostom and Aphrahat. The murdered Abel, too, is identified with Jesus, and the fact that Abel was replaced by Seth is taken to represent the Resurrection of Christ. Moreover, the wanderings of Cain were seized on as symbolic of the dispersion of the Jews after the destruction of their Temple. The Christian poet Prudentius (348–c.410) expresses this aspect as follows: 'From place to place the homeless Jew wanders in ever-shifting exile, since the time when he was torn from the abode of his fathers and has been suffering the penalty for murder and having stained his hands with the blood of Christ, whom he denied, paying the price of sin' (Prud. *Apotheosis* 541–5).

Thus the alleged persecutions of Christians by Jews had no basis in historical fact, but were part of the mythical picture by which the Christians ordered their world. James Parkes has subjected to careful analysis the mass of tales that have been preserved about the early Christian martyrdoms.[8] In many of those of the second and third centuries a peripheral Jewish element has been introduced (usually Jewish members of the crowd jeering at the dying martyr or dissuading other members of the crowd from offering help or sympathy). In the great majority of these later stories, however, there is no Jewish element at all. Jews are given more prominence and initiative in stories of martyrdoms of the first century, which however are largely modelled on stories in the New Testament itself, or else are legendary and contradicted by incompatible stories about the same martyr (some of whom, indeed, never existed at all, but were based on pagan legends). All in all, the conclusion is that Christian martyrs suffered at pagan hands (because they were held to be disloyal in not offering incense to the Roman Emperor, and did not have the special dispensation in this respect enjoyed by the Jews). Jewish participation was minimal or non-existent.

The lack of evidence in the martyrology thus stands in stark contrast with the generalized statements of the early Christian writers blaming

The Church and the Jews

the persecutions chiefly on the Jews. Parkes therefore ascribes these generalizations to theological considerations, and thinks that in many cases they were not even meant to be taken literally. Yet modern Christian historians have mostly taken them at face value. Thus Harnack writes that the Jews 'systematically and officially . . . scattered broadcast horrible charges against the Christians which played an important part in the persecutions as early as the reign of Trajan; they started calumnies against Jesus; they provided heathen opponents of Christianity with literary ammunition; unless the evidence is misleading, they instigated the Neronic outburst against the Christians, and as a rule wherever bloody persecutions are afoot in later days, the Jews are either in the background or the foreground.'[9] Similar judgments are made by the Church historians H. Leclerq and M. Allard. The myth of the ever-malevolent Christ-killing Jew is thus perpetuated by seemingly objective historians, who based their pronouncements not on the evidence but on the theologically motivated generalizations of the early Christian writers.

The mythical picture of the Jew as Christ-killer and Christian-killer achieved its most horrific form in the medieval 'blood-libel' accusations, which brought about the torture and death of countless Jews and of whole Jewish communities. The tenor of this totally imaginary accusation was that the Jews captured and killed Christian children for ritual purposes (the phrase 'ritual murder' is sometimes used to characterize this alleged crime). The whole matter was investigated thoroughly by Hermann Strack, a Christian scholar (1848–1922), who wrote *Das Blut im Glauben und Aberglauben der Menschheit* (1891; eighth edition 1911), which was translated into English by H. Blanchamp as *The Jew and Human Sacrifice: Human Blood and Jewish Ritual* (1909). Strack's argument was that not only were the Jews guiltless of the charges made against them (which were still frequent, especially at Easter-time, in the period when he wrote), but that such charges arose from blood-superstitions that existed in *Christian* culture and were notably absent in Jewish culture. Strack himself was a convinced Christian, coming from a long line of Protestant pastors, and was even active in missionary activity directed towards the Jews. He considered that the baseless accusations were a great hindrance to Christian missionary efforts, as well as being a terrible blot on the Christian record, for which he wished to make amends. His book was successful, but brought upon him much vilification from anti-Semitic sources. He was accused of having been bribed by the Jews, or of being a Jew himself, and of being ignorant of Hebrew, though he was in fact the greatest non-Jewish Talmudic scholar of all time, and his *Introduction to the Talmud* is used to this day as an indispensable text-book by Jews and Christians alike. The official Catholic publi-

Contemporary representations of late medieval ritual-murder stories: left, a Jew conjures the Devil from the blood collected in crucifixions he has carried out; right, Jews are tortured to 'confess' to the ritual murder of Simon of Trent. (Woodcuts, 1575 and 1475 respectively.)

cation *La Civiltà Cattolica* virulently supported the ritual murder charge from the foundation of the periodical in 1849, though popes of previous generations had dismissed the charge as groundless. In general, it was the lower clergy throughout the centuries who had the greatest hand in spreading the charge, especially in their sermons, in spite of attempts by many popes and emperors to deny the truth of the accusations. There was thus something in the fabric of Christian belief that encouraged, even demanded such an accusation and made it inevitable. It corresponded so well to the conformation of the Christian imagination that rational attempts to control it were in vain.

We can discern two phases in the history of the 'ritual murder' accusation.[10] In the first phase, the accusation was modelled closely on the New Testament story of the Crucifixion of Jesus; it was alleged that the Jews regularly or from time to time abducted a Christian child and crucified him in a manner that was a repetition of the death of Jesus. In this phase, the accusation is associated with the Christian festival of Easter, *not* with the Jewish festival of Passover; it was at Easter-time that these alleged crimes took place, so that the Crucifixion could be imitated in every particular, including the time of its occurrence. In the second phase, however, the emphasis was laid not on Easter but

The Church and the Jews

on Passover. It was alleged that the Jews used the blood of the murdered Christian child in their Passover ceremonies, by mixing it with their unleavened bread. In this phase, once the notion of the use of blood had entered the picture, all kinds of wild, bizarre fancies were introduced: that the Jews needed to drink Christian blood because, owing to their sin, Jewish men menstruated like the women, and needed to replenish the lost blood; or that they needed blood to compensate for the blood lost in circumcision. The blood-fantasies that now proliferated were derived, as Strack pointed out, from European folklore, with its rank growth of tales about vampires, bloodsucking witches, etc. Such tales are absent in Jewish folklore, to which a preoccupation with blood is in any case alien.

It is the first phase of ritual murder accusations, beginning in the twelfth century, that is more relevant to our present enquiry, since in this phase the Jew is envisaged as continuing his role as sacrificer. In the second phase, the Jew is regarded not as a sacrificer, but as a kind of demon or werewolf or vampire; the ancient identification of the Jews as the people of Satan here amalgamated with Christian and pagan nightmares about bloodsucking demons. The long indoctrination had at last reached the level of the popular imagination, and the Jews were incorporated into the pre-conscious fear-system of the people. At the same time, this demonization of the Jews reinforced the theological picture and aroused a horror and loathing appropriate to a people who had performed the divine sacrifice. The introduction of blood-fantasies was thus welcomed by the lower clergy as a new weapon in the armoury against the Jews.

It may be asked why this particular development took place when it did, in the twelfth and thirteenth centuries, and not earlier, or later (of course, it has continued to our own day, but the present enquiry is about the historical origins of the accusation in its first and second phases).

We may also ask why the ritual murder accusation specifically concerned the murder of a *child*, never of an adult. This was an entirely new feature of the myth, for the Christ-figure in all the centuries before this time had always been thought of as a young adult male. As such, he had been easily assimilated, in ancient times, to other dying-and-resurrected gods, such as Attis and Adonis. The figure of a child, in these religions, had never been associated with scenes of death, but rather with an idyllic mother-and-child scene, as in the worship of Isis. There had evidently been a significant psychological shift in the twelfth and thirteenth centuries in Christendom, since the Crucifixion myth was by then so frequently fantasised as involving a child-victim. This psychological shift entails also a shift in the way in which Jew as sacrificer was envisaged.

The Church and the Jews

There is some interesting evidence that the shift had taken place before it began to have an effect on the Christian image of the Jew. In the twelfth century, before the first blood-libel accusation, we find mention of alleged appearances of Christ at Holy Communion in the form of a child (sometimes in the form of a lamb[11]). It seems that the popular imagination had begun to see the Christ-child as present in the wafers of the Eucharist, rather than the body of an adult Christ. One popular preacher of the thirteenth century, Berthold von Regensburg, was asked the question, 'Why does not Christ visibly appear in the Holy Communion?', and he answered that this was to spare the susceptibilities of the congregation, who would not much care to bite into the Communion wafer if they could see that they were actually biting off the head, hands and feet of a little child[12] (*Predigten*, Vienna, 1880). This almost incredible answer was given at a time when the ritual murder accusations against the Jews were in full swing. It shows that the Christian imagination of the time, at a hardly preconscious level, was full of fantasies about cutting up and eating a small child. This was essentially a religious act performed in fantasy by the Christians themselves, but it was easily displaced and imputed to the Jews, who thus once more became the bearers of Christian guilt about their sacrificial modes of handling spiritual problems.

The first case brought against the Jews was that of William of Norwich, in 1144. It was alleged that the Jews had 'bought a Christian child before Easter and tortured him with all the tortures wherewith our Lord was tortured, and on Long Friday hanged him on a rood in hatred of our Lord.' It was alleged that this was an annual event at Easter, and that an assembly of rabbis met every year to choose the place for the sacrifice. This charge was not believed, and no Jews were convicted of the alleged crime on this occasion, but the charge struck such a chord that it was repeated on very many occasions throughout Europe in the subsequent years, and gradually more and more credence was given to it. Jews were tortured to 'confess' the crime, and inevitably some gave way under the torture and said what their torturers wanted. Jews and Jewish communities began to be executed or wiped out, and the long medieval nightmare had begun.

A famous case was that of Hugh of Lincoln (1255). The body was found in a cesspool, after the child had been missing for over three weeks. The obvious explanation was that the child had fallen into the cesspool and drowned, but the fact that there was an unusually large number of Jews in Lincoln at the time to attend a wedding suggested a ritual murder accusation. An account of the trial was written by Matthew Paris. The indictment stated that 'the child was first fattened for ten days with white bread and milk, and then almost all the Jews in England were invited to the crucifixion.'[13] The alleged fattening of the child was an unusual detail, and has been related to a libel told by the ancient anti-Semitic writer Apion that the Jews sacrificed a Greek in the Temple once a year after fattening him.[14] It is unlikely that the people of Lincoln had such a parallel in mind; the detail rather attests the unconscious cannibalism of their fantasy, and is related to the fantasies surrounding the Eucharistic meal. A Jew called Copin was tortured until he 'confessed' that the boy Hugh had been crucified by the Jews, and nineteen Jews, including Copin himself, were then hanged.

The story of Hugh of Lincoln was the model for Chaucer's 'Prioress's Tale' in *The Canterbury Tales*, written about 1385. In Chaucer's time there were no Jews in England, since they had been expelled in 1290 with indescribable sufferings. The absence of Jews, however, did not prevent Chaucer from loathing Jews like a good Christian; indeed Jew-hatred often reaches greater intensity in countries where there are no actual Jews to moderate the excesses of the Christian imagination. Chaucer's 'Prioress's Tale' has often been extolled by literary critics as 'charming' and 'exquisite'. Such critics are as oblivious to the sinister aspects of the story as was Chaucer himself, and, indeed, as was the Prioress, who was so gentle that (the Prologue tells us) she could not bear to witness the death of a mouse and wept piteously for the imagined death of her little martyr, while contemplating with cheerful satisfaction the torture and execution of the Jews – the only part of the story that is based firmly on fact.

Chaucer's version of the blood-libel, however, is interesting in that it is not a ritual murder story. It is not alleged that the Jews in the story kill the child in order to crucify him, or even to make ritual use of his blood. It is a killing out of pure malice, because the Jews cannot bear the purity of the child. The story is thus more basic than the ritual murder stories which allege that the Jews perform an imitation of the murder of Christ; here the murder is itself a kind of Christ murder, rather than an imitation; the motives are the same as those for which the original Christ murder was allegedly performed, a Loki-like hatred of the Light. But there is also another element in Chaucer's story, which is of great importance, and may give us a clue to our question about why Christ has become a child, rather than a young adult, during this era. This is the introduction of the theme of the Virgin Mary. (It should be noted, by the way, that Chaucer did not invent his story, but adapted it from a German tale that can be traced back for about two centuries before him. His version, therefore, is not a late transmutation, but based on possibly the earliest and most revealing version of all.)

It has not been sufficiently noticed that medieval stories and ballads about alleged Jewish murders of children often also involve the Virgin

The Church and the Jews

Mary. Usually the story comes into not only the category of the 'Jewish child murder' stories but also that of the 'Miracles of Our Lady' stories. In Chaucer's story it is not just the innocence and purity of the child that arouses the hatred and aggression of the Jews, but the fact that he is a devotee of the Virgin Mary. It is his song in honour of the Virgin that moves the Jews to fury. In general, too, the Jews are portrayed in stories, even those not involving child murder, as the special enemies of the Virgin Mary, who is portrayed as also detesting them.[15]

Here we have a new development of the anti-Jewish theme, for the honour, not to say worship, paid to the Virgin Mary was not an early element in Christianity, but a product of the eleventh century at the earliest. Before then the Virgin Mary had no very prominent place in the Christian imagination; but it is not too much to say that from this time onward she became a goddess. In particular, she became the chief focus of Christian concepts of *forgiveness*. The reasons for this are complex. One important reason is that Jesus himself was no longer thought of as a forgiving figure. One of the images of Jesus found in the New Testament is that of Judge at the Last Day, separating the sheep from the goats,[16] and this image had come to supersede that of Jesus as all-forgiving advocate of the sinner against the severity of God the Father. Indeed, Jesus had himself become a father-figure of terrifying severity, superseding and taking the place of the father-god of the Old Testament as seen by Christians (though not by Jews, to whom the father-god of the Old Testament was an altogether more kindly figure). In these circumstances, the role of all-forgiver, so essential to Christianity precisely because of the terror of God the Father, was taken over by a female figure, the Virgin Mary, whose role was to intercede for the sinner and circumvent the implacable processes of judgment. Henry Adams has described how the Virgin Mary became the 'greatest goddess in history', the indispensable standby of sinners and the unfailing support of all who gave her honour – even burglars prayed to her before embarking on their night's work – but a dangerous enemy to those who failed to give her due honour.[17]

The reappearance of the female-figure in religion, after so many centuries of repression, was part of a general movement of thought and feeling in Europe, a movement that included such groups as the troubadours, the Albigensian heretics and even the Jewish Kabbalists. It has been argued, indeed, by Denis de Rougemont and others,[18] that the cult of the Virgin Mary arose as a counter-attraction to the cult of the female-figure in heretical groups that were making dangerous inroads into orthodox Christian allegiance. Mariolatry, at any rate, was taken up with such enthusiasm and swiftness that it evidently met a profound need. It has been hailed as a great advance, since it marked a revulsion against the oppression and belittling of women, and it certainly had this aspect. On the other hand, however, it took the form in Christianity of a psychological regression to the condition of infant at its mother's breast, and such regression cannot be regarded as an advance except in cases where it is a preliminary to a new form of adult awareness and sexual orientation. The cult of the Virgin Mary failed to be such a preliminary, but became fixated in an infantile attitude of dependence on the mother-figure. In particular, the cult gave rise to more infantile and primitive forms of oral aggression than had previously occurred in the history of Christendom.

The relationship of the worshipper to the Virgin Mary was of an ecstatic and sentimental kind. It was indeed a highly sexual relationship, but any explicit thought of sex was utterly banned. More accurately, it was adult sex that was banned, and only the generalized, free-floating sexual feeling of the child at the breast was allowed. Thus, though the Virgin Mary was a supreme sexual object of fantasizing, enormous stress was laid on her virginity. Adult sex was interdicted as utterly wicked, and thus the adoration of the Virgin Mary had no real effect on the status of actual women engaged in real sexual activities, who were regarded as more degraded than ever.

The goddess: the Virgin Mary, with an infant at her breast and the moon beneath her feet. (Woodcut by Dürer.)

The Church and the Jews

It is not at all surprising that the infant Jesus should now have acquired such importance. The cult of the infant Jesus arose simultaneously with the cult of the Virgin Mary, having previously been of no importance. The picture of the Virgin Mary with the infant Jesus on her lap became the greatest image of Christianity, since the male worshipper now identified himself with Jesus in infant form, rather than, as previously, with Jesus in adult form. Jesus became two figures instead of one: the adult Jesus, a stern, judging figure, and the infant Jesus, a symbol, together with his mother, of the availability of forgiveness for every sin.

Since the Mass was regarded as a sacrifice through which the forgiveness of sins was effected, the requirement of the worshipper to envisage Jesus as substantially present in the bread and wine of the Mass, which became magically transmuted into his body and blood, became a ceremony in which the forgiving *infant Jesus* was cut up, eaten and drunk; by eating the infant the worshipper became himself an infant. The adult Jesus, being a figure of judgment, was no longer concerned in the Mass. The displacement of responsibility for the sacrifice of Jesus on to the Jews thus now involved elements previously absent: the dismemberment and eating of a child and the drinking of its blood. Previously, it was only the sacrifice of the Crucifixion for which the Jews were made responsible: now the cannibalistic fantasy which accompanied the eating of the Mass aroused such feelings of unconscious guilt, especially now that the victim was pictured as a child, that this sacrifice too had to be attributed to the Jews, who were pictured as doing in reality what the Christian worshipper was doing in fantasy, i.e., killing a child and drinking its blood.

There is thus a strong historical and psychological connection between the rise of the Virgin Mary cult and the rise of the ritual murder and blood-libel accusations against the Jews. It was only from this period that the Jews began to be regarded as sub-human, bestial and demonic. Previously, with all their imputed guilt, the Jews retained something of the residual dignity of the Sacred Executioner. From now on, however, the word 'Jew' became synonymous with 'vampire'. Many Christians came to believe that Jews had cloven feet and a tail, and that they suffered from an innate bad smell and from diseases of the blood, for which they sought remedies in vampirism.[19] For the Jews were now seen by Christian believers as the enemies of the ecstatic cult of the holy mother and child (the Jews themselves hardly knew that a change had come over the Christian cult, except that they were aware of an increased hostility). Even the stories that now arose about the Jews stealing the Host and desecrating it by cutting it to pieces should be understood in relation to the cult of the

The Church and the Jews

A fifteenth-century representation of alleged desecration of the Host by Jews. (Woodcut, 1492.)

infant Jesus, who was regarded as incarnate in the bread of the Host. To be the murderers of the adult Jesus had been bad enough, but at least this had been done with the dignity of a trial and execution. When the Jews were reduced to the level of child-murderers, however, they were no longer thought of as cruel but impressive father-figures, decreeing death on the son-figure, but as furtive creatures of the dark, awaiting their opportunity to snatch a Christian infant and do him to death with bestial, demonic rites.

Yet the Jews still retained enough of their adult, father-like status to be regarded as the special enemies of the sexless sexuality that was characteristic of the Christian mother and child cult. It is significant that in earlier versions of the story on which Chaucer built his 'Prioress's Tale' the song sung by the little child was 'Gaude Maria', a song in which the Jews were reproached for not believing in the virginity of Mary, and for saying that Jesus was born by the normal reproductive process.[20] It was quite true that the Christian emphasis on celibacy and virginity was quite foreign to the Jews, who regarded sexuality as the gift of God, and regarded a virgin as someone to be pitied rather than admired. This difference in sexual attitude between Christianity and Judaism is closely bound up, psychologically, with

The Church and the Jews

the different importance placed in the two religions on the concept of sacrifice. Christianity is a religion in which sacrifice is primary; only through the sacrifice of Jesus is the believer saved. This argues a deep sexual guilt, which the sacrifice removes. If the sacrificer is fantasized as performing his deed, not out of desire to help the believer, but from evil motives of his own, as in the Christian myth, then it is natural that the sacrificer should be identified with the evil sexuality that the sacrifice is designed to expiate. Thus the Jews were regarded as representatives of the carnal sexuality which the Virgin Mary miraculously transcended, and as sneering at the Christian ideal of virginity by spreading the slander that the Virgin Mary was not a virgin at all.

The desexualizing of woman in the Virgin Mary cult actually shows a great fear of women, who are admired and worshipped, in the person of Mary their representative, only on condition that their adult sexuality is removed. It is no accident that the worship of the Virgin Mary was accompanied by terrible denunciations of women in general as a snare and temptation, and by fantasies of women as witches and succubi. The fear of woman underlying the cult is not entirely absent even from the portrayal of Mary herself, who, in many stories and ballads, is a fearsome figure when her will is crossed. It is also significant that, in the only ballad version of the Jewish child murder story in which the Virgin Mary does not appear, the murder is performed not by a Jew, but by a Jewess, who is portrayed as a sexual seducer of the child's father, and, in general, as the 'Eternal Feminine' at its most dangerous.[21] Just as the male Jew is a surrogate for the terrifying father-god who demands the death of the son-god, so, when the goddess reappeared in the form of the Virgin Mary, an awareness approached consciousness that it was the goddess herself who originally demanded the sacrifice of the son-god; and a female surrogate for this blood-ravening goddess had to be supplied in the form of a Jewish murderess and seductress.

The role of the Jew as Sacred Executioner thus underwent some startling changes in the Middle Ages as Christianity itself suffered regression and changed its picture of the sacrificial figure, Jesus himself. As this picture became more infantile, and as the Mass, rather than the Crucifixion, became the centre of oral-aggressive fantasies of killing and eating the sacrificed god, the figure of the Jew, on to whom these fantasies were displaced, degenerated into a loathsome bogyman. As the figure of the mother, divested of all sexuality, assumed the centre of the stage, the Jew became the enemy of all tenderness and infantile bliss, and the threat of a reconstitution of the banned or exorcised cruel father. As such, he became the focus of ferocious rage, commensurate with the supposed blissfulness of the holy mother-infant relationship which he was conceived as threatening, and was treated with increasing cruelty and contempt. The Prioress's 'tender pity' is thus only the other side of the coin in relation to her pleasure at the torture and execution of the Jews.

At the same time, the more traditional picture of the Jew as cruel, judging father-figure continued alongside that of the Jew as bestial bogy-man. It is in the more traditional picture, based on the Gospels with their severe, judging Pharisees and condemning Sanhedrin, that the Jew retains some of the dignity required for the Sacred Executioner; for, together with the task of taking the blame for the sacrifice, there is always some residual need for the Executioner to endow the sacrifice with a degree of awesomeness and holiness. In the next chapter, we shall see how this need re-asserted itself. Here, just one more detail may be added to our account; that in many Christian countries, Jews were forced to act as public executioners.[22] No fact could be more expressive of the character of Christianity, and of its concept of the role of the Jew. In contrast to Jewish law, in which the chief witnesses for the prosecution must take the chief part in the actual execution (Deuteronomy 13: 10), Christianity sees a necessary killing as something for which the responsibility must be shifted; and to whom could it be better shifted than to the Jew, who was (allegedly) responsible for the most necessary killing of all?

Chapter Thirteen

The Sacred Executioner in the modern world

The medieval world provided the reservoir of loathing and contempt of the Jew that enabled the Nazis to carry through their policy of extermination. It was in those countries where the medieval picture of the Jew was strongest that the policy could be implemented with the tacit and, in some cases, active support of the populace. Yet the Nazi theory of Jew-hatred was in some important respects different from the theologically derived medieval theory. This is shown by the very fact that the Nazis embarked on a plan of complete extermination, for, as we have seen, Christendom did not want the Jews to disappear from the world, since they played an essential role in the Christian mythical economy. The Nazis abandoned the idea of the Jews as necessary carriers of guilt for the community and thought of them as an entirely expendable nuisance, which could be obliterated without ill effects like a plague of rats. While the Nazis used every anti-Jewish weapon in the medieval armoury, their stance had shifted. Instead of being satisfied with continual persecutions, expulsions, pogroms, limited periodical massacres, all of which took for granted the continued presence of Jews in Christendom, the Nazis were able to envisage a world without Jews – a world, in other words, in which the sacrificial role of the Jews was unnecessary. It is of some importance to trace how this shift took place, without ever losing sight of the continuity between Nazi anti-Semitism and its Christian background, without which the former would never have come into existence.

The medieval world provided a number of different images of the Jew, some of which might seem at first sight to have little to do with the function of the Jew as Sacred Executioner, though all of which contributed to the Nazi anti-Jewish stereotype. There was the Jew as 'sorcerer', the Jew as 'usurer' and the Wandering Jew legend. The apparent independence of these images from the sacrificial role of the Jews, was, however, illusory, and cannot be regarded as supplying separate archetypes to the Nazis.

The Jew as sorcerer was intimately bound up with the concept of the Jew as earthly representative of the Devil. Since the Crucifixion of Jesus was brought about chiefly by the Devil, it is natural that his earthly minions should be credited with special favour from the Devil in the form of knowledge of the black arts. At the same time, the possession of such knowledge procured a grudging admiration of the Jews. They were believed to have knowledge of all forms of illicit science, a belief that had much foundation in fact, since Jews were prominent in scientific discovery and in medical knowledge. From this arose popular stories such as 'The Jew's Beautiful Daughter' story, in which a Christian youth works as sorcerer's apprentice to a Jew, learns his secrets and finally makes off with his treasure and his beautiful daughter.[1] This story shows to what extent the Jews were regarded as powerful father-figures by Christians. The story is really a variant of ancient legends and folk-tales (such as the tale of Jason or Theseus) in which a young stranger outwits the powerful king and wins his treasure, both material and sexual. At a time when the Jews were in fact helplessly weak and oppressed, they figured in the Christian imagination as dangerous and powerful. The father-figure status of the Jews derives from several sources: from identification with the 'bad father' himself – the Devil; from identification with God the Father, the centre of worship in Jewish religion; but chiefly from identification with the purposes of both good and bad father in bringing about the death of the son.

The Jew as usurer is more subtly connected with the Jews' sacrificial role. For a certain period, the Jews were in historical fact strongly associated with usury, or lending money on interest, but not by their personal choice. They were forced into this role by being excluded from all other professions. The Jews had previously been great merchants, opening up trade with far countries and travelling adventurously between them. The growth of the guilds, which excluded Jews, meant the end of large-scale trading for the Jews of Europe, and their exclusion from all other honourable professions (except medicine, in which secular rulers continued to employ them illicitly despite papal fulminations) meant that they were able to use their capital only by lending it at interest. To lend money at interest is actually forbidden between Jews by Biblical law,[2] and also between Jew and Gentile by Talmudic law,[3] except in conditions of dire necessity – which were in fact adjudged to obtain in this instance. The historical process can be seen in two anti-Jewish plays: Marlowe's *Jew of Malta*, in which the Jewish villain is a great merchant; and Shakespeare's *Merchant of Venice*, in which the Jewish villain is a great money-lender. Shakespeare's picture was already becoming out of date, for the growth of Christian banking was already thrusting the Jews out of large-scale money-lending as they had been thrust out of large-scale trading before. The era of the poverty-stricken Jewish pedlar and pawnbroker had begun.[4]

A Nazi poster of 1924: the Jew was made the scapegoat of all the ills of German society; here, as a wealthy businessman who has made money out of banking and speculating on the stock exchange, he rides on the back of a worker – an image readily accepted by a brainwashed population.

During the period in which lending money on interest was regarded as completely forbidden by Christian law (an idea mainly derived from the Hebrew Bible though without the realistic qualifications introduced by the Talmud), the Jews were not only allowed to lend money on interest, but actually encouraged to do so. The possession of Jews was regarded as a great asset by secular rulers, who often protected their Jews from annihilation, though they practised great extortions and cruelties of their own on the Jews whom they regarded as their personal slaves. The Jews were in fact performing an essential function in society by acting as bankers, but, since banking or 'usury' was regarded as a deadly sin, it was most convenient that a class of people existed which was damned in any case, and which was regarded as practised in the role of committing necessary sins. The

The Sacred Executioner in the modern world

'usury' of the Jews was thus just like their enforced role as public executioners. They did the dirty work of the Christian community, not, like the serfs (or the Untouchables in Hindu society), in the physical realm, but in the moral realm. To be usurers, therefore, was simply an extension of the Jews' general sacrificial role, a logical corollary of their position as the performers of the great but necessary crime of the Crucifixion.

All this, nevertheless, did not prevent the Jews from being vilified for their 'detestable usury' and from being massacred, on occasion, for this reason alone. Indeed, there is a strong link between usury and the blood-libel accusation, for many of the cases of blood-libel were instigated by Christians, often of the upper class, who wished thereby to avoid paying their accumulated debts to the Jews. Moreover, the image of the Jew as usurer, with its concomitant metaphors of 'bloodsucking', coalesced with the blood-libel to form a picture of the Jews as parasites on society, performing no useful labour, but draining the life out of the hardworking Christian peasantry. This is an image which survived into the modern world despite the entry of the Jews into all the professions previously barred to them, and despite even the growth of a Jewish peasantry in Israel. Anti-Semites such as Ezra Pound equated usury with the Jews though banking and the stock exchange had become the preserve of the Christian upper-class.[5] To the Nazis, the banks were all Jewish; one Jewish banking family, the Rothschilds, became synonymous with world usury, though they formed an insignificant banking unit compared with the great non-Jewish banks.

The legend of the Wandering Jew[6] also contributed to the Nazi anti-Semitic image, though, in some of its versions at least, this legend was the least hostile of the Christian fantasies about the Jews. The legend has roots in early Christian times, but it first became widely popular only as late as the seventeenth century. In its most amiable form the legend concerns a Jew called Ahasuerus, who was a shoemaker in Jerusalem at the time of Jesus's Crucifixion. While Jesus was carrying his cross, he stopped for a rest outside the cobbler's shop, but Ahasuerus drove him on with harsh words, or, in some versions, with a push. Jesus said, 'I go, and you will wait for me until I return.' Ahasuerus was thus condemned to live until the Second Coming of Christ. He is always restless and cannot stay in one place for long. He longs for death, but cannot die; even if he throws himself into a river, the waters refuse to drown him. He has long ago repented of his sin, and become a convinced Christian; and by telling his story wherever he goes he witnesses to the truth of Christianity, having been an eye-witness of the Crucifixion and personally assured by Christ of the Second Coming. (See frontispiece.)

The Sacred Executioner in the modern world

In this form, the legend clearly embodies a Christian wish-fulfilment. It expresses the desire that the Jews will accept the role assigned to them in the Christian myth. The push given to Jesus by Ahasuerus symbolizes his participation in the execution and his involvement in the guilt of the Jewish people. The Wandering Jew, therefore (as has always been realized) symbolizes the Jewish people as a whole, and his wanderings are nothing less than the weary exile of the Jews, with their constant expulsions even from places like Spain where they had made a priceless contribution to the culture and well-being of the host nation. The prolonged life of the Wandering Jew symbolizes also the miraculous survival of the Jews, ascribed by Christians not to the strength of Jewish identity and culture, but to the desire of God to prolong their agony until the time of the millennium. But these two elements – the wandering and the prolongation of life – are, as we have seen, features of the Sacred Executioner. Cain, too, was a wanderer, and was given a charmed life. For the early death of the Sacred Executioner would remove his saving power; there would be no-one to bear the sins of the community, and particularly to bear the guilt arising from the continuing efficacy of the divine sacrifice.

Finally, the 'waiting' of the Wandering Jew for the Second Coming of Jesus echoes the waiting of the Jews in the Christian myth, in which the millennium cannot occur without their participation. This aspect no doubt accounts for the sudden popularity of the legend in the seventeenth century, a time of millennial expectations throughout Europe (even among the Jews themselves). The proliferating stories of the appearances of the Wandering Jew in various European towns would heighten the hopes of the imminent Second Coming of Christ.

But in Christian eyes the legend of the Wandering Jew was more than merely a symbol of the sufferings of the Jews themselves: there was also the idea of the Wandering Jew's belief in Christianity. This was the expression of a fervent wish, not merely that the Jews would become converted, but that, like the Wandering Jew, they would acknowledge their guilt for the death of Jesus and accept as deserved the consequent sufferings heaped upon them in Christendom. If this were to happen, the time for the millennium would have arrived – not that the conversion of the Jews would actually bring about the millennium, but it would show that the millennium was at hand. For the millennium, as we shall see shortly, is that period in which the function of the Jews as Sacred Executioner is no longer necessary.

But before pursuing this important aspect, it must be pointed out that the version of the Wandering Jew legend just described is not the only one. Other versions existed (especially in Germany) which lacked the positive hope of reconciliation. In those negative versions, the sufferings of the Wandering Jew are seen merely as just punishment for his depravity. He is not a convert to Christianity, but an unregenerate Jew, with evil magic powers derived from his long experience of life and his association with the Devil. It was this negative version that gave rise to the nineteenth-century anti-Semitic stereotype, taken up with enthusiasm by the Nazis, of the Jew as a 'rootless cosmopolitan' – an interpretation that sometimes took the form of a theory that the Jews were essentially nomads, who had invaded Palestine from the desert and remained at heart creatures of the desert.[7] This was something of a twist, since in this development the wanderings of the Wandering Jew became part of his nature rather than his punishment. In the negative Christian stereotype (which the Nazis were giving a would-be anthropological interpretation) the restlessness of the Wandering Jew is a kind of neurotic affliction which impels him from country to country, an idea partly derived from the figure of Herod in the medieval Passion Plays, who was presented as suffering from an inability to remain still, his whole body continually in motion. This portrayal of Jews persists as far as the nineteenth-century novel.[8]

In these negative versions, the wanderings of the Jews were held against them as indicative of their evil nature. But the Jews did not actually wander because they wanted to, or because they were in the grip of a neurosis, but because they were forced to. In Germany, in particular, the Jews were not allowed to remain in any place for long, but were continually harried into moving on. Yet it was particularly in Germany that the Wandering Jew was portrayed as an inveterate nomad. The wanderings of the Jews are the antithesis of the wanderings of a nomadic people such as the Gypsies. The Jews regarded themselves as in exile, from their settled home Palestine, to which they would eventually return when they had expiated the sins for which the exile was a punishment. Their intense love of home showed itself in their love for any place where they were allowed to settle for any length of time, so that when the inevitable expulsion eventually came it was experienced as an exile within the great exile. The nostalgia of the Jews for Spain, for Poland, and even for Germany, remains even today – even in Jews who have returned to the Promised Land! The Jews, indeed, have always been great travellers, but there is a great distinction to be made between travellers and nomads. The aim of a traveller is always to return home.

In the negative versions of the Wandering Jew legend, the prolonged life of the Wandering Jew was also given a hostile connotation: it meant that the Jew was an eternal plague. In Germany the immortality of the Jew was stressed, rather than his wandering, in the appellation *'der ewige Jude'*; but the question that it posed was, 'Will this nuisance never have an end?'

The Sacred Executioner in the modern world

In the positive version of the Wandering Jew legend, a happy outcome of the Jewish problem is envisaged. Because he has acknowledged his guilt for the Crucifixion, the Wandering Jew can be regarded by the Christian clientele of this legend without hatred, even with a certain reverence. The Wandering Jew is in all respects an example of the Sacred Executioner, but one who willingly embraces his misery and thus functions as the perfect bearer of the guilt of the Christian community. He contrasts remarkably with the medieval picture of the Jew as a ghoulish, demonic figure abducting Christian children, mutilating the Host or poisoning wells. The hatred expressed in the medieval picture may arise partly from the refusal of the Jews to accept the role assigned to them in the Christian myth, whereas the Wandering Jew legend gives conscious expression to the way that, in Christian eyes, the Jews ought to behave. This kind of penitent, sad Jew, meekly accepting his sufferings as his destined and deserved lot, could be regarded by Christians with something approaching friendliness. The actual Jews, however, who insisted on pursuing their own life and religious culture in complete oblivion to Christian requirements, seizing with both hands any temporary respite and opportunity for happiness and prosperity, and wondering only why Christians would not let them alone, had to be persecuted and degraded and regarded as fiends, since they wilfully refused to understand the part they were supposed to play. Even the positive version of the Wandering Jew legend, therefore, does not really offer much hope of satisfactory Jewish-Christian relations, since it demands of the Jews a drastic change in their self-image, by which they would regard themselves as primarily actors in the Christian myth rather than as the bearers of a religious tradition and myth of their own where *they* are the principal actors and heroes, not the foil and repentant villain. Some Christians today have seized on an image not unlike that of the Wandering Jew as a means of avoiding anti-Semitism: the Jews are to be regarded with pity and awe as enacting a God-given role within the Christian myth.[9] Such an attitude, however, is only too likely to revert to the crudest hostility when it is realized that the Jews are not in the least interested in the offered role.

It was mainly the positive version of the Wandering Jew legend that was the basis of the treatment of the Wandering Jew in Romantic literature. Yet the Wandering Jew, as found in Romantic poetry from Christian Daniel Schubart to Shelley, or in the novels of Monk Lewis, Godwin, Bulwer Lytton and Sue, has little to do with the present study. The Romantic writers were not interested in the sacrificial aspects of the Wandering Jew, seeing him as a victim rather than as a sacrificer. They saw him as one more example of the Romantic hero – a wandering hero, isolated from normal society, expiating some crime

The Sacred Executioner in the modern world

which, in the last resort, was a praiseworthy act of rebellion against tyrannous authority. Thus Shelley sees the Wandering Jew as a kind of Prometheus and even denounces the Crucifixion as a fraud by which two divine tyrants, father and son, impose their authority on mankind.[10] Alternatively, the Romantics might see the Wandering Jew as guilty of a real crime, but one that had heroic quality, since it introduced him to a new dimension of knowledge beyond the range of ordinary mankind. This is to assimilate the Wandering Jew to Adam, or Teiresias, or Faust, heroes who buy knowledge at the expense of some degree of damnation. Thus the Romantic writers take the Wandering Jew outside his true context of the Christian myth and the conflict between Christianity and Judaism. By universalizing him they falsify him, and make him just one more peg for the concept of the anti-bourgeois hero, like the Flying Dutchman or Byron's Corsair. They turn him into an individualist who has sharpened his sense of individuality through sin, while it is the essence of the Wandering Jew in the authentic legend that he is not an individualist, however lonely his suffering, but a figure that has an expiatory role in relation to the Christian community. (Actually, the Romantic character that is nearest to the authentic Wandering Jew is Coleridge's Ancient Mariner).

There is an interesting exception to be found in T. S. Eliot's poem 'Gerontion', in which the figure of the 'jew' is almost certainly modelled on the *negative* version of the Wandering Jew legend. The 'jew' is a wanderer, a 'rootless cosmopolitan', 'spawned in some estaminet of Antwerp,/Blistered in Brussels, patched and peeled in London.' The old age of the 'jew' is compared to the dilapidated state of the decaying house and is regarded not as something miraculous, but negatively, as Jewish remoteness from the values of youth, symbolized in the youthful death of Christ and in other images of youthful violent death ('the hot gates', that is, Thermopylae, where the army of young Spartans died a sacrificial death). Thus, in Eliot's poem the Wandering Jew with his inability to die is not a Romantic hero, as in Shelley, but the exact opposite, a symbol of anti-Romanticism, the withering of the soul that comes from the refusal to accept the revivifying force of sacrificial death. Eliot was well aware of the connections between Christianity and pagan cults of human sacrifice, and also of the connections of both with the youth-worship of Romanticism.[11] His version of the Wandering Jew has much in common with that of a movement that must be regarded as belonging to the darker side of the history of Romanticism, namely, Nazism.

It was certainly the negative version of the Wandering Jew legend that was adopted in nineteenth-century anti-Semitism and in its successor, Nazism. The possibility of regeneration for the Jews

The Sacred Executioner in the modern world

through repentance, found in the positive version, was ruled out completely by the racialist doctrine. The Wandering Jew was a wanderer in the sense that he had no attachment to any human group, but was the common enemy and scourge of mankind in all his settled habitations. The detailed picture of the Jew was built up from medieval sources: the blood-sucking usurer, the murderer of children, the enemy of chastity, the poisoner of wells, the fiend in barely human shape. In addition there was the fantasy of the Elders of Zion, according to which the Jews had a highly organized international network, governed by a central body, the Elders of Zion, dedicated to the overthrow of all Gentile civilization and to the domination of the whole world by the Jews, to which end different policies were employed in different contexts, so that the Jews could be accused of being the moving force of both capitalism and communism.[12] Even this fantasy of a worldwide Jewish conspiracy had its medieval source in the blood-libel stories which portrayed the Jews as meeting in international conclave to decide where and when the next child sacrifice would take place.

Yet in general it can be said that nineteenth-century racialist anti-Semitism has departed from its Christian origins in providing no safeguard or loophole for Jewish survival. It was the hope of the millennial conversion of the Jews that preserved them in Christendom at times when they came close to annihilation. Thus modern anti-Semitism has all the negative aspects of Christian anti-Semitism without any of its restraints. From Christianity it derived the picture of the Jews as the people of the Devil; but it jettisoned the Christian idea that the Devil too has his place in the scheme of things. Thus, dangerous as Christianity was to the Jews, the move from Christian to post-Christian society was even more dangerous. For post-Christian society, while believing itself to be secular, retains all the deepest and most irrational prejudices of Christianity while freeing itself of the moral and mythopoeic checks by which Christianity exerts some moderating influence on these prejudices.

Yet is it quite true to say that Christianity itself provided no model for the plan of completely exterminating the Jews? While it is true that the scenario of the millennial conversion of the Jews rules out such a plan, medieval and Renaissance Christianity contained an alternative scenario that did indeed contemplate the extermination of the Jews. This is the myth of the Antichrist. Here we have a picture of what would happen at the time of the millennium that contradicts the eirenic concept of the conversion of the Jews and its attendant legend of the Wandering Jew, and substitutes a paranoiac, dualistic scheme which implements the hysterical medieval Jew-phobia and foreshadows the mass extermination programmes of the Nazis.

The Sacred Executioner in the modern world

The apocalyptic fantasy of the Antichrist, in its most influential form, runs as follows.[13] In the last days, a man would appear who would lead the armies of the Devil against the armies of Christ. This man, the Antichrist, would be a Jew, and his chief supporters would be the Jews. He would be a kind of demonic parody of Christ himself, for he would be born through the impregnation of a Jewish harlot by the Devil himself. He would be born in Babylon, but would proceed to Palestine where he would be instructed in the black arts. He would achieve great success, and would rebuild the Jewish Temple and reign over a Jewish empire which would comprise the whole world. But at the point of his greatest success the Second Coming of the true Christ would occur. Christ would lead the Christian armies against the Antichrist, who would be defeated, and all his supporters including the entire Jewish people would be annihilated. Part of the demonic forces thus defeated would be the Lost Ten Tribes of Israel, who would appear from their remote retreat to take part in the triumph of the Jewish empire and be defeated in its ultimate overthrow.

This extraordinary vision of future events had its main adherents among the populace rather than among the leading thinkers of Christendom. Indeed, the belief in the coming of the Antichrist was sometimes turned against the official leadership of Christendom, for popular movements of discontent sometimes identified the pope himself as the Antichrist and the officials of the Church, rather than the Jews, as his army. But the prevailing theory was that it was indeed the Jews who would form the army of the Antichrist, and this belief became particularly strong at times of millennial excitement. The widespread massacres of Jews by a frenzied populace at the time of the Crusades, for example, were partly actuated by the identification of the Jews with the Antichrist. The Muslims too, against whom the Crusaders fought, were regarded as armies of the Antichrist, but to the Christian populace the Muslims were hardly differentiated from the Jews, and were even widely regarded as the Oriental hordes of the Lost Ten Tribes (the 'Red Jews') who formed one of the nightmare images in the medieval mind. Even Christian leaders were not above such fantasies, as was shown by the almost incredible episode of the impostor David Reubeni, who in 1524 was given audience by the pope and treated with great fear and honour, on the pretence of being the ambassador of an Oriental Jewish empire – the realm of the Lost Ten Tribes.[14]

The myth of the Antichrist was thus a millennial notion based on a belief in the Jews as a powerful, dangerous political entity. The Wandering Jew legend, on the other hand, was based on the much more factual premise that the Jews were helpless and downtrodden,

The Sacred Executioner in the modern world

beaten into submission by their sufferings. Both myths were visions of the millennium, but of very different kinds: one envisaged a time of reconciliation, while the other a time of violence, worldwide battles and the final annihilation of a fearsome enemy. Both, it may be added, envisaged a time when the continued existence of the Jews would not be necessary: in the Wandering Jew legend because the Jews would be allowed to expiate their sin at last and find oblivion in the bosom of the Church, and in the Antichrist myth because the reign of the Devil would at last be over, and his allies the Jews would share his downfall and disappearance. In the Antichrist myth, the necessary role of the Devil as Sacred Executioner is lost sight of; he is regarded as merely the old power of evil, engaged in perpetual combat with the Light, but destined eventually to be defeated by it. This is essentially a Gnostic conception. The Wandering Jew legend, however, retains the idea that the existence of the Jews is necessary: the Wandering Jew is an essential witness and a harbinger of the millennium. Though his sin itself is not consciously acknowledged to be necessary, the sympathy and awe with which he is regarded give him the aura of the Sacred Executioner. Christianity, as we have seen, was formed by a combination between Gnosticism and the salvation doctrine of the mystery religions. This double strand persists throughout the history of Christianity. When the salvation doctrine of the necessary sacrifice predominates, the Jew retains some sanctity. When the sheer dualism of Gnosticism predominates, the Jew becomes a demon, and his annihilation becomes a desideratum. He is no longer in any sense a representative of the Christian community.

Even the Gnostic Christian, however, may regard the Jew as a necessary evil, like the Devil himself, in the sense that evil in this world is inevitable. But once it is believed that the millennium has already started, the last vestige of this necessity vanishes. That is why millennial movements associated with the doctrine of the Antichrist soon lead to massacres of Jews of a radical kind. The massacres at the time of the Crusaders were on a scale hitherto unknown in Christendom.[15] They should be regarded as the precursors of the mass extermination programme of that modern millennial movement, Nazism.

Yet there was nothing new, at the time of the Crusades, about the doctrine of the Antichrist; it was just that it had never been associated before with a populist movement. The requirements for an extermination programme seem therefore to be mass hysteria in a populist movement fomented by a charismatic leader, combined with the doctrine of the Antichrist.

The Antichrist doctrine itself was as old as Christianity. Its originator was the originator of everything else that is distinctive in

The Sacred Executioner in the modern world

Christianity – Paul. The whole idea (except the actual name Antichrist, which is found first in the Epistles of John) is in the Second Epistle to the Thessalonians (Chapter 2). Here is found the idea which has been hailed as further proof of the 'genius of Paul', namely that the chief eschatological opponent of Christ would not be a great Gentile empire, such as the Greek Empire in the Book of Daniel or the Roman Empire in the Book of Revelation, but the Jews, who would be punished for their lack of faith in Jesus by misplaced faith in the Antichrist. This idea shows the 'genius of Paul' because it enabled Christianity to 'break its ties with Judaism and establish itself in the world of the Roman empire.'[16] So Paul is the source of *both* eschatological doctrines about the Jews, that of their millennial conversion and that of their millennial annihilation. The Antichrist doctrine thus has very respectable antecedents, and can be supported from the works of many leading Christian theologians,[17] though it tended to be out of favour with the rulers of Christendom because of its tendency to encourage mob enthusiasm and millennial hopes that were dangerous to established power.

It should be noted that in an important sense *both* millennial doctrines postulated the annihilation of the Jews in the last days, for even the view that they would be converted implied their disappearance as a distinct entity. The millennium, then, is by definition the time when the continued existence of the Jews is unthinkable, because the problem of evil will have been solved. From the Gnostic point of view, the Jews will be swept away together with the Devil and all his works, while, from the sacrificial mystery-religion point of view, the sin of Adam will have been quite washed away, the soteriological sacrifice of Jesus will no longer be required, and therefore the role of Sacred Executioner will be abolished and the Jews will be able to sink thankfully into nonentity.

An important difference, however, between the conversion doctrine and the Antichrist doctrine is that the latter acknowledges Judaism as a *religious* rival, and a formidable one, to Christianity, while the conversion doctrine sees Judaism as a mere obdurate clinging to an empty shell of a religion: at the time of the millennium this almost miraculous (because baseless) obstinacy melts away. In the Antichrist doctrine, on the other hand, it is realized that the Jews have a rival Messianic hope of their own. This hope is allowed considerable weight: a Jewish Messiah would actually come, and would for a time seem to be the complete fulfilment of Jewish hopes. The Jews are here seen not in the pathetic guise of the Wandering Jew, but as a rival faith that would be displaced only after a world war.

It will be seen, then, how many and how great are the similarities between Nazism and the Antichrist doctrine that was always such a

The Sacred Executioner in the modern world

persistent thread in the history of Christian thought. Nazism was essentially a millenarian doctrine, though formulated in secular terms. Its very slogan, the 'thousand-year Reich', is taken directly from the vocabulary of the millenarian movements (itself taken from Revelation 20:4-6). The term the 'Final Solution', which the Nazis applied to the policy of liquidation of the Jews, has strong apocalyptic overtones. It was conceived as the purging away from humanity of racial contamination and the inauguration of an era of racial purity, in which the Master Race would rule over inferior races, while the poison in the blood of humanity, the Jews, would cease to exist altogether. Only the Jews were scheduled for extermination. 'Inferior' races, such as the Slavs, were to be deprived of their cultural pretensions by the liquidation of their leaders and cultural élite, but were then to be allowed to live as slaves to the Master Race. The Gypsies, for example, were not scheduled for extermination, as is often wrongly said; only those who insisted on preserving their 'anti-social' nomadic way of life were sent to the extermination camps, and many Gypsies, having adopted a sedentary way of life, actually served in the German armed forces.[18] The status of Hitler himself, as a semi-divine figure, was that of saviour, corresponding to the figure of Christ in his Second Coming. It was thus part of his role, as in the myth of the battle of Christ against Antichrist, to rid the world completely of the forces of evil, namely the Jews.

The Nazis thus expressed in racialist terms the concept of the final overcoming of evil that formed the essence of Christian millenarianism. The choice of the Jews as the target arose directly out of centuries of Christian teaching, which had singled out the Jews as a demonic people dedicated to evil. Anti-Semitism was thus a potent political weapon, since it made a deep appeal to a populace that had been conditioned by one of the most effective educational processes in history to regard the Jews as the source of all evil. But even the Final Solution of the extermination of the Jews had strong Christian antecedents in the Antichrist myth, which also provided the concept of the Jews as a worldwide organized force with a powerful leadership of its own. Thus the Nazis, in sending helpless, unarmed people out of their own citizenry to be murdered by gas, starvation or a bullet in the back of the neck, imagined that they were fighting against a powerful organized threat (I leave out of account here those Nazi leaders who did not really believe the Nazi myth, but used it cynically, knowing that it enabled them to draw on an unfailing supply of mass hysteria).

Nazism, as a millenarian movement, contained only the figure of the triumphant Christ (i.e. Hitler) and not the figure of the sacrificed Christ. If the millennium has arrived the divine sacrifice and therefore the Sacred Executioner are no longer required.

Chapter Fourteen

Theoretical problems and conclusions

In the foregoing pages, a group of myths has been isolated and studied, and it has been argued that they are linked to the ancient ritual practice of human sacrifice, and especially to the position in that ritual of the person who actually performs the sacrifice on behalf of the community. A number of theoretical questions have no doubt occurred to the reader in the course of the argument, especially where the methods and assumptions used may seem to run counter to recent views on the function of myths and their relationship to ritual. Some clarification is required; and it is also necessary to make more explicit the ways in which anthropological and psychological considerations may be relevant to the study of myths and to the figure of the Sacred Executioner.

It should be noted, first, that it is not intended here to provide a general theory of myth. In particular, it is not asserted that all myths arise from rituals. This is the exaggerated theory chiefly associated (not quite correctly) with Frazer and developed by Gilbert Murray, Jane Harrison, A. B. Cook and F. M. Cornford in relation to the Greek myths.

On the other hand, there has been a tendency, in the reaction against monolithic theories of myth, to underplay the relationship between myth and ritual. The monumental work of Frazer showed that there is indeed a strong link between certain important myths and the ritual practice of human sacrifice. This was shown not directly (for the myths in question do not explicitly mention human sacrifice) but through a mass of circumstantial evidence, including folk-customs in many lands at times of sowing and harvest.[1]

The relationship between the ritual and the myth, however, is more complex than Frazer envisaged. He noted correctly, for example, that the Norse myth about the death of Balder was linked to a ritual of human sacrifice carried out for purposes of promoting fertility, and the evidence he presents can only be regarded as incontrovertible. But he did not consider why the myth conveys the details of the sacrifice in such a distorted form. He would have said, no doubt, that the myth was intended, originally, to validate the ritual by telling the story of how it first came to be performed. In the course of time, the ritual fell

Theoretical problems and conclusions

into disuse, but the story continued to be told for its own sake. Since its original purpose had been forgotten, it became distorted or rather changed in the interests of intelligible and affecting narrative; instead of being a story about a human or divine sacrifice, it became a tale full of pathos about how the most beloved of the gods met with an accidental death and was deeply mourned.

This is to underestimate the role of guilt in the formation of both rituals and myths. The example of the Athenian Bouphonia sacrifice may serve to show how *pretence* was apt to play an important part in the ritual of sacrifice. The bull was slain, but the sacrificing priests fled from the altar to express their denial of responsibility. Then a trial was held in which the knife was found guilty of the slaying. It seems too that the bull himself was a vicarious bearer of guilt, for the first step in the ceremony was to coax the bull to the vicinity of the altar on which lay some sacred barley-corns, which the bull ate; and his death was then regarded as deserved for this sacrilege. Thus the guilt of agriculture itself was expiated through an intermediate animal sacrifice, which then itself had to be expiated and distanced by blaming an inanimate perpetrator. So the indirectness and inexplicitness of a myth, such as that of Balder, are not due to increasing detachment in the course of time from the originating ritual, but are reflections of the ritual itself. Indeed, it may be that the function of the myth is not to validate the ritual but to reinforce those elements of the ritual that absolve the community from direct involvement in it, though of course the two aims can be attained simultaneously, and the myth can be said more accurately to validate the attainment of contradictory aims, the performance of the sacrifice and absolution from the guilt of performing it.

Some of the arguments used recently to undermine the connection between ritual and myth are consequently beside the point, since they are based on an over-simple concept of what it means for a myth to 'validate' a ritual. Only direct, explicit links are allowed to count, and the symptomatic, tell-tale clue is reduced to the status of a mere fortuitous, unmeaning detail. If detectives were not allowed to use the concept that criminals tend to cover up their crimes, not many criminals would ever be detected.

As a concrete example, we may take the myth of the death of Neoptolemus, the son of Achilles. Neoptolemus, it is told, offered repeated insults to Apollo at his shrine of Delphi and to the inspired priestess of Apollo, the Pythoness, through whom the Delphic oracles were pronounced. One day, when Neoptolemus was at Delphi and tried to appropriate Apollo's animal sacrifices for himself, his death was pronounced by the Pythoness, and he was killed by Machaereus, a Phocian, who used his sacrificial knife to cut him down. Upon this, the Pythoness gave orders that Neoptolemus should be buried beneath the threshold of the new sanctuary (the previous one having been burned down by Neoptolemus on a previous visit). Despite his bad behaviour, Neoptolemus, having been a famous warrior, would guard the new shrine, as a ghostly presence, and would preside over sacrifices made in honour of heroes.

The comment of G. S. Kirk on this story[2] is that it should not be regarded as proving any connection between ritual and myth: 'If Achilles' son Neoptolemus was killed with a sacrificial knife in a brawl at Delphi, that was a minor invention that drew on the ritual use of knives there in an unimportant way'. This ignores the important clues and does not allow for the need for disguise in matters of human sacrifice. The detail that Neoptolemus was killed with a sacrificial knife is revealing. There could be no motive for adding such a detail to a story which was merely about a brawl. When one directs one's attention to the man who is alleged to have wielded the knife, the detail becomes even more significant. The name Machaereus is a personification of the knife itself, since the Greek for knife is *machaera*. We have here another instance of the device used in the Buophonia sacrifice, i.e. blaming the knife for the slaying. That Neoptolemus was killed with a sacrificial knife is therefore the clue by which the sacrificial nature of the slaying is covertly preserved. An important methodological tool is the incongruous detail that goes against the grain of the narrative. Here the whole story is telling us, 'Neoptolemus was *not* killed as a sacrifice. His body may have been put under the threshold like a foundation sacrifice, and this may have happened just at the time when a new shrine was being built, but this was just an afterthought. Neoptolemus was killed because he insulted the god and his priestess.' Then comes the incongruous detail – he was killed with a sacrificial knife – as if to say, 'Don't take this explanation too seriously. Appearances are after all not misleading. He *was* killed as a sacrifice.' Giving due weight to the incongruous details corresponds to the maxim in textual criticism *lectio difficilis melior*, 'the difficult reading is better'; i.e. when one has two readings one of which is smooth and easy and the other difficult and puzzling, it is the latter that is more likely to be the true reading, because it is much more probable that a difficult reading was changed to read smoothly than that a smooth reading was changed into a difficult one. Here, too, it is much more likely that the sacrificial knife survives from an earlier stratum of the story than that it was added as a 'minor invention'.[3]

This particular myth does not contain a Sacred Executioner because it uses an entirely different way of distancing the slaying: it puts the blame on the victim. We have seen reason to believe that a number of myths about the slaying of monsters are based on this device.[4] There is

Theoretical problems and conclusions

a tension or contradiction in this method between the desire to show that the victim deserved his death and the desire to display him as worthy of the great role of sacrificial victim. This leads to an awkward transition when Neoptolemus has to change from being a boorish villain into a great hero, so that he can act, after death, as tutelary deity of the shrine. A corresponding tension exists in the Sacred Executioner solution, where the blame is laid on the slayer. The slayer alternates between being a murderer and being a sacred person, so that the innocence of the community and the efficacy of the sacrifice can be alternately stressed. The basic contradiction, in both cases, is between the community's desire for salvation and its desire to repudiate the means by which salvation is attained. The myth could thus be said, in the vocabulary of Lévi-Strauss, to 'mediate' between these two contradictory desires, though since the contradiction, in Lévi-Strauss's mode of analysis, is always drained of emotional content and guilt, it would be more relevant to cite the terminology of Freud, with his notion of a neurosis or a dream mediating a 'conflict', and enabling an impulse to be simultaneously gratified and inhibited. Part of the 'evil' pole of the victim in the Neoptolemus story may be the name Neoptolemus itself. For Neoptolemus was known to have had a grudge against the god Apollo because of the latter's part in the death of his father Achilles (either by prompting Paris to shoot Achilles, or, in some versions, by impersonating Paris and shooting Achilles himself). Neoptolemus was thus a suitable person for the role of burning down Apollo's shrine and trying to confiscate Apollo's sacrifices, actions necessary in order to justify his slaying at the command of the Pythoness.

We may conclude that the story is a foundation myth (probably not associated originally with Neoptolemus) commemorating the building of a new shrine at Delphi. The earlier shrine was probably burnt down by accident, but such an event would have aroused great alarm and guilt, and therefore a foundation sacrifice would have been felt necessary when the shrine was rebuilt. Since the victim was identified with the hostile power who had caused the temple to be burnt down, the sacrifice had the effect of winning over that power to become an ally of the presiding god, Apollo, instead of his enemy.

In the case of a foundation sacrifice, the role of an accompanying myth is particularly important, because the function of the sacrifice is continued, not merely reinforced, by the telling of the myth. On the other hand, a ritual, whether sacrificial or not, that is regularly performed may or may not be accompanied by a myth. Such a myth, if it exists, has a function, in that it validates the ritual and ensures that it will continue to be performed; but this is a kind of afterthought, rather than an integral contribution to the efficacy of the ritual, and such

Theoretical problems and conclusions

afterthoughts, as G. S. Kirk has shown, may often be casual or trivial aetiologies, having little relation to the true meaning of the ritual. Many important rituals had no accompanying myth. The foundation myth, on the other hand, perpetuates the memory of an event that can never be repeated (though it can be renewed at special moments of danger or catastrophe), and the telling of the myth is itself a way of preserving the cohesion and sense of identity of the community. Indeed, it is not strictly necessary that the foundation sacrifice should actually occur as a historical event, as long as a story exists to say that it did. It may be doubted whether Rome was really founded by twin brothers called Romulus and Remus, one of whom slew the other. But this is the kind of story that was felt to be suitable for the foundation of a city, and such a story demonstrates the link between ritual and myth just as well as if we could prove that the ritual was actually performed, for the myth could not have come into existence without at least the idea of a sacrificial ritual. A more subtle instance is the foundation myth of Christianity, where the death did actually occur, but not in the way that the myth required: a political execution was transformed in the myth into a sacrificial execution, though none of the people concerned (Pilate, the High Priest, the Jewish people, Judas) knew that they were taking part in a sacrificial rite. On the cosmic plane, however, the act functioned as a sacrifice, and the acceptance of its sacrificial character by initiates is what clinches its ritual efficacy. It is interesting, however, that the regularly performed sacrificial ritual of Christianity, the Mass, is *not* a repetition of the Crucifixion, but a quite different kind of sacrifice in which God is eaten by the community who thus achieve oneness with Him. This regular ritual is validated by a little myth of its own: the story of Jesus's sharing of bread and wine at the Last Supper and his instructions to perform the Mass in memory of this occasion. This myth is of the perfunctory aetiological kind, and does not convey the essence of the ritual, which was derived from the mystery religions and through them from the prehistoric totem feast.

The relationship between ritual and myth thus cannot be characterized in any simple way. In foundation myths, the myth acts as what Malinowski would have called a 'charter' for the tribe, showing that it was founded in a way acceptable to the god or gods. Even the pretence that the ritual killing embodied in the myth happened by accident is a kind of tribute to the god, since it would not do to admit that such a cruel sacrifice was demanded by or pleased him. So the tribe has paid to the god his due tribute of human life without offending him by putting the blame for the killing upon him. But this does not mean that all myths are charters. Even those that are charters usually perform other functions as well. For example, the myth of

Theoretical problems and conclusions

Noah and Canaan's curse acts as a charter for the Israelite conquest of the land of Canaan, but it also validates norms of Israelite society by its portrayal of father-son relationships, by its rejection of wine orgies and in other ways. Other myths that have no link with ritual do this more directly. For example, the Babylonian myth traces the origin of mankind to the sin of a rebellious god whose body was sliced up to form the human race; man's main object in life was thenceforth to expiate the sin of their ancestor by service to the gods; this myth tells us a great deal about Babylonian society and its attitudes to morality and freedom. In contrast, the Hebrew myth of the origin of man describes how God made the first pair by an act of free creation, endowed them with power over nature and exhorted them to populate the earth and cultivate it; a myth that breathes humanism and universal brotherhood. This is a charter for humanity, but, by being so, is also an ethical programme. To say that a myth is a charter tells us something: but we still have to ask what kind of charter.

Myths in general are the stories that characterize a given society and demand a sociological explanation which is not confined to considerations of individual psychology (which may be the same everywhere in a given phase of development) nor to abstract sociological explanations (which may be true of every society). Structuralist analyses of myths stay on the abstract sociological level and discuss problems and anxieties that are felt in all societies without venturing into the content and colour of individual societies. Lévi-Strauss admits that he is not concerned with the content of myths, only with their structure, and he regards his method as applicable only to primitive societies in which the content is unknown to us, not to 'hot' societies in which we become involved in the content and cannot confine ourselves to the structure.[5]

But such involvement is precisely what we need for full understanding. We cannot understand a myth if we strip ourselves of the tools of moral evaluation. For the myths themselves are concerned with moral evaluation in that they provide answers to the question, 'What is the good society?' Even if they confine themselves to the apparently non-moral question, 'How can a society be set up in such a way that it is likely to survive?', the answers always present themselves for moral evaluation, since they depend on the degree of courage or hope with which a society begins and which act as its spiritual capital; a society whose solutions are provided by fear and despair is headed for tyranny and cruelty.

Each distinctive civilization has its basic myth which is rooted in the circumstances in which that civilization was born. Thus the basic myth of Greek civilization is that of the victory of the Olympian gods over the crude, barbaric Titans, reflecting the historical victory of the

Theoretical problems and conclusions

Hellenes over the aboriginals of Greece. In the type of polytheism of Greece lies its ideal of aristocratic individualism, characteristic of militaristic invaders (such as the Normans). The basic myth of the Jewish civilization was of the liberation of a nation of slaves, pitted against all the oppressive régimes of the world by a unitary and unifying pact with a single God, who refused to co-exist with the gods who had betrayed mankind into slavery. The basic myth of Rome was identical with its foundation myth: a triumphant Cain-figure, Romulus, leader of a band of desperate outlaws, given the omen of a flight of vultures to show that his descendants would prey on mankind like vultures, or like the wolves by whom Romulus was nurtured. Virgil, however, tried to change this myth into that of the story of Aeneas, so that the Romans could regard themselves as Hellenes, with a civilizing mission; since Rome became a cultural vassal of Greece, this new myth was to some extent successful, but only after the Roman vulture, somewhat disguised as an eagle, had assembled all the loot of Europe and the Near East into Rome. The basic myth of the Christian civilization, again, identical with its foundation myth, was of the liberation of mankind from sin and from the misery of this world, which was given over to tyranny; this myth arose in the wretched conditions of the Greco-Roman Empire among masses who had lost all civic identity and attachment to the earth because of the demoralizing conquests of Macedonian Greeks and their imitators the Romans; because of the retention of the Old Testament, however, the humanism and attachment to the earth of Judaism remained as a strand within Christianity, contradicting its major trend. The basic myth of Islamic civilization is of the choice of the Arab people as the people of God; this is a transplantation of the Jewish myth, with the difference that it regards the values of the desert as superior to the values of the sown, while Judaism regards the desert as only a preparation for the Promised Land; and Islam, somewhat like Greece, envisaged an aristocratic rule by successful invaders, who, at heart, remained men of the desert, which is their real Promised Land and centre.

A myth, therefore, forms a culture, and once the myth has set and become established in the minds of the people, the outlines of the culture are determined. The entire set of myths of a particular culture form a single system, and no single myth can be understood fully except in relation to the other myths in the system. Lévi-Strauss has understood this, and his work on the interrelatedness of myths, and of the importance of taking into account various versions of the same myth in order to grasp its total meaning within the system of the tribe, is valuable. For each version explores a particular aspect to the detriment of other equally important aspects; an example is the set of myths about Judas explored above. This means that the listing of

Theoretical problems and conclusions

parallels between one culture and another can often be misleading. What appears to be an identical mythological theme can have very different meanings in different cultures, even if based on the same text, as, for example, the theme of Adam's sin, which has a different significance in the Jewish and the Christian cultures. Yet to decry the exploration of parallels altogether as 'parellelomania' is to forgo an important tool of research; for the parallels provide the basic psychological, sociological and technological problems which different cultures treat in their own way. To point out the parallels is thus the beginning of the study; the sequel should be not to relapse into a comfortable conviction that human predicaments and their solutions are the same everywhere, but to explore the variety of human approaches to a solution, some of which are far more valuable than others. Awareness of the dangerousness of superficial parallel-pointing, however, too often goes along with a relativism that, by insisting on the unbridgable differences between one culture and another, ultimately reduces them all to sameness again, since a generalized tolerance of differences minimizes their significance and importance.

The relationship between mythology and literature may be clarified in the light of the above remarks. Some investigators would wish to confine the term 'myth' to orally transmitted material. Lévi-Strauss, for example, regards his theory of myth as applying only to such material. The criterion, however, should be how far the story in question has sunk into the mentality of the mass of the community. This means in practice that oral transmission is of primary importance, for it is the way a story is told by parents and teachers that has a lasting effect on the psyche of the individuals that make up the community, rather than the literary form a story may have assumed through the individuality of a writer. It is important in the study of Greek myths, for example, to detect and discount *literary* variants that were of little communal significance. Nevertheless, literary versions of a myth can be of great importance too in centralizing and fixing a myth so that its continued effect is greater than ever on the mass of the people. The Bible and Homer are great examples of this. Both these works became canonical, i.e. were the subjects of myths of their own, but even a purely literary work, such as Aeschylus' *Oresteia* or Shakespeare's *Merchant of Venice*, can give new impetus to a myth by giving it fresh relevance to the time of the artist.

A myth, then, essentially belongs to a particular community or culture and cannot be understood outside the context of that culture. The history of the culture is thus highly important in the assessing of its myths, especially the conditions in which it first originated. These conditions give their stamp to the culture for all its subsequent

Theoretical problems and conclusions

history, so that the history of the culture may be regarded as the working-out of the solution offered to the problem of the originating conditions, and subsequent failures or stagnation or cultural collapse can be traced to flaws in that original solution. There are, however, various transcultural aspects in every mythological system, that is, levels at which it copes with problems common to all cultures. These may be listed as follows: (i) the technological aspect, for example, the transition from Stone Age to Iron Age, or from nomadic hunting to agriculture; (ii) the psychological aspect, that is, the relations between child and parents and the problems associated with maturation and sexual adjustment; (iii) the political aspect, that is, the problem of power within the community, and how the rulers are related to the governed; (iv) the class aspect, a more generalized version of the political aspect, in that the relations between power groups are considered from an economic standpoint and the groupings caused by the division of labour; (v) the sex-power aspect, comprising the problems arising from the division of mankind into biological groups, male and female, and the resulting power struggle; (vi) the aspect of cultural plurality or nationality, that is, the problems involved in relations with groups of mankind outside the community concerned and the preservation of a separate communal identity. These transcultural aspects comprise the material with which a mythological system has to deal and which it moulds into a ruling orientation for a particular community born at a particular conjunction of circumstances in history. Some of the above transcultural aspects have themselves been used as the basis of monolithic theories of myth. The results have often been valuable, but in fact all the aspects have to be taken into account and moulded into a specific characterization for each separate culture; and it is also important to note that the aspects are not independent of each other.

One of the above aspects to which great attention has been given in this book may seem questionable. This is (v), which has appeared largely in relation to the conflict between matriarchy and patriarchy, a conflict regarded by many recent investigators as non-existent. The swings in anthropological fashion are hard to predict, but the importance of this conflict cannot long be ignored. By 'matriarchy' I do not mean the *political* rule of women, which seems hardly ever to have occurred. Even Bachofen, the originator of the matriarchal theory,[6] did not claim that women had held political power in pre-patriarchal communities. To substitute the term 'matrilineal' for matriarchal, however, as some propose, is also misleading, for this change of terminology does not convey the real spiritual ascendancy enjoyed by women at this period of the history of human society, when physical power did not co-exist with magical and religious authority. That such

Theoretical problems and conclusions

an era of female authority did take place, when the chief deities and their ministers were female and personal identity and honour were reckoned through the female line, can be shown by evidence that is far too copious and various to be ignored.[7] The change from the rule of goddesses to the rule of gods is thus one of the most momentous revolutions in the history of mankind and must play an important part in the interpretation of myths. Certainly Aeschylus thought so when he made it the subject of his stupendous trilogy of plays, the *Oresteia*.

This is not to say that certain Women's Liberation theorists are right in regarding matriarchy as a Golden Age in the past from which the growth of patriarchal institutions has been a sad decline. Matriarchy was in many ways savage and cruel, and rational systems of justice and civilized codes of behaviour have developed largely thanks to patriarchy – though patriarchy too has had its characteristic forms of cruelty and injustice, including notably the oppression of women. The relationship between matriarchy and patriarchy is very like that between infancy and adolescence in the life of an individual. This does not mean that we must adopt a mystical organicist theory of the stages of development of a society, for there are good reasons for making the analogy. In its early stages, human society depends on the earth for its sustenance, and food is gathered or killed without the need for cultivation or forethought. In this stage, the thought processes of mankind are like those of an infant at the breast, and the forms of religion centre on the mother. In the stage of early agriculture, the role of the man in fertilizing the female and working the earth attains more recognition and the gods appear as consorts of the goddesses. In late agriculture when technological advances minimize the importance of magic and enhance male confidence, the era of subduing the female begins, and the sky-god, fertilizing the earth with his semen or rain, takes over the leadership of the pantheon. The more confidence man attains in manipulating the world around him, the more the male predominates, since his physical superiority ceases to be overawed by female magic. But this is not necessarily progress in the absolute sense, though it is undoubtedly a process of maturation. To return to childhood is not a solution either, and in general the problems become more complex as the organism matures. The interpretation of a myth must always bear in mind the stage of human development at which the myth occurs; for example, the myth of Attis in the context of the middle-agriculture period is quite different from the same myth in the context of Greco-Roman mystery religion.[8]

The myths studied in this book have been traced to the institution of ritual human sacrifice, which existed in both matriarchal and patriarchal societies, but had different meanings in each. In matriarchal society the death and resurrection of young men promoted by sym-

Theoretical problems and conclusions

pathetic magic the fertility of the fields. In patriarchal society human sacrifices were an expression of submission to an angry male god. They were thus an expression of guilt which was itself the creation of patriarchal society. But violent solutions to the problem of guilt are self-defeating, for they create new guilt for the violence required by the solutions themselves. The present book has studied the ways in which this secondary guilt is handled by what I have called distancing devices. By the use of these devices, the community shifts its guilt for its violent guilt-removing rites to a scapegoat or whipping-boy who is blamed for the violence without which the community cannot remove its primary guilt. The prime example of this technique is anti-Semitism, by which the modern world perpetuates modes of feeling that originated in the sacrificial rituals of the ancient world.

A straightforwardly dualistic religion like Zoroastrianism projects evil outside from the start; Christianity, however, internalizes evil but in such a way that the individual cannot cope with it, and needs a divine sacrifice to atone for it. The Sacred Executioner takes the responsibility for the sacrifice, but must be regarded as evil, so that the saved person can be absolved from the guilt of the sacrifice. By continual identification with the sacrifice (such as by a ritual of incorporation, eating and being eaten by the god), the saved person is able eventually to feel so completely saved that he has purged all evil from his system; at this point the millennium can begin. Evil has been exteriorized again, and the Sacred Executioner can disappear (be converted), or, alternatively, he can be regarded solely in his aspect as destroyer of the good and can thus become the chief focus of the exteriorization of evil. At this point the massacre of the Jews begins, whether by the crazed Crusading populace, by the millenarians fighting the Antichrist, or by the Nazis in their death-camps.

Perhaps a deeper understanding of the atavistic nature of anti-Semitism and of its unbroken historical connection with rites of human sacrifice will help to eradicate this evil from the world, and will further the efforts of modern man to shoulder the burden of his own guilt, avoiding all devices by which guilt may be shifted to his fellow-man. In this way, we may even turn to the task of reversing and improving the behaviour and qualities which make us feel so guilty, while eschewing the chimera of achieving absolute moral purity and perfection.

Notes

1 The Sacred Executioner

1 See p. 178 and Yerkes, 1953, pp. 68–74, where the rite is reconstructed from somewhat conflicting accounts by Androtion, Theophrastus, Pausanias and Porphyry.
2 See, for example, Campbell, 1959, pp. 334–47, on the palaeolithic bear sacrifices.
3 See Milgrom, 1981.

2 Cain

1 The fullest version of the legend of Romulus and Remus is in Plutarch's *In Romulum* (other versions may be found in Dionysius Halicarnassus, 1–2; Livy, I, 4; Valerius Maximus, III, 2–3; Pliny, XV, 18; Virgil *Aeneid*, II, 342, 605; Ovid, *Metamorphoses*, XIV, 616, 845; *Fasti*, IV; and other authors). In one variation, Remus is killed not by Romulus but by one of his companions, Celer, who then fled to Etruria, thus enacting the role of the Sacred Executioner, and relieving Romulus of his Cain-like role.
2 Human sacrifices are attested all over the world not only for the foundation of cities, but for the building of bridges, houses, palaces, temples and fortresses ('foundation sacrifices'). See, for example, for Polynesia, Ellis, 1831, i, p.346; for Melanesia, Codrington, 1891, p.301; for N. America, Boas, 1895; for S. America, Liebrecht, 1879, p.287; for Siam, Frazer, 1911, p.90; for Japan, *Encyclopaedia of Religion and Ethics*, iv, p.856b. Many legends and folk-ballads point to the former existence of the rite (e.g. the Balkan ballad of the Bridge of Arta), recounting the immolation of the builder's wife or a child to keep the bridge from falling down (such legends are found in Germany, Eastern Europe, India, Western Asia, North Africa, Celtic parts of British Isles; see *Encyclopaedia of Religion and Ethics*, ii, p.850). Old houses pulled down in England and on the Continent are frequently found to have the body of a cat walled up in them. Christian legends tell of monks buried alive under monasteries (e.g. Oran, a companion of Columba, in Iona). Sometimes statues were substituted for live sacrifices. Sometimes the foundation stone was laid on a person's shadow, and it was believed that the person would die within a year. In Oldenburg, it is reported that children were buried alive as late as the seventeenth century to make the dikes secure (L. Strackenjan, 1908, i, pp.127ff.). In the Near East, archaeologists have frequently found the bodies of children buried under floors in such a way as to make the hypothesis of foundation sacrifice highly probable, though recently attempts have been made to explain these as burials of stillborn infants. The account in I Kings 16:34 of the death of the sons of Hiel on the occasion of the rebuilding of Jericho has been widely held to refer to a foundation sacrifice, though the deaths are attributed to a curse. That the story of Romulus and Remus is a disguised account of a foundation sacrifice was suggested by several scholars.

For archaeological evidence of a human sacrifice at the building of a city see De Vaux and Stève, *Revue biblique*, LVIII, 1951, pp. 401–3, in connection with Tell al-Fara, near Nablus.
3 The first gladiatorial combats were introduced by the Bruti upon the death of their father (264 BC) to take the place of the human sacrifices of slaves previously made to appease the ghosts of the dead (see Valerius Maximus, ii, 4, 7).
4 In Genesis 15:19, the Kenites are included among the tribes whom God promises to dispossess in favour of descendants of Abraham. This is the only such reference, and is in contradiction to other passages where the Kenites are described as allies of the Israelites. There was evidently some ambivalence in the

Notes

Israelite attitude to the Kenites before it became one of settled friendship. The ambivalence is shown also in the Bible's reticence about the special relationship between Israelite and Kenite culture.

5 See Stade, 1887, i, pp.130ff.; Budde, 1899, 1; Rowley, 1950, pp.149–60; Vischer, 1929; Eerdmans, 1947, pp.14ff.; Morgenstern, 1927.

6 This relationship was first noticed by Buttman, 1828, i, pp.170ff.

7 This pattern has been worked out in various ways, but is thought to comprehend various epochs culminating in the foundation of Solomon's Temple. See especially Bousset *Zeitschrift für die Alt-testamentliche Wissenschaft*, xx, pp.136–47, and Skinner, 1930, p.135. The numbers given in the Septuagint and the Samaritan Bible, are, however, different from those in the Masoretic text.

8 Scholars, however, have generally preferred to derive the Sethian line from the list of ten Babylonian antediluvian patriarchs given by Berossus, though the names have almost nothing in common.

9 There are many Greek legends of purification following exile after a homicide, and some of these legends show strong traces of having been originally stories of human sacrifice. Two interesting examples are the following: (i) In Theophrastus' version of the Bouphonia ceremony at Athens, the origin of the rite is explained by a story. The original bull was killed by a man called Sopatros, who fled to Crete as one under a curse. Yet later, by the instructions of the Delphic oracle, it was he who set up the regular Bouphonia sacrifice, thus averting a famine, and the curse on Sopatros was lifted. Since the bull, when killed, was eaten raw by the people, this story goes beyond human sacrifice back to a period when the totem animal was held to be more sacred than any human. The whole story, which is very complicated, deserves detailed study. For our present purposes, it displays the flight and curse (or impurity) of the sacrificer, together with his sanctity and privileged status. (ii) The Stepteria rite recorded by Plutarch shows similar elements. Every ninth year a hut representing a king's dwelling was suddenly attacked and set on fire. Those involved fled from the scene without looking back, and afterwards one of them went to Tempe for purification, but then returned in triumph to Delphi, wearing a crown. This rite evidently represents the ninth-year sacrifice of the king, and the flight, purification and triumph of his sacrificer and successor. (See Plutarch *Why Oracles are Silent*, 15.)

10 There were, in fact, other sacrifices which were performed, partly at any rate, 'outside the camp', and it is noteworthy that in all these, the officiant became unclean (whereas no such uncleanness attached to the performance of sacrifices within the Temple). These are: the bull and two goats of the Day of Atonement (Leviticus 16), and the sin-offering bulls sacrificed to atone an unwitting sin by the High Priest or by the community as a whole (Leviticus 4). The Bible does not explicitly mention uncleanness in relation to the last two, but Jewish tradition repairs the omission; see Babylonian Talmud, Yoma 68a.

11 This is contrary to the usual view, which builds on the parallel between the seventh position of Enoch in the Sethite chronicle and the seventh position of Evedoranchus (corruption of Enmeduranki) in the list of Babylonian antediluvian patriarchs given by Berossus, since Enmeduranki is described on a tablet in the library of Asshurbanipal as one who was 'initiated into the mysteries of heaven and earth', though there is no mention of an early death or translation to heaven. On this view, it is the Cainite line, as given in the Bible, that has displaced Enoch from seventh to third, and the order of the Sethian line is primary. The motivation of the alleged displacement from seventh to third is obscure. More likely is a displacement the other way, in an attempt to adapt the Cainite line to the structure of the Babylonian patriarch list.

12 An interesting parallel to Enoch may be found in Greek legend. The founder of Athens, Kekrops, had a son by Aglauros (another name for the goddess Athene) called Erysichthon. This name means 'protector of the land'. It is not told how he protected the land, but only that he died early and had no issue. In Olympia, there was the figure of Sosipolis ('saviour of the city'), who was a divine boy in the form of a serpent. In Thebes, the foundation story concerns the slaying of a great serpent by the founder, Cadmus. Serpents, as well as being

Notes

figures of evil, were holy figures, representing city-founders themselves or their surrogates (Kekrops was represented as half-serpent). It may be, then, that a foundation myth about the slaying of a serpent is a disguised form of a foundation myth about the sacrifice of a divine serpent-boy. To disguise the serpent as a figure of evil is one more distancing device by which the nature of the slaying is obscured. (See Kerenyi, 1959, p.213.)

3 The Israelite account of Cain

1 Examples of possible human sacrifice in early strata of the Bible are the cases of Achan (Joshua 7), Jephtha's daughter (Judges 11), and Hiel's sons (I Kings 16), and the dedication of cities to destruction (e.g. Jericho, Joshua 6; Ai, Joshua 8). An indubitable human sacrifice is by Mesha, king of Moab in II Kings 3:27, to which the verse seems to accord a certain validity. The final redaction of Genesis was probably in the sixth century BC, when human sacrifices had long been regarded with detestation.
2 See Milgrom, 1981.
3 See, for example, Hooke, 1956, p.67.
4 The earliest occurrence of this theory is in Midrash Genesis Rabbah 22.
5 See Exodus 29:13, and *Shulhan Arukh*, Yoreh De'ah, 64.
6 See Hooke, 1947, p.42.
7 See Hooke, 1956, p.68.
8 I owe this interpretation to my father, the late E. M. Maccoby.
9 See Babylonian Talmud 59b, commenting on Genesis 1:29.
10 See Numbers 35:31. Money compensation for murder was allowed among the Greeks (*poine*), and among the Germans (*wergild*). The Koran also allows it (2:178f.). See Milgrom, 1971: 'The notion that homicide cannot be commuted is the foundation of criminal law in the Bible: human life is invaluable, hence incommutable. This concept is not found in any other law corpus in the ancient Near East.'
11 See Genesis Rabbah 22.
12 In Greek mythology, the wanderings and sufferings of Orestes, accursed by female deities but supported by the male god Apollo, are a good example of the fate of one who commits a heroic crime, though this is not an instance of sacrifice, but of rebellion against matriarchal law, by which Clytemnestra should have been exempt from punishment. Close to our theme is the case of Athamas, who sacrificed his sons Learchus and Melicertes (allegedly under the influence of madness) and then was condemned to wander for a period in the wilderness, after which child sacrifice of a member of the royal family of Alus, in Thessaly, became a regular institution (see Frazer, *The Golden Bough*, 'Sacrifice of the King's Son'). In Africa, the Matiamvo, or Emperor, of Angola, was sacrificed at the end of his sacred reign by the hand of an executioner sent from the neighbouring hostile tribes. The executioner buried the dismembered corpse of the Matiamvo secretly, and then the head of the executioner himself was struck off. Negotiations then commenced for the return of the corpse from the hostile tribes, and a splendid State funeral ensued. Here, the tribe disclaims responsibility for the sacrifice by the device of accomplishing it through putative enemies, so the executioner does not acquire sufficient sanctity to justify a period of exile and an eventual return.
13 Genesis Rabbah 22.
14 E.g. Smith, 1903, p.251.
15 The Septuagint translates *azazel* as *tragos apopompaios*, taking the word to mean 'the goat that departs', and the Vulgate follows suit. The rabbinical translation (Yoma 67b) is 'hard rock'.
16 In Enoch, Azazel is the name of a rebel angel. T. H. Gaster objects that scapegoats are never offered to demons. Azazel may be a name originally given to the Sacred Executioner himself.
17 See Mishnah, Yoma 6:6.
18 See Hooke, 1956, p.70.
19 See Mishnah, Yoma 6:3, 'All were eligible to lead it away, but the priests had established the custom not to suffer an Israelite to lead it away.'
20 See Harrison, 1980, pp.149–50.
21 See Mishnah, Yoma 6:8.
22 See *ibid*. 6:6 and 8.

4 Lamech

1 See, for example, J. Skinner, 1930, p.121, following F. Lenormant and J. Wellhausen.
2 This line of thought was initiated by Herder, who invented the name 'Sword Song' for Lamech's utterance.
3 It has been pointed out that the life-

Notes

span of Lamech in the Sethian line is given as 777 years (5:*31*), a figure which suggests some relationship with the expression 'seventy-seven-fold' used by the Lamech of the Cainite line (4:*24*). This is certainly a curious coincidence, which increases the probability that the Sethite chronicle depends on the Cainite chronicle and not vice-versa. A vivid and poignant detail of the Cainite chronicle has been transformed into a mundane chronological note in the Sethite chronicle. The opposite process is unlikely.

4 See chapter 6, n.11.

5 Confirmation of the archetypal quality of the story is the long history it has had in European art. See Mellinkoff, 1981.

6 See Frazer, *The Golden Bough*, 'The Myth of Balder'.

7 See Freud, 1955.

8 In a somewhat similar fashion, the name Christ (Hebrew, 'Messiah'), which had been a title of every Davidic monarch, became a divine title in Christianity when attached to a sacrificial figure, though the Christian type of salvationism meant that this could happen only once.

9 The order is unequivocal at least in Genesis 5:*32*, 6:*10* and 9:*18*. There is some doubt, however, as we shall see, in 10:*21*.

10 The Septuagint on 10:*21* translates 'the brother of Japheth the elder'.

11 *Yuval* and *yaval* appear once each, not as names, but as variants of a noun meaning 'stream' (Isaiah 30:*25* and Jeremiah 17:*8*).

12 See p.55.

5 The Kenites and the Rechabites

1 See Speiser, 1962, p.236: 'The Table of Nations . . . is an ambitious undertaking, the first of its kind known from anywhere.'

2 For the Kenites in Amalek, see I Samuel 15:*6*; in Galilee, Judges. 4:*11*, 5:*24*; in the Negev (S. Judaea), I Samuel 27:*10*. A place called Cain is listed in Joshua 15:*57*, in the territory of Judah.

3 See Doughty, 1888, i, pp.280ff.

4 A fresco painting in the 12th-dynasty tomb of Khnumhotep III at Beni Hasan (Bani Hasan) in Egypt represents Semitic nomads entering Egypt, and includes a group held to be metal-workers, since their donkeys carry bellows (see *Encyclopedia Judaica*, vi, p.494, ill.). The period is about 1890 BC.

5 Frazer, 1957, p.112. See also Frazer, 1918, ii, p.21 for the Wachaga tribe.

6 See Pauly, 1912, p.337.

7 These are the so-called Torque Bearers of the early Bronze Age, who were organized in a special cult with a deity of their own.

8 For the Chalybes, see Herodotus, i, 28, and Xenophon, *Anabasis*, 4. More mythical are the groups which combined magic with metal-working, the Corybantes, the Dactyloi, and the Couretes; but the legends about them give evidence of the relationship between metal-working and mystical secret societies with special rites (see Thomson, 1946, p.110).

9 See Budde, 1896 and 1899; Meyer, 1906, pp.88–9, 129–41; Friedlaender, 1910, pp.253–7; Flight, 1923, pp.158–226; Schmökel, 1933, pp.212–29; Nyström, 1946; Gautier, 1927, pp.104–29.

10 The clan names of the Rechabites (Tithrathites, Shimeathites, Sucathites) have not been satisfactorily explained. They may derive from place-names.

11 The Targum of Jeremiah 35:*19* interprets the expression 'stand before the Lord' to refer to Temple service. The Septuagint superscription of Psalm 70 (Hebrew 71) is '[A Psalm sung by] the sons of Jonadab', suggesting that the Rechabites sang among the Levites.

12 Another possible survival of the Kenites is the Jewish tribe of Medina, the Banu Qaynuqa, who, unlike the other two main Jewish Arabian tribes with whom Muhammad clashed, the Nadir and the Quragga, owned no land and were metal-workers.

13 For example, the Nabataean ascetics mentioned by Diodorus Siculus (xix, 94), who, like the Rechabites, eschewed wine and lived in tents.

14 Babylonian Talmud, Bava Batra, 58b: 'Wine is the greatest of all medicines: drugs are necessary only where wine is lacking.'

15 Babylonian Talmud, Ta'anit 11a.

16 Jewish tradition held that the sons of Adam procreated by marrying their twin-sisters, so Lot's incest would not have been disgraceful in such circumstances. The Talmud excuses Lot's daughters on the ground that they thought the disaster was worldwide; this is a possible echo of the original form of the story.

17 See Genesis Rabbah 36:*7*; Babylonian

Notes

Talmud, Sanhedrin, 70a; Yalqut Shimoni, Noah, 61.

18 For human sacrifices, accompanied by orgies, to the earth goddess, among the Khonds of Bengal, see Frazer, 1957, ii, pp.571–5, and Campbell, 1962, pp.160–3. Each family obtained a shred of the victim for its field. These sacrifices continued until the nineteenth century.

19 See Kirk, 1970, pp.214–20.

20 See Pope, 1977, pp.507–8, commenting on various Ugaritic texts.

21 The Biblical narrative shows uncertainty about the identity of the slayer/castrator/voyeur, since it ascribes this role to Ham, while laying the resultant curse upon Canaan. This is because the Bible wishes to detach the story from its character as a Canaanite foundation myth, though this aspect survives in the drastically changed form of a curse against the Canaanite nation. Canaan has been transformed from the hero of the story into the villain, though his dislodgment from the central role makes this transformation problematic; and as founder of the Canaanite nation, he transmits a curse to it that justifies its conquest by the Israelites.

22 The story of the voyage of Dionysus, when he was captured by pirates, but made vines grow all over the ship and filled the ship with animals, finally turning the pirates into dolphins, is told in the Homeric Hymn to Dionysus, pp.6ff.; Apollodorus, iii, 5.3, and Ovid, *Metamorphoses*, iii. 577–699. On Dionysus and Deucalion, see Graves, 1960, ii, p.141.

6 Abraham and Isaac

1 Micha Joseph Bin Gorion (Berdyczewski) put forward this view in his *Sinai und Garizim*, 1926. In a Phoenician myth recounted by Eusebius (*Praeparatio Evangelica*, i, 10, 29), Kronos sacrificed his only son Ieoud to his father Uranus.

2 Apollodorus, *Bibliotheca*, i, 9, 1; Herodotus, vii, 197; Plutarch, *De superstitione*, 5.

3 Euripides, *Iphigenia at Aulis*, 1540; *Iphigenia in Tauris*, 20.30–783; Aeschylus, *Agamemnon*, 1534; Ovid, *Metamorphoses*, 12.245 sq.

4 See Green, 1975, pp.99–102.

5 Pausanias, *Graeciae Descriptio*, i, 5, 2; Jerome, *Adversus Jovinianum*, 1, 41 (Migne, PL, xxiii, col. 270).

6 Pausanias, *Graeciae Descriptio*, iv, 9:4.

7 Judges 11:30–40.

8 See Noth, 1958, pp.157–9; Moore, 1895, pp. 299–305; Boling, 1975, pp.206–10; Reinke, i, pp.419ff.

9 Jubilees 18:12.

10 Genesis Rabbah 56:7.

11 Spiegel, 1967, p.57: 'We would have here, as occasionally also elsewhere in the Midrashim of early generations, some leftovers of belief before the beliefs of Israel.' Also, pp.116–17: 'What survived from the heritage of idolatry which in Judaism remained peripheral grew to become dominant in the Christian world.'

12 See Midrash ha-Gadol on Genesis 22:19 for Isaac's visit to Paradise, and Paaneah Raza, 29a, and Yalkut Reubeni, Va-yera, for the healing of his wound. See also Hadar Zekenim, 10b, and Minhat Yehudah, Toledot, Genesis 25:27.

13 Leviticus Rabbah 20:2.

14 See Spiegel, 1969, p.47, on Mekhilta de-R. Simeon ben Yohai (ed. D. Hoffmann) p.4. Spiegel refers to a quarter of a *log* of blood as 'the amount required to keep a man alive'. This is somewhat misleading, however. A quarter of a *log* (*reviit*) is equivalent to a volume of only 1½ eggs, so the loss of this amount of blood is hardly dangerous to life. Spiegel, in a note, points out that certain Talmudic texts seem to say that a human being contains only one quarter-*log* of blood, an anatomical absurdity. An explanation given by Tosafot (Sotah 5a) is that this refers only to the heart's blood. Another explanation is that it is an infant that contains only one quarter-*log* of blood. These explanations are cited by Spiegel. But Isaac was not an infant, and it is unlikely that the Mekhilta means that Abraham drew Isaac's heart's blood. So the Mekhilta refers to a less serious wound than Spiegel suggests. The matter is not improved by Spiegel's translator's policy of sometimes referring to a quarter-*log* of blood as 'a quarter of his blood'.

15 Shibbolei ha-Leket, 9a–b. See also Spiegel, 1969, p.37, on Cambridge University Library MS Or. 1080, Box I: 48, for the most explicit version.

16 Midrash ha-Gadol on Genesis 22:19: 'Though he did not die, Scripture regards Isaac as having died and his ashes having lain on the altar'. See also Sifra, ed. Weiss, p.102c: 'God regards the ashes of Isaac as though they were piled upon the altar.'

Notes

17 For example, Vermes, 1973, p.205–8, where passages referring to the actual shedding of blood are quoted alongside 'as if' passages.
18 See Kierkegaard, 1941. See also Simon, 1958.
19 See pp. 160ff.

7 Moses and Circumcision

1 The ceremony of passing between the severed halves of an animal was common in the ancient world, and among savage tribes in later times, as a means of ratifying an agreement or covenant (see Frazer, 1918, i, pp.391–428). The meaning of the rite is superficially, 'May I be severed like this animal if I break this agreement', but, more profoundly, the rite signifies the union between the two parties in the spiritual body of the sacrificed animal, as Frazer shows, building on the work of W. Robertson Smith. The only other Biblical example of the rite is in Jeremiah 34:17–20. Abraham, while accepting God's promise to give him a son on trust, required a formal covenant to ratify God's promise of the Land, which involved a transfer of property from the Canaanites and therefore required unimpeachable title. Thus explained, there is perhaps something prosaic about the Covenant between the Pieces; but the ordeal suffered by Abraham in his watch and conflict with the swooping birds of prey has the atmosphere of an initiation ordeal (cf. Jacob's struggle with the angel). There is an interesting parallel to this in Virgil's account of the ordeal of Aeneas and his companions when their sacrifice of cattle to Jupiter was attacked by the female Harpies (Aeneid, iii, 219–57). This is a conflict between patriarchal god and supplanted female deities, whose curse, however, remains effective. Abraham's treaty with God, the father-god, for control of the Land also has to contend with the wrath of swooping female deities, representing the abrogated divine status of the Land itself, which has become a passive piece of property in the control of the father. Abraham fights off the last traces of goddess-worship in order to become the devotee of the father-god, and enter into possession and control of the Promised Land. It is perhaps significant that the birds set aside for the sacrifice were 'not divided', and, in a sense, reappear as the attacking birds of prey.
2 See Morgenstern, 1963, pp.35–70, and Morgenstern, 1927, pp.51–4, where it is argued that Exodus 4:24–8 is derived from a Kenite source. Morgenstern holds, however, that circumcision was never a puberty rite.
3 See Mekhilta on Exodux 18:3, Exodus Rabbah, 5:8, Babylonian Talmud, Nedarim, 31b–32a. For Targumic, Apocryphal and other comments, see Vermes, 1973, pp.178–92.
4 Jubilees 48:1–4.
5 The verb *pagash* found here is usually translated as 'to meet', but Hosea 13:8 shows that it can have the meaning 'to attack'. The cognate verb *paga'* can have the meaning 'to afflict with madness' in late Hebrew, but that this is the meaning here is only conjectural, and is not strictly necessary for the argument.
6 See Numbers 3:44–51.
7 See Wellhausen, 1957, pp.340–1.
8 See Bettelheim, 1955, pp.154–64, citing Australian myths about women originating circumcision with flint knives (see also Roheim, 1945, p.78). He also cites the case of Zipporah (p.159). See also Barton, *Encyclopaedia of Religion and Ethics*, iii, p.680. Gennep (1960), however, denies any sexual factor in circumcision, attributing the custom to the propensity of savages to chop off projecting portions of their body as identifying signs!
9 Bettelheim, 1955, pp.159–64, cites various examples, including the Western Arunta.
10 See Frazer, 1907, pp.220–1.
11 Most of the ancient Semites practised circumcision. Exceptions were the Babylonians and the Assyrians. The Philistines, a non-Semitic people, were uncircumcised. The rite is widespread in tribes of Africa, Australia and America.
12 The goddess Hera was not originally the wife of Zeus, but an independent goddess with a subordinate spouse, Heracles. Her marriage to Zeus represents a compromise between patriarchy and matriarchy, but their continual quarrels show that the arrangement was precarious. See Thomson, 1946, p.30.
13 See Yashar, Va-yera, 44a–47a; Yalkut, i, 98–9; Tanhuma, Va-yera, 23.
14 See I Maccabees 1:60–1, showing

Notes

circumcision by women in hard times. In the Falasha tribe of Ethiopia, circumcision is performed regularly by women.

8 The sacrifice of Jesus

1 For the 'Original Murder' by which agriculture came into being, see Campbell, 1962, p.4.
2 Koran, Sura 37:*100–11*, gives an account of the sacrifice of Abraham's son. Though the name Ishmael is not given here, the passage precedes the account given of the birth of Isaac (*112–13*). Islamic tradition thus assumes that it was Ishmael who was the victim required by God. See Torrey, 1967, pp. 102–4.
3 See Crone & Cook, 1977, pp.122–3, where it is argued that the doctrine of the Arabs as a holy nation coexisted with contrary notions. I cannot see, however, that Muslim ideas about converts differed from those of Judaism; both religions allow converts from any nation; converts become members of the holy nation.
4 See Maccoby, 1980, for arguments supporting this paragraph.
5 The doctrine of eternal torment for the wicked does not appear in the Old Testament. It first appears in Enoch (probably through Iranian influence). Ben Sira denies the doctrine (41:4), as did Jewish mainstream religion, except in the case of desperate sinners (Babylonian Talmud, Rosh ha-Shanah, 16b–17a). The doctrine of eternal torment features prominently in the New Testament (e.g. Luke 16:23, Matthew 13:42 and 50), and it became a dogma of the Church, elaborated by the scholastics.
6 See Braude, 1940.
7 See Frazer, 1957, ii, p.579, on the annual slaying of a priest as the embodiment of Attis, and ii, pp.768–75 for the divinity of the human sacrifices in Aztec religion.
8 See Maccoby, 1966.
9 See Frazer, 1957, ii, p. 643.
10 See Delehaye, 1912, pp.11ff.
11 The late Father Thomas Corbishley at a dialogue organized by the National Book League in London in 1973.
12 Galatians 2:*21*: 'If righteousness comes by law, then Christ died for nothing.' Galatians 3:*13*: 'Christ bought us freedom from the curse of the law.'
13 See Maccoby, 1980, pp.55–65, 97–8, 210–15.
14 See Mishnah, Pesahim 9:5.
15 See Sanders, 1977, pp.165–8; Moore, 1927, i, p.505.
16 Milgrom, 1981.
17 '. . . The backward half-look/Over the shoulder, towards the primitive terror.' T. S. Eliot, 'The Dry Salvages'.

9 Christianity and Hellenistic religion

1 See Jacobs, 1964, pp.398–454.
2 That God suffers in sympathy with the sufferings of mankind, however, is a well-established Jewish doctrine (e.g. Bava Batra, 73b). This Jewish view, however, was denounced as blasphemous by Christian theologians (e.g. at the Disputation of Paris, 1240) as akin to the Patripassian heresy, the orthodox Christian view being that God the Father was 'impassible', and even the Son of God could suffer only in the flesh. See Maccoby, 1982.
3 Among those who have argued against the connection are, in ancient times, Justin Martyr and Tertullian, and, in modern times, Cardinal Newman, C. Colpe, W. D. Davies, W. Meeks, A. Schweitzer, G. H. C. MacGregor, H. G. Marsh, A. D. Nock, W. Manson, C. A. A. Scott. Christians of the school of Bultmann, however, have affirmed the influence of mystery religion and Gnosticism on Christianity.
4 See Ezekiel 8:*14*: 'There sat women weeping for Tammuz.' See Frazer, 1907, p.189.
5 See Frazer, *The Golden Bough*, for the case of the priest of Diana at Nemi, which he relates to the deaths of Hippolytus, Adonis, Attis, all 'mortal youths who paid with their lives for the brief rapture of the love of an immortal goddess'. In practice, the consort of the earthly representative of the goddess was sacrificed yearly, e.g. at Iolcus, Thessaly; see Graves, 1952, p.127.
6 Plato, *Gorgias*, 497c; Hippolytus, *Philosophumena*, 5, 8; Otto, 1940, pp.99–106; Campbell, 1969, pp.185–7.
8 See Reich, 1950.
9 See Cumont, 1903; Campbell, 1964, pp.255–61.
10 Plutarch, *On Isis and Osiris*; Frazer, 1907, pp.267–400; Campbell, 1969, pp.424–7.
11 *Carmina*, lxiii, 'Attis' (edition of W. Kroll, Leipzig, 1923).
12 Lucretius, ii, 598 sqq; Frazer, 1907, pp. 217–65.

Notes

13 Vellay, 1904; Frazer, 1907, pp. 3–216.
14 For example, Zoroastrianism regarded agriculture with the highest reverence. See *Encyclopaedia of Religion and Ethics*, xii, p.865.
15 M. Krause, 1964, pp.215–23. MacRae (1976, p.618) writes, 'The Nag Hammadi library cannot yet be said to prove conclusively the non-Christian origin of Gnosticism, but it adds a great deal of probability to this classic position.'
16 In Hellenistic thought, the expression 'Son of God' appears in the Logos philosophy. Plato (*Timaeus*) refers to the world-organism as 'the only-begotten son of God'. Philo uses the same expression about the Logos (*De opificio mundi*, 21). The expression was common in the soteriological cults, and was applied to charismatic cult-founders such as Apollonius of Tyana. It was also a title of the Roman emperors and of the Ptolemaic kings of Egypt.
17 For anti-Semitism in the Gnostic cults, see *Encyclopaedia of Religion and Ethics*, ix, p.500.
18 Judas of Galilee, Theudas and Athronges all go without mention in the Talmud. The sparse references to Jesus in the Talmud are responses to Christian missionary activity of the third and fourth centuries AD, and are not based on preserved traditions.
19 Acts 5:33–9. See Maccoby, 1980, pp.67–8, and (for Paul) pp.179–83.
20 See the Ebionite account of Paul quoted by Epiphanius, *Heresies*, xxx, 16.
21 Pelagius, a British monk (perhaps Welsh or Irish) came to Rome about AD 400 and attacked Augustine's views on Original Sin and the inefficacy of good works, on the ground that they precluded free will and the possibility of morality. Pelagius's views were condemned in 416, and Pelagius himself was excommunicated.
22 Marcion was excommunicated in AD 144. He regarded the God of the Old Testament as the Demiurge, an inferior and despotic god who had created the world and given the Torah, being a god of law, unlike the Highest God, who was a god of love. Jesus had been sent by the Highest God in order to overthrow the God of Judaism.
23 See Galatians 3:19.
24 See Hatch, 1890, p.291f. Justin Martyr describes the Eucharist of the Mithras cult (*Apology*, i, 66). See also Tertullian, *De praescriptione haereticorum*, 40. See Robertson, 1911, p.307.
25 This view has been challenged in recent years (e.g. J. C. O'Neill, *Paul's Letter to the Romans*, 1975) but without justification. See the correspondence in *Commentary*, April 1977, pp.13–16.
26 The explanation is that of Rabbi Meir (Babylonian Talmud, Sanhedrin, 46b). Another rabbinical interpretation is that the verse refers to the punishment of a blasphemer. The translation, on this view, would be: 'He is hanged on the tree because he cursed God.' Here, too, there is no question of the man himself suffering from a curse because he has been hanged; on the contrary, his punishment expiates his crime of cursing God. See Mishnah, Sanhedrin 6:4, and Babylonian Talmud, Sanhedrin, 45b.
27 Frazer, 1907, p.244.

10 Judas Iscariot

1 See Haugg, 1930; Lake, 1933; Wells, 1971, p.130; Maier, 1933. That Judas never betrayed Jesus was first proposed by Bruno Bauer, 1842, iii, pp.235ff.
2 Most scholars agree that John is the latest of the Gospels. See Smith, 1965. For the pseudepigraphic aspect of the Gospel, see discussions of John 21:24, e.g. Black, 1962.
3 See Maccoby, 1980, pp.201–3.
4 John 7:4.
5 See Galatians 1:19, where James is called the 'Lord's brother'. The theory of Joseph as an elderly widower with children first appears in the Protevangelium of James, and is current in the Eastern Churches. Another view is that James was Jesus's cousin; this is current in the Roman Catholic Church.
6 See Maccoby, 1980, pp.159–68.
7 Twins in mythology are Iphiclus, twin to Tirynthian Hercules; Pollux, twin to Castor; Lynceus, twin to Idas; Calais, twin to Zetes; Remus, twin to Romulus; Demophoon, twin to Triptolemus; all these are associated with alternating or joint reigns over a kingdom. Cain and Abel are regarded as twins in Midrashic tradition. Other rival Biblical twins are Perez and Zarah, and Jacob and Esau. Sometimes the twins are portrayed as great friends, but deeper investigation reveals a grimmer reality. Thus Castor and Pollux

Notes

are companions in battle; but one is mortal, the other immortal, and as a compromise they spend six months alternately in Hades. This myth expresses an alternation of kings called alternately Castor and Pollux, each dying at the hand of the incoming king after a reign of six months. Of course, the identity of slayer and slain is an expression of primitive philosophy, not merely a way of escaping the guilt of homicide; for this aspect, see Campbell, 1964, p.235.

8 In the Acts of Thomas, Judas Thomas is regarded as the twin of Jesus.

9 For Nebuchadnezzar as God's instrument, see, for example, Jeremiah 19:21–3.

10 A much more likely etymology of 'Iscariot' is from the Latin *sicarius*, ('knifeman') a name given to a group of revolutionaries. This is supported by the fact that in some MSS, Judas is called Judas Zelotes, i.e. Judas the Zealot (Latin MSS of Matthew 10:3, and Sahidic version of John 14:22).

11 Propp, 1958.

12 Kermode, 1979, pp.84–95.

13 See Maccoby, April 1980.

14 By the ransom theory of atonement held by Hilary of Poitiers, Augustine, etc., Satan had acquired rights over man through the Fall of Adam. The death of Christ acted as a ransom. The trick consisted of deceiving Satan into thinking that Jesus was only human, so that when Satan accepted Jesus's death as ransom for humanity, he did not realize that Jesus would escape death by resurrection. This 'deception' theory was first advanced by Gregory of Nyssa, and was accepted by Augustine, Gregory the Great, Bernard of Clairvaux and Peter Lombard. Peter Lombard describes the Cross as a mousetrap baited by the blood of Jesus.

15 See Maccoby, 1970, pp.65–7.

16 There is also a non-mythical, sectarian aspect of the treachery of Judas, an aspect that it shares with the milder treachery of Peter and with the crass incomprehension portrayed in the other disciples. The Gospels were written by Paulinists, who supported Paul in his quarrel with the Jerusalem elders – survivors of Jesus's original band of Apostles. A denigration of that band, therefore, served Paulinist purposes. It may even be that this historical motif was the germ out of which the mythic role of Judas developed.

17 For the identity of sacrificer and sacrificed, see the mythical case of Odin (Frazer, 1907, p.244), and the actual cases of divine kings who, at the end of their term, cut themselves to pieces: 'He takes some sharp knives, and begins to cut off his nose, and then his ears, and his lips, and all his members, and as much flesh off himself as he can; and he throws it away very hurriedly until so much of his blood is spilled that he begins to faint, and then he cuts his throat himself' (Frazer, 1957, p.362).

11 The role of the Jews in the New Testament

1 See Matthew 8:12: 'Those who were born to the kingdom will be driven out into the dark, the place of wailing and gnashing of teeth.' See Eusebius, *Demonstratio Evangelica*, 1:1; Hippolytus, *Contra Judaeos*, 6; Augustine, *Adversus Judaeos*, 5(6), 7(10); *ibid.*, *De Civitate Dei*, xvii, 19 and xviii, 46, etc.; Justin Martyr, *Dialogue*, 16; Tertullian, *Adversus Judaeos*, 3; Irenaeus, *Adversus Haereses*, ii, 16:1. See Ruether, 1974, pp.144–9.

2 The Romans are referred to in the Scrolls under the name Kittim (or Chittim), taken from the Biblical prophecies (e.g. Daniel 11:30). This name had previously been applied to the Macedonian Greeks; see I Maccabees 1:1.

3 See Maccoby, 1980, pp.45, 70, 154–7.

4 See *ibid.*, 1980, pp.19–20, 160–4.

5 Romans 13:1.

6 Black (1962), however, asserts the genuineness of the passage as follows: 'Paul's strong words are perfectly explicable as an outburst of exasperation . . . the Jews . . . were beginning to show their teeth.'

7 See Maccoby, 1980, pp.117–18 and pp.217–18.

8 See Dodd, 1961, pp.4–5.

9 See Maccoby, 1976.

10 See Ruether, 1975, pp.90–5. See Mark 12:1–12 (the 'Parable of the Vineyard'), and parallels e.g. Acts 7:51–2, and Matthew 23:29–35. The accusation that the Jews killed nearly all their prophets seems to be an exaggeration of II Chronicles 36:16, 'misused His prophets' and of Nehemiah 9:26 'and they killed Thy prophets'. Extra-Biblical tradition represented some of the prophets as having

suffered martyrdom, e.g. Isaiah, at the hands of Menasseh. This was a reflection of the preoccupation with martyrdom during the Hellenistic period (see Fischel, 1947). The New Testament picture, however, cannot be fully explained on these lines; as Ruether argues, it is motivated by Christian theology.
11 See Ruether, 1974, pp.124-31, 'Jewish History as a Trail of Crimes', citing Lactantius, Eusebius, Aphrahat, Chrysostom, Prudentius, Ephrem, Augustine.
12 See Ruether, 1974, pp. 133-4, citing Aphrahat ('the father of the Jews was not Abraham, but Cain'), Ephrem ('the Jews stand among the nations ashamed, as Cain was, at their unnatural deed'), Tertullian, Chrysostom, Augustine.
13 See Maccoby, 1980, pp.13-21, 159-68.
14 See Maccoby (1968) for the view that Barabbas, called Jesus Barabbas in some MSS, was the same person as Jesus of Nazareth, but split off in the Gospels in order to obviate the awkward fact that the Jerusalem crowd called for Jesus's release. See also Maccoby, 1980, p.164.
15 The draft prepared by Cardinal Bea in 1960 was 'unrecognizably watered down' (Hans Wirtz) in the versions of 1964 and 1965. The sentence clearing the Jews of 'deicide' was omitted in the final version of 1965, on the insistence of Arab clergy (who saw in it a legitimation of Israel) and of Eastern Orthodox and conservative Catholic clergy (who thought it contradicted the Gospel account). See Gilbert, 1968, p.179. The expression 'wicked generation' is used in the 'Explanations' of the changes made in the final version. (Gilbert, 1968, Appendix E). In the 'Explanations', too, the view that the destruction of the Temple and Jerusalem was a punishment for the death of Jesus was reaffirmed.
16 Ruether, 1974, p.113.

12 The Church and the Jews

1 See Hare, 1967, pp.20-43; Parkes, 1934, pp.121-51.
2 See Hare, 1967, pp.20-30; Simon, 1958; Gealy, F. D., *Interpreter's Dictionary of the Bible*, 'Stephen', iv, pp.441-2.
3 Ruether, 1974, p.88.
4 See Hare, 1967, pp.130-45.
5 For the abusive *Adversus Judaeos* tradition in the Church, see Williams, 1935; Ruether, 1974, ch. 3; Heer, 1967, ch.

5; Flannery, 1965, pp.39-63; Hay, 1950, ch. 1.
6 Origen, *On Psalm xxxvii*, PG, xii. p.1322.
7 Psalms 37:12: 'The wicked plotteth against the just, and gnasheth upon him with his teeth.'
8 Parkes, 1934, pp.125-50.
9 Harnack, 1908, i, pp.58ff. See Parkes, 1934, p.125.
10 See Strack, 1909; Baron, xi, pp.146-57; Trachtenberg, 1966, chs. 9-10.
11 See Strack, 1909, p.34, quoting Paschasius Radbertus and Germanus.
12 Strack, 1909, from Regensburg, 1880, ii, p.270.
13 Paris, 1872-83, v, p.518. See Trachtenberg, 1966, p.131.
14 Josephus, *Contra Apionem*, 2:*89-102*.
15 'In spite of her own origin, she disliked Jews, and rarely neglected a chance to maltreat them.' Adams, 1905, p.263.
16 See Matthew 25:31-46: 'When the Son of man shall come in his glory, and all the holy angels with him, then shall he sit upon the throne of his glory; and before him shall be gathered all nations: and he shall separate them one from another, as a shepherd divideth his sheep from the goats . . . And these shall go away into everlasting punishment: but the righteous into life eternal.' See also Mark 8:*38*, Matthew 16:*27*, Luke 9:*26*. See Henry Adams, 1905, pp.249-81, on the fear of Jesus as Judge, and the recourse to Mary as intercessor; he quotes Peter Abelard, 'All of us who fear the wrath of the Judge, fly to the Judge's mother, who is compelled to sue for us, and stands in the place of a mother to the guilty.'
17 Adams, 1905, p.251.
18 De Rougemont, 1956.
19 See Trachtenberg, 1966, ch. 3, 'With Horns and Tail', especially p.50.
20 The hymn 'Gaude Maria' contains these words: 'Erubescat Judaeus infelix, qui dicit Christum Joseph semine esse natum.'
21 The ballad is 'Sir Hugh, or the Jew's Daughter', Child, 1882-98, iii, p.233 (no.155). See Child's valuable introduction to this ballad.
22 See Trachtenberg, 1966, p.129; Starr, 1939, pp.22ff., p.202. No.149; Roth, 1943, p.102; Starr, 1942, pp.68, 74ff. Starr, in the last citation, describes the graciousness of the Doge of Venice, who, while refusing to relieve the Jewish executioner of his

Notes

duties, excused him from officiating on Sabbaths and festivals.

13 The Sacred Executioner in the modern world

1 See Maccoby, 1970 (2).
2 Exodus 22:24.
3 Babylonian Talmud, Bava Metzi'a, 70b–71a. See Stein, 1955.
4 See Baron, 1967, xii, pp.69–197; Roth 1943, ch. 19.
5 See Maccoby, 1976 (2).
6 See Gaer, 1961; Rosenberg, 1961; Anderson, 1965.
7 For example, Werner Sombart, who argued that the alleged desert philosophy of the Jews was responsible for modern capitalism. See Sombart, 1913, pp.324–51, where all the ingredients of this type of anti-Semitic theory can be found.
8 See Rosenberg, 1961, pp.320–4.
9 As argued above (p.137), this attitude was initiated by Paul in Romans 11:28, 'they are treated as enemies for your sake'. This is called by Paul a 'secret', or 'mystery'. Modern exponents of the view are Leon Bloy, Nicholas Berdyaev and Malcolm Muggeridge. There has been a temptation to some Jews to accept the offer of this role as awesome, wandering bearers of the guilt of mankind (e.g. Disraeli, George Steiner, Leo Abse), since such a romantic posture seems preferable to the boring, if realistic, position of being the irritated victim of paranoid fantasies.
10 See Shelley's *Queen Mab*, Canto vii, and *Hellas*; also his earlier treatment of the theme in *St Irvyne* and 'The Victim of the Eternal Avenger'.
11 See Maccoby, 1969.
12 See Cohn, 1967.
13 See Bousset, 1893; *ibid.*, 1908; *ibid.*, 1947; Preuss, 1906.
14 See Roth, 1963; Adler, 1930; *Encyclopaedia Judaica*, xiv, pp.114–16.
15 See Baron, 1957, iv, ch. 21; Poliakov, 1974, i, Part Two.
16 See Bousset, 1947, p.61.
17 Irenaeus, *Adversus Haereses*, v; Hippolytus, *de Antichristo*, and *Commentary on Daniel*; Lactantius, *Divinae Institutiones*, vii, 14ff.
18 See Bauer, 1978, p.36.

14 Theoretical problems and conclusions

1 In *The Golden Bough*, Frazer shows the affinities between the *myths* of Hippolytus, Adonis, Attis, Dionysus, Osiris, etc. and the *rites* of human sacrifice of sacred kings, incarnate gods, scapegoats (or their substitutes) and the *folk-customs* in which human sacrifice is symbolically performed.
2 Kirk, 1974, p.247.
3 There is a resemblance between the slaying of Neoptolemus for eating sacrificial meat and the slaying of the bull in the Bouphonia for eating sacrificial corn.
4 See chapter 2, n.12.
5 See Charbonnier, 1969, p.33.
6 See Joseph Campbell's Introduction to Bachofen, 1967, pp.xxxi–xxxii.
7 See the massive evidence collected by Schmidt, 1912–55. For a useful summary of Schmidt's work, see Campbell, 1969, pp.318–23.
8 See Frankl, not yet published (which I have had the privilege of seeing in MS).

Bibliography

Adams, Henry, *Mont-Saint Michel and Chartres*, Boston, 1905.
Adler, E. N., *Jewish Travellers*, London, 1930.
Albright, W. F., *From Stone Age to Christianity*, Baltimore, 1904.
Anderson, G. K., *The Legend of the Wandering Jew*, Providence, 1965.
Ante-Nicene Christian Library (ed. Roberts and Donaldson), Edinburgh, 1868–72.
Augustine, *The City of God*, 2 vols, New York, 1945.
Bachofen, J. J., *Das Mutterrecht*, Stuttgart, 1861.
——, *Myth, Religion and Mother Right: Selected Writings of J. J. Bachofen* (tr. Ralph Manheim, with a preface by George Boas and an introduction by Joseph Campbell), London, 1967.
Baron, Salo W., *A Social and Religious History of the Jews*, 16 vols, New York, 1952–75.
Barton, G. A., 'Circumcision (Semitic)', *Encyclopaedia of Religion and Ethics*, iii, pp. 679–81.
Bauer, Bruno, *Geschichte der Synoptiker und des Johannes*, Berlin, 1842.
Bauer, Yehuda, *The Holocaust in Historical Perspective*, London, 1978.
Bertholet, A., *Der Sinn des kultischen Opfer*, Berlin, 1942.
Bettelheim, Bruno, *Symbolic Wounds*, London, 1955.
Bin Gorion (Berdyczewski), Micha Joseph, *Sinai und Garizim*, Berlin, 1926.
Bishop, Carl W., 'The Beginnings of Civilization in Eastern Asia', Supplement to the *Journal of the American Oriental Society*, No. 4, Dec. 1939.
Black, Matthew (ed.), *Peake's Commentary on the Bible*, rev. ed., London, 1962.
Bloch, Joseph S., *Israel and the Nations*, Berlin-Vienna, 1927.
Bloy, Léon, *Le salut par les Juifs*, Paris, 1892.
Boas, Franz, *Indianische Sagen von der nord-pacifischen Küste Amerikas*, Berlin, 1895
Boling, Robert G., *Judges* (Anchor Bible), New York, 1975.
Bousset, Wilhelm, *Der Antichrist in der Überlieferung des Judentums, des neuen Testaments und der alten Kirche*, Göttingen, 1893. Eng. tr. *The Antichrist Legend*, London, 1896.
——, 'Das Chronologische System der biblischen Geschichtsbücher', *Zeitschrift für die Alt-testamentliche Wissenschaft*, XX (1900), pp. 136–47.
——, 'Antichrist', *Encyclopaedia of Religion and Ethics*, i, pp. 578–81, 1908.
——, 'Antichrist', *Encyclopaedia Britannica*, ii, p. 61, 1947.
Braude, William G., *Jewish Proselyting in the First Five Centuries CE*, Providence, 1940.
Briffault, R., *The Mothers*, London, 1927.
Bright, J., *A History of Israel*, Philadelphia, 1959.
Budde, K., *Das nomadische Ideal in AT*, Giessen, 1896.
——, *The Religion of Israel to the Exile*, London, 1899.
Bultmann, Rudolf, *Das Evangelium des Johannes*, Göttingen, 1950. Eng. tr. *The Gospel of John: A Commentary*, London, 1971.
——, *Primitive Christianity in its Contemporary Setting*, London, 1956.
Buttman, P. C., *Mythologus, oder gesammelte Abhandlungen über die Sagen des Alterthums*, Berlin, 1828.
Campbell, Joseph, *The Masks of God: Primitive Mythology*, New York, 1959.
——, *The Masks of God: Oriental Mythology*, New York, 1962.
——, *The Masks of God: Occidental Mythology*, New York, 1964. (See also Bachofen, J. J.)
Charbonnier, George, *Conversations with Lévi-Strauss*, London, 1969.

Bibliography

Child, F. J. (ed.), *English and Scottish Ballads*, 8 vols, Boston, 1882–98.

Codrington, R. H., *Melanesians*, Oxford, 1891.

Cohn, Norman, *The Pursuit of the Millennium*, London, 1957.

——, *Warrant for Genocide: the myth of the Jewish world-conspiracy and the Protocols of the Elders of Zion*, London, 1967.

Colebrook, R. and Wilson, H., 'On the Sacrifice of Human Beings', *Journal of the Royal Asiatic Society*, XXIII (1926), pp. 96–109.

Conway, M. D., *The Wandering Jew*, London, 1881.

Cornford, F. M., *From Religion to Philosophy*, London, 1913.

Crone, Patricia, and Cook, Michael, *Hagarism: The Making of the Islamic World*, Cambridge, 1977.

Cumont, Franz, *The Mysteries of Mithra*, London, 1903.

——, *Les Religions Orientales dans le paganisme romain*, 4th ed., Paris, 1929.

Davies, W. D., *Paul and Rabbinic Judaism*, London, 1948.

Delehaye, H., *Les Origines du culte des Martyrs*, Brussels, 1912.

De Rougemont, Denis, *Passion and Society*, London, 1956.

De Vaux, R., 'La troisième campagne de fouilles à Tell El-Far'ah, près Naplouse', *Revue Biblique*, LVIII (1951), pp. 401–3.

Dieterich, A., *Eine Mithrasliturgie*, Leipzig, 1903.

——, *Mutter Erde*, Leipzig-Berlin, 1905.

Dodd, C. H., *The Parables of the Kingdom*, New York, 1961.

Doughty, C. M., *Travels in Arabia Deserta*, 2 vols, Cambridge, 1888.

Eerdmans, B. D., *The Religion of Israel*, Leiden, 1947.

Eissfeldt, Otto, *Molk als Opferbegriff im punischen und hebraïschen und das Ende des Gottes Moloch (Beiträge zur Religionsgeschichte des Altertums, Heft 3)*, Halle, 1935.

Ellis, W., *Polynesian Researches*, 2nd ed., London, 1831.

Fischel, H. A., 'Martyr and Prophet', *Jewish Quarterly Review*, 37 (1947–8), pp. 265 ff. and 363 ff.

Flannery, Edward H., *The Anguish of the Jews*, New York, 1965.

Flight, J. W., 'The Nomadic Idea and Ideal in the Old Testament', *Journal of Biblical Literature*, XLII (1923).

Foucart, P., *Les Mystères d'Eleusis*, Paris, 1914.

Frankfort, Henri, *Kingship and the Gods*, Chicago and London, 1948.

Frankl, George, *The Failure of the Sexual Revolution*, London, 1974.

——, *The Psychoanalysis of Society* (unpublished).

Frazer, Sir J. G., *The Golden Bough*, 3rd ed.: Part III, *The Dying God*, London, 1911; Part IV, *Adonis Attis Osiris*, London, 1907; Part VI, *The Scapegoat*, London, 1913. Abr. ed. in 1 vol., London, 1922.

——, *Folk-lore in the Old Testament*, 3 vols, London, 1918. Abr. ed. in 1 vol., London, 1923.

Freud, Sigmund, *The Interpretation of Dreams*, London, 1955.

Friedlaender, I., 'The Jews of Arabia and the Rechabites', *Jewish Quarterly Review*, I (1910).

Gaer, J., *The Legend of the Wandering Jew*, New York, 1961.

Gardner, P., 'Mysteries (Greek)', *Encyclopaedia of Religion and Ethics*, ix, pp. 77–82.

Gaster, T. H., *Thespis: Ritual, Myth and Drama in the Ancient Near East*, rev. ed., New York, 1961.

——, 'Sacrifices', *Interpreter's Dictionary of the Bible*, New York, 1962.

Gautier, L., 'À propos des Rékabites', *Études sur la religion d'Israel*, Lausanne, 1927.

Gennep, Arnold van, *The Rites of Passage*, New York, 1960.

Gilbert, Arthur, *The Vatican Council and the Jews*, Cleveland and New York, 1968.

Graetz, H., *Geschichte der Juden*, 11 vols, Leipzig, 1897–1911.

Graves, Robert, *The White Goddess*, 3rd ed., London, 1952.

——, *The Greek Myths*, 2 vols, rev. ed., Harmondsworth, 1960.

Gray, G. B., *Sacrifice in the Old Testament*, Oxford, 1924.

Grayzel, Solomon, *The Church and the Jews in the Thirteenth Century*, New York, 1966.

Green, A. R. W., *The Role of Human Sacrifice in the Ancient Near East*, Missoula, Montana, 1975.

Gugliemo, A., 'Sacrifice in the Ugaritic Texts', *Catholic Biblical Quarterly* XVII (1955), pp. 196–216.

Hare, Douglas A. R., *The Theme of Jewish*

Bibliography

Persecution of Christians in the Gospel according to St. Matthew, Cambridge, 1967.
Harnack, A., *The Mission and Expansion of Christianity*, New York, 1908.
Harrison, Jane Ellen, *Themis*, Cambridge, 1912.
——, *Prolegomena to the Study of Greek Religion*, 3rd ed., London, 1922.
Harrison, R. K., *Leviticus*, Leicester, 1980.
Hartland, E. Sidney, 'Foundation', *Encyclopaedia of Religion and Ethics*, vi, pp. 109–15.
Hastings, J. (ed.), *Encyclopaedia of Religion and Ethics*, Edinburgh, 1908–18.
Hatch, E., *The Influence of Greek Ideas and Usages upon the Christian Church*, London, 1890.
Haugg, D., *Judas Iskarioth in den neutestamentlichen Berichten*, Berlin, 1930.
Hay, Malcolm, *The Foot of Pride*, Boston, 1950.
Heer, Friedrich, *God's First Love*, London, 1967.
Hepding, Hugo, *Attis: Seine Mythen und sein Kult*, Giessen, 1903.
Hocart, A. M., *Kingship*, Oxford, 1927.
Hooke, S. H., *Myth and Ritual*, Oxford, 1933.
——, *In the Beginning*, Oxford, 1947.
——, *The Siege Perilous: Essays in Biblical Anthropology*, London, 1956.
——, *Middle Eastern Mythology*, Harmondsworth, 1963.
Hubert, H. and Mauss, M., *Sacrifice: Its Nature and Function*, London, 1964.
Jacobs, Louis, *Principles of the Jewish Faith*, London, 1964.
——, *A Jewish Theology*, London, 1973.
James, E. O., *The Origins of Sacrifice*, New York, 1971.
James, M. R. (ed.), *The Apocryphal New Testament*, Oxford, 1953.
Katz, Jacob, *Exclusiveness and Tolerance*, London, 1961.
Kaufmann, Y., *The Religion of Israel*, Chicago, 1960.
Kennedy, H. A. A., *St. Paul and the Mystery-Religions*, London, 1913.
Kerenyi, Karl, 'Die orphische Kosmologie und der Ursprung der Orphik', *Eranos-Jahrbuch 1949*, Zurich, 1950.
——, *The Heroes of the Greeks*, London, 1959.
Kermode, Frank, *The Genesis of Secrecy: On the Interpretation of Narrative*, Cambridge, Mass., and London, 1979.
Kierkegaard, Soren, *Fear and Trembling*, London, 1941.
Kirk, G. S., *Myth: its Meaning and Functions in Ancient and Other Cultures*, Cambridge, 1970.
——, *The Nature of Greek Myths*, Harmondsworth, 1974.
Klein, Melanie, *The Psychoanalysis of Children*, 3rd ed., London, 1950.
——, and Riviere, Joan, *Love, Hate and Reparation*, London, 1967.
Krause, M., 'Das literarische Verhältnis des Eugnotosbriefe zur Sophia Jesu Christi', in *Mullus: Festscrift Theodor Klauser*, Jahrbuch für Antike und Christentum, Ergänzungsband, I, 1964, pp. 215–23.
Lake, K., 'The Death of Judas', in F. J. Foakes-Jackson and K. Lake (eds), *The Beginnings of Christianity*, v (1933), pp. 22–30.
Leipoldt, J., *Sterbende und auferstende Götter*, Leipzig, 1923.
——, *Dionysos*, Leipzig, 1931.
Lévi-Strauss, Claude, *The Savage Mind*, London, 1966.
Levy, G. R., *The Gate of Horn*, London, 1963.
Liebrecht, F., *Zur Volkskunde*, Heilbronn, 1879.
Loisy, A., *Les mystères païens et le mystère chrétien*, 2nd ed., Paris, 1930.
Maass, E. W. T., *Orpheus*, Munich, 1895.
Maccoby, Hyam, 'Two Notes on Ash Wednesday', *Notes & Queries*, Nov. 1966.
——, 'Jesus and Barabbas', *New Testament Studies*, xvi, pp. 55–60, 1968.
——, 'A Study of the "jew" in "Gerontion"', *Jewish Quarterly*, 17, 2 (1969).
——, 'The Figure of Shylock', *Midstream*, 16, 2 (1970) (1).
——, 'The Delectable Daughter', *Midstream*, 16, 9 (1970) (2).
——, 'The Legend of the Wandering Jew: a New Interpretation', *Jewish Quarterly*, 20, 1 (1972).
——, 'The Anti-semitism of T. S. Eliot', *Midstream*, 19, 5 (1973).
——, 'Is the Political Jesus Dead?', *Encounter*, Feb. 1976 (1).
——, 'The Jew as Anti-Artist: the Anti-semitism of Ezra Pound', *Midstream*, 22, 3 (1976) (2).
——, 'Gospel and Midrash', *Commentary*, April 1980, pp. 69–72 (1).

Bibliography

———, *Revolution in Judaea*, New York, 1980 (2).

———, *Judaism on Trial: Christian-Jewish Medieval Disputations*, East Brunswick, 1982.

MacCulloch, J. A., *The Religion of the Ancient Celts*, Edinburgh, 1911.

MacRae, George, 'Nag Hammadi', *Interpreter's Dictionary of the Bible* (Supplementary Volume), Abingdon, 1976.

Maier, F. W., 'Judas Iskarioth', *Lexikon für Theologie und Kirche*, v, col. 671–2, Freiburg im Breisgau, 1933.

Malinowski, Bronislaw, *The Family among the Australian Aborigines*, London, 1913.

———, *Sex and Repression in Savage Society*, London, 1960.

Mellinkoff, Ruth, *The Mark of Cain*, California, 1981.

Meyer, Eduard, *Die Israeliten und ihre Nachbarstämme*, Halle, 1906.

Migne, I. P., *Patrologia Latina*, Paris, 1844.

Milgrom, J., 'Bloodguilt', *Encyclopedia Judaica*, iv, p. 1118, 1971.

———, 'Cult and Conscience: the Asham and the Priestly Doctrine of Repentance, Leiden, 1976.

———, 'Sacrifices, Offerings, Old Testament', *Interpreter's Dictionary of the Bible* (Supplementary Volume), Abingdon, 1976.

———, 'The Paradox of the Red Cow', *Vetus Testamentum*, XXXI, 1 (1981), pp. 62–72.

Money-Kyrle, R. E., *The Meaning of Sacrifice*, New York, 1965.

Moore, George Foot, 'Judges', *International Critical Commentary*, Edinburgh, 1895.

———, *Judaism in the First Centuries of the Christian Era*, 2 vols, Cambridge, Mass., 1927.

Moret, A., *Mystères Égyptiens*, Paris, 1913.

Morgenstern, J., 'The Oldest Document of the Hexateuch', *Hebrew Union College Annual*, iv, 1927, pp. 1–138.

———, 'The "Bloody Husband" (?) (Exod. 4:24–26) Once Again', *Hebrew Union College Annual*, 1963, pp. 35–70.

Murray, Gilbert, *Five Stages of Greek Religion*, London, 1935.

———, Edition of Aeschylus' *Oresteia*, London, 1946.

Noth, M., *History of Israel*, London, 1958.

Nyström, Samuel, *Beduinentum und Jahvismus*, Lund, 1946.

Oesterley, W. O. E., *The Labyrinth*, London, 1935.

———, *Sacrifices in Ancient Israel*, London, 1937.

Otto, Walter, 'Der Sinn der eleusinischen Mysterien', *Eranos-Jahrbuch 1939*, Zurich, 1940.

Paris, Matthew, *Chronica Maiora*, 7 vols, ed. H. R. Luard, London, 1872–83.

Parkes, James, *The Conflict of the Church and the Synagogue*, London, 1934.

Pascal, Blaise, *Pensées*, London, 1931.

Pauly, A., *Realencyclopädie der klassischen Altertumwischenschaft*, Stuttgart, 1842–66.

Pausanias, *Description of Greece*, tr. with annotations by J. G. Frazer, 6 vols, London, 1890.

Poliakov, Léon, *The History of antisemitism*, 3 vols, London, 1974.

Pope, Marvin, *The Song of Songs*, New York, 1977.

Prescott, W. H., *Conquest of Peru*, London, 1908.

Preuss, H., *Die Vorstellung von Antichrist im späteren Mittelalter*, Leipzig, 1906.

Pritchard, James B., *Ancient Near Eastern Texts*, Princeton, 1955.

Propp, Vladimir, *Morphology of Folktale*, Bloomington, 1958.

Railo, Eino, *The Haunted Castle: A Study of the Elements of English Romanticism*, London, 1927.

Regensburg, B. von, *Predigten*, Vienna, 1880.

Reich, Wilhelm, *Character Analysis*, London, 1950.

Reik, Theodor, *Ritual: Psychoanalytic Studies*, New York, 1957.

Reinach, A. J., 'La Lutte de Jahve avec Jacob et avec Moise et l'Origine de la circoncision', *Revue des Études Sémitiques*, I (1908), p. 351.

Reinach, S., *Orpheus: histoire générale des religions*, Paris, 1909. Eng. tr. *Orpheus*, London, 1931.

Reitzenstein, R., *Die hellenistische Mysterienreligionen*, 3rd ed., Leipzig-Berlin, 1927.

Rivers, W. H. R., 'Mother Right', *Encyclopaedia of Religion and Ethics*, viii, pp. 851–9.

Robertson, J. M., *Pagan Christs*, 2nd ed., London, 1911.

Robinson, J. (ed.), *The Coptic Gnostic Library*, Leiden, 1975–.

——— (ed.), *The Nag Hammadi Library in English*, Leiden, 1977.

Bibliography

Roheim, Geza, *The Eternal Ones of the Dream*, New York, 1945.

Rosenberg, Edgar, *From Shylock to Svengali: Jewish Stereotypes in English Fiction*, London, 1961.

Roth, Cecil, *A Short History of the Jewish People*, rev. ed., Oxford, 1943.

——, 'David Reubeni', *Midstream*, 9 (1963), pp. 76–81.

Rowley, H. H., *From Joseph to Joshua*, London, 1950.

Ruether, Rosemary, *Faith and Fratricide*, New York, 1974.

Sanders, E. P., *Paul and Palestinian Judaism*, London, 1977.

Schmidt, W., *Der Ursprung der Gottesidee*, 12 vols, Munster in Westfalia, 1912–55.

Schmökel, H., 'Yahweh and the Kenites', *Journal of Biblical Literature*, lii (1933).

Simon, Ernst, 'Kierkegaard and the Akedah', *Conservative Judaism*, 12 (Spring 1958), pp. 15–19.

Simon, M., *St. Stephen and the Hellenists in the Primitive Church*, London, 1958.

——, *Verus Israel*, 2nd ed., Paris, 1964.

Skinner, John, *Genesis*, 2nd ed., International Critical Commentary, Edinburgh, 1930.

Smith, D. M., *The Composition and Order of the Fourth Gospel*, London, 1965.

Smith, W. Robertson, *Kinship and Marriage in Early Arabia*, 2nd ed., London, 1903.

——, *The Religion of the Semites*, 3rd ed., London, 1927.

Sombart, Werner, *The Jews and Modern Capitalism*, London, 1913.

Soustelle, Jacques, *Daily Life of the Aztecs*, London, 1961.

Speiser, E. A., 'Man, Ethnic Divisions of', *Interpreter's Dictionary of the Bible*, iii, 1962, pp. 235–42.

——, *Genesis* (Anchor Bible), New York, 1964.

Spencer, B. and Gillen, F. J., *The Native Tribes of Central Australia*, London, 1899.

Spiegel, Shalom, *The Last Trial*, New York, 1969.

Stade, Bernhard, *Geschichte des Volkes Israel*, Berlin, 1887.

Starr, Joseph, *The Jews in the Byzantine Empire*, Athens, 1939.

Starr, Joshua, 'Jewish Life in Crete under the Rule of Venice', *Proceedings of the American Academy for Jewish Research*, xii (1942), pp. 59–114.

Stein, S., 'The Development of the Jewish Law on Interest', *Historia Judaica*, xvii (1955), pp. 3–4.

Strack, Hermann L., *Das Blut im Glauben und Aberglauben*, 8th ed., Munich, 1911. Eng. tr. H. Blanchamp, *The Jew and Human Sacrifice*, London, 1909.

Strackenjan, L., *Aberglaube aus dem Herzogtum Oldenburg*, 2nd ed., Oldenburg, 1908.

Thomson, George, *Aeschylus and Athens*, 2nd ed., London, 1946.

Torrey, Charles Cutler, *The Jewish Foundation of Islam*, USA, 1967.

Trachtenberg, Joshua, *The Devil and the Jews*, New York, 1966.

Van Buren, E. D., 'Foundation Rites of a New Temple', *Orientialia* (New Series), No. 21 (1952), pp. 293–306.

Vellay, Charles, *Le culte et les fêtes d'Adonis-Thammuz dans l'Orient antique*, Paris, 1904.

Vermes, Geza, *Scripture and Tradition in Judaism: Haggadic Studies*, Leiden, 1973.

Vischer, Eberhard, *Jahwe der Gott Kains*, Berlin, 1929.

Watt, W. M., *Muhammad at Medina*, Oxford, 1956.

Wellhausen, Julius, *Prolegomena to the History of Ancient Israel*, New York, 1957.

Wells, G. A., *The Jesus of the Early Christians*, London, 1971.

Williams, A. L., *Adversus Judaeos*, Cambridge, 1935.

Yerkes, R. K., *Sacrifice in Greek and Roman Religions and Early Judaism*, London, 1953.

Zirus, Werner, *Der ewige Jude in der Dichtung, vornehmlich in der englischen und deutschen*, Leipzig, 1928.

Index

Page numbers in italics refer to illustrations

ABEL 9, 11–15, 42, 126, 132, 141, 142; murder of 20; a human sacrifice 20; and Enoch 23–4; meaning of name 24; conflict with Cain 29; identified with Jesus 151
Abelard, Peter 196
Abraham 9, 15, 20, 58, 74–86, 94, 97, 99, 134; and Cities of the Plain 84; and circumcision 87
Achan 189
Achilles 177, 179
Adah (wife of Lamech) 48, 57, 93
Adam 15, 16, 18, 67, 99, 170; sons of 190
Adams, Henry 157, 196
Adler, E. N. 197
Adonis 65, 66, 107–8
Aeneas 182, 192
Aeolus, king of Athamas 76
Aeschylus 77, 191; *Oresteia* of 94, 183–4
aetiology in myths 180
Agamemnon 77
Aglauros 188; *see also* Athene
Ahasuerus 166
Ajigarta 77
Akedah 79, 83, 84, 87, 88, 96, 99, 105; in Islam 135
Akhnaton 17
Albigensians 157
Ali 97
Allard, M. 152
Alus 189
Amalek 59
Amalekites 15
Ammon 64
Ammonites 78
Ancient Mariner 7, 170
Anderson, G. K. 197
Androtion 187
angels, as source of Torah 116; as givers of the Torah 148
animals, subordination of to man 31

animal sacrifice 45, 74 ff.; in Old Testament 10; earlier than human sacrifice 8; meaning of 27; and repentance 27; superiority of to vegetable sacrifice 28–9
'Antagonist' 130
Antichrist 172
Antioch 150
anti-Semitism 113, 163–75; in Gnosticism 112; and sacrifice 186
Antonio 131
Aphrahat 150
Aphrodite 66
Apion 156
Apocrypha 116
Apollo 76, 119, 177, 179, 189
Apollodorus 76, 191
Arabs 97
Aristodemus 78
Arta 187
Artemis 77
Arthur, King 114
Arunta 192
Astarte 110
Athamas 189
Athene 67, 94, 96
Athens 78, 188
Athronges 194
Attila 129
Attis 65, 66, 92, 107–9, 118, 132; communion of 116
Augustine 115, 150–1, 194
Azazel 35, 189
Aztecs 7, 23, 100, 101

BAAL 126
Babylon 172
Babylonia, influence of on Bible 58
Babylonian New Year festival 21, 37
Bacchus 65
Bachofen, J. J. 184
Balaam 15, 16

Balder 49–50, 66, 76, 100, 121, 137, 143–4, 176
Banu-Qayin (tribe) 62
Banu Qaynuga 190
Barabbas 142–4, 196
Baron, Salo W. 196, 197
Bauer, I. 197
Bea, Cardinal 196
bear sacrifices 187
Beloved Disciple 125, 126
Beni-Hassan 59, 190
Benjamin, tribe of 115
Berdyaev, Nicholas 197
Berdyczewski, M. J. *see* Bin Gorion, M. J.
Berossus 188
Bettelheim, B. 192
Bin Gorion, M. J. 75, 191
Black, M. 194, 195
Blanchamp, H. 152
blood fantasies 154
blood-libel 152–9
Bloy, Leon 197
Boas, Franz 187
Boling, R. G. 191
Bouphonia 8, 177, 178, 188
Bousset, W. 188, 197
Braude, W. G. 193
'bridegroom of blood' 95
Bruti 187
Budde, K. 188, 190
Bultmann, Rudolf 111, 193
Bulwer-Lytton, E. G. E. L. Lord 169
Buttman, P. C. 188

CADMUS 188
Caesarea 148
Cain 7, 9, 11 ff., 74, 126, 132, 137, 142, 151, 167; meaning of name of 13; line of 18; and Adam 24; and Eden 25; wife of 26; cause of conflict of, with Abel 29; not punished by death 33; a Sacred Executioner 33; and blood-feud

203

Index

34; and metal-working 42; killed by Tubal-Cain 48, and Lamech 44
Cainan 55–6
Calchas 77
Campbell, Joseph 187, 191, 193, 195, 197
Canaan (land) 87
Canaan (son of Ham) 63, 67, 68; curse of 134, 181
Canaanites 61–2, 87
Castor 133
Catullus 110
cedar 39
Celer 187
Chalybes 60, 190
Charbonnier, George 197
Chaucer 160; 'Prioress's Tale' of 156
Child, F. J. 196
child-murder, charge of 154–6
Christ 190
Christian Church, as true 'Israel' 134; and the Jews 147–62
Christianity 97, 107 ff.
Chrysostom 150
Church Fathers 142, 145
circumcision 87 ff.; and animal sacrifice 90; pre-marital 91; as ordeal 92; of infants 93
Civiltà cattolica (periodical) 153
Class-struggle 184
Clytemnestra 189
Codrington, R. H. 187
Cohn, Norman 197
Columba, Saint 187
Communion (Eucharist) 116, 117; Christ-child in 155
Cook, A. B. 176
Cook, Michael 193
Copin 156
Corbishley, T. 193
Cornford, F. M. 176
Corybantes 190
Couretes 190
Covenant, the 187
'Covenant between the Pieces' 87, 192
Crone, Patricia 193
Cronus 65, 66, 68, 70, 95; *see also* Kronos
Crucifixion the, *117*, 180; history of 120; imitation of in blood-libel 152–3; not martyrdom 101–2
Cumont, Franz 193
Cybele 92, 110, 118

DACTYLOI 190
Damascus 115
David 30, 97
Day of Atonement 21, 105
Delehaye, H. 193
Delphi 177
Demeter 108
Demiurge 112–13, 116, 194
De Nantes, Abbé Georges 139
De Rougement, Denis 157, 196
Deucalion 69, 191
De Vaux, R. 187
Devil 86, 164; not found in Hebrew Bible 30
Diodorus Siculus 190
Dionysius Halicarnassus 187
Dionysus 65, 66, 69, 116, 191
distancing devices 50, 97
Docetism 113
Dodd, C. H. 195
Doughty, C. M. 190
drama, origin of 108
dualism, in Gnosticism 111

EASTER 152
Ecce Homo 143
Eden, Garden of, Isaac in, 83; Cain in 25
Eerdmans, B. D. 188
Egypt, cicumcision in 92
El (god) 67
'Elders of Zion' 171
Eleusinian mysteries 108
Eliezer 88
Eliot, T. S. 100, 170, 193
Ellis, W. 187
Enmeduranki 188
Enobarbus 131
Enoch 12, 16, 18, 188; in Christian Church 22; death of 22, in Synagogal tradition 22; and sun-worship 23; meaning of name of 23; in Cainite and Sethite chronicles 23
Enosh 18
Epiphanius 194
Erinnyes (Furies) 67
Erysichthon 188
Essenes 115
Ethiopian Church 122
Eucharist 64; *see also* Communion
Euripides 77, 191
Eusebius 191
Eve 15, 18, 67; subordination of to Adam 31

FALASHAS 192

Fall of man, due to serpent not Satan 30
Fan (tribe) 59
Faust 170
'Field of Blood' 131
Final Solution 175
Flannery, Edward H. 196
Flight, J. W. 190
flint knife 95
flint sickle 66
Flood, the, symbolic meaning of 69
Flying Dutchman 170
foundation myths 97; of Christianity 180
foundation sacrifices 27–8, 179, 187
Frankl, George 197
Frazer, Sir James 12, 50, 51, 59, 176, 187, 189, 190, 191, 192, 193, 195, 197
Freud, Sigmund 17, 50, 80, 84, 94, 179, 190
Friedlaender, I. 190
Frigg 49–50

GAER, J. 197
Gamaliel 115, 145, 148
Gaster, T. H. 189
'Gaude Maria' 160, 196
Gautier, L. 190
Ge 95
Gealy, F. D. 196
Genealogy of Nations (Biblical) 58
Gennep, Arnold van 192
Germanus 196
Gershom 88
Gilbert, Arthur 196
Girgashites 87
gladiatorial combat 12, 187
Gnosticism 110–13, 173; history of 111
gnosis 112, 116
God, absolved of cruelty 81
God the Father, double role of in Christianity 99
Godwin 169
Graves, Robert 191, 193
Greece, sacrifice in 77–8
Greek civilization 181–2
Green, A. R. W. 191
Gypsies 59, 168, 175

HAM 18, 43, 58, 63, 68, 74, 86; in Kenite saga 53; and Hammath 61; castration of Noah by 65

204

Index

Hammath 61, 68
hanged sacrifice 119–20
Hare, Douglas A. R. 148, 196
Harischandra 77
Harnack, A. 152, 196
Harrison, Jane 176
Harrison, R. K. 189
hatan 91
Hatch, E. 194
Haugg, D. 194
Hay, Malcolm 196
Heber the Kenite 14, 60
Hebrews, Epistle to 22, 104, 105
Heer, Friedrich 196
Hellenes 182
Hellenistic religion 107–20
Hephaestus 59
Herder, Johann Gottfried von 189
Herod 168
Herodians 145
Herodotus 76, 190, 191
Hiel 187
High Priest 147, 180; a Sadducee 103; a Roman appointee 115; tool of the Romans 135
Hillel 145
Hippolytus 197
Hitler, Adolf 150, 175
Hittites 87
Hivites 87
Hobab 14
Homer 77, 183
Hooke, S. H. 29, 189
Hother 50, 76, 123, 137, 139
Hugh of Lincoln 155–6
human sacrifice 7, 74 ff.; in Old Testament 10; execration of in Bible 27; of daughters 78; divinity of victims in 100
hyssop, for sprinkling 39

IAGO 131
Ieoud 191
Iphigenia 77
Irad 18
Irenaeus 197
iron-working 59
Isaac 9, 74 ff., 79, 87, 94, 97, 99, 135; 'blood' and 'ashes' of 83; in medieval tradition 83
Iscariot, derivation of 195
Ishmael 87, 91, 97, 135, 193
Isis 66, 109; worship of, and Christianity 109
Islam 97, 134; ban on wine in 63; basic myth of 182

Isorni, Jacques 139
Israel 20; as first-born 90
Israelites 15, 16; and agriculture 69–70; a 'nation of priests' 90

JABAL 18, 42, 57
Jacob 20, 50, 91
Jacobs, L. 193
Jael 60
James (brother of Jesus) 127
Japheth 18, 43, 58, 63, 190; in Kenite saga 53
Jason 164
Jebusites 87
Jehu 61
Jephtha 78, 189
Jeremiah 60
Jericho 187, 189
Jerome 191
Jerusalem Church 127
Jesus 9, 97 ff.; Crucifixion of 76; and Satan 81; soteriological role 103; as reformer 103–4; a historical person 113; not a Christian 114; a hanged god 119; and Judas Iscariot 121–33; brothers of 127; as victim of Jews 134–46; in infant form 158; and Wandering Jew 166
Jethro 14, 16, 19, 59, 88; in Jewish tradition 22
Jewess, as sexual seducer and murderess 162
Jewish civilization, basic myth of 182
Jewish priesthood 22
Jews 7; as collective Sacred Executioner 9, 122, 132; and Crucifixion 76; mythologization of 120; in Christian myth 134; in New Testament 134–46; 'blindness' of 137; vilification of in Christian writings 149; as vampires 159; as public executioners 162; as sorcerers 163–4; as usurers 163–4; as travellers 168; as nomads 168
'Jew's Beautiful Daughter' story 164
Job 16; Book of 30, 80
Johanan ben Zakkai 145
John the Baptist 97
John the Evangelist 116
John, Gospel of 111; on Eucharist 117; on Judas 124–5; diabolization of Jews in 145–6

John (son of Zebedee) 126
Jonadab (son of Rechab) 60, 61
Joseph (father of Jesus) 127
Joseph (son of Jacob) 32
Josephus 142, 196
Joses (brother of Jesus) 127
Joshua 91
Jubal 18, 42, 57, 59
Jubilees, Book of 80
Judaism, pluralism of 99; sacrificial system of 104 ff.
Judas the Apostle 126; split off from Judas Iscariot 126
Judas (brother of Jesus) 126
Judas Iscariot 51, 81, 121–33, 130, 180, 182; action of fated 123; designated by Jesus 124; as Jesus's twin-brother 128; motives of 130; death of 131–3
Judas of Galilee 194

KABBALISTS 157
Kadmonites 87
Kain (town) 60
Karaism 103
Kekrops (Cecrops) 188
Kenan 18
Kenites 14, 87, 190; influence on Israelite religion 19; and Rechabites 60–2; scattered residence of 60; and agriculture 69
Kenite saga 20, 21; on Cain 39; the Flood in 41; after the Flood 55–6, 57
Kenizzites 87
Kerenyi, Karl 189
Kermode, Frank 130, 195
Keturah 15
Khonds 191
Kiddush 117
Kierkegaard, S. 84, 192
King, Martin Luther 102
Kirk, G. S. 178, 180, 191, 197
Kittim 195
kohen 16
Koran 189, 193
Krause, M. 194
Kronos (Cronus) 191
Kumarbi 67
kurios 116

LACTANTIUS 197
Lake, K. 194
Lamech 18, 41 ff., 49, 74, 93, 137, 189; the Kenite Noah 43; 'vengeful tribesman' theory of 44; and Cain 44; sacrifice of son by 47

205

Index

laghon shes zehorit 38
Last Supper 117, 125, 180
Lazarus 114
Learchus 189
Leclercq, H. 152
Lenormant, F. 189
Leos 78
leper, purification ceremony of 38
Lévi-Strauss 179, 181, 182, 183
Levites, and Rechabites 62; substitutes for first-born sons 90
Lewis, Monk 169
Liebrecht, F. 187
Livy 187
Loki 7, 50, 51, 76, 80, 121, 123, 131, 137, 139, 144
Lost Ten Tribes 172
Lot, drunkenness of 64; daughters of 190
lots, use of, for sacrifice 36
Lucretius 193
Luke 115; on Judas 124

MACCABEES 32
Maccoby, E. M. 189
Maccoby, Hyam 193, 194, 195, 196, 197
Machaereus 177
Macrae, H. 194
Maenads 66
Mahalalel 18
Maier, F. W. 194
Malinowski, Bruno 180
Marcion 106, 115, 194
Mark, on Judas 124; on parables 138
Marlowe, Christopher 164
Marsyas 119
martyrdom, distinguished from human sacrifice 101
Mass, the 159, 180
Mastema 80, 89
Matiamvo of Angola 189
matriarchy 184–5
matriarchal attitudes, return of, in patriarchal society 85–6
Matthew, on Judas 124; on parables 138; imprecation of, against Jews 141
Mehujael 18
Meir, Rabbi 194
Melchizedek 16, 112; in Christianity 77
Melicertes 189
Mellinkoff, Ruth 190
Mesha (king of Moab) 189

Mesopotamian Church 128
Messiah 97, 103, 113
Metatron 22
Methuselah 18, 22
Methushael 18
Meyer, Eduard 190
Midian 15, 59
Midianites 16
Midrash, containing material earlier than Bible 47; on Isaac's sacrifice 82–3; on Moses and circumcision 88–9
Migne, I. P. 191
Milgrom, J. 105, 187, 189, 193
mistletoe 50
Mithraism 109; Communion of 116
Moab 64
monotheism 69
Moore, G. F. 191, 193
Morgenstern, J. 188, 192
Moriah, Mount 83
Moses 14, 15, 16, 87 ff., 116; as liberator 19; as saviour 107
Mot 126
mother goddess (earth) 132
Mount of Olives 114
mourning, for a god 107
Muggeridge, Malcolm 197
Muhammad 97, 135
Murray, Gilbert 176
Muslims 172
mystery cults, matriarchal elements in 109
mystery religions 107–10, 173
myths, and ritual 176–8; aetiological 180; as 'charters' 180; Babylonian 181; structuralist theory of 181; moral dimension of 181; basic myths of various civilizations 182; and literature 183

NAAMAH (sister of Tubal-Cain) 57
Nabataeans 190
Nadir 190
Nag Hammadi 111, 194
Nazarenes 114, 115, 147
Nazirites 62, 64
Nazis 163–75; and anti-Jewish propaganda 165
Nebuchadnezzar 129
Neoptolemus 177–8, 179
Newman, Cardinal 193
New Testament, regression in 10
Noah 15, 16, 18, 86, 181;
sacrifice by 45, 46; meaning of name of 54; drunkenness of 63 ff.
Nod, land of 25–6
Normans 182
Noth, M. 191
Nyström, Samuel 190

ODIN 195
Oedipus 94, 142
Oldenburg 187
Old Testament, and ritual sacrifice 9
Olympia 188
Olympian gods 181
O'Neill, J. C. 194
oral aggression 158
Oran 187
Orestes 189
Origen 149
Original Sin 99
Orpheus 66
Orphism 108
Osiris 65, 66, 107–8, 126; castration of 66
Otto, W. 193
Ovid 187, 191

PALESTINE 168
Palm Sunday 128
Paphos 66
parables, of Jesus 137–8; of Pharisees 139
'parallelomania' 183
Paris (hero) 179
Paris, Matthew 155, 196
Parkes, James 151–2, 196
Paschal Lamb 104
Paschasius Radbertus 196
Passion Plays 168
'Passover sacrifice of Egypt' 104
patriarchal society, psychological mechanisms of 85
patriarchy 184–5
Patripassian heresy 193
Paul 98 ff., 104, 114–20; Epistles of 111; and mystery religions 116; on Deut.21:22–3 118; anti-Jewish stance of 136–7; and Gnosticism 136; pro-Roman stance of 136–7; as Saul, persecuting Christians 147; supported by Pharisees 148; and Antichrist 174
Pauly, A. 190
Pausanias 187, 191
Pelagius 115, 194
Pentheus 66